Mometrix
TEST PREPARATION

DSST®

Organizational Behavior Exam

Exam Secrets Study Guide

I0892272

DEAR FUTURE EXAM SUCCESS STORY

First of all, **THANK YOU** for purchasing Mometrix study materials!

Second, congratulations! You are one of the few determined test-takers who are committed to doing whatever it takes to excel on your exam. **You have come to the right place.** We developed these study materials with one goal in mind: to deliver you the information you need in a format that's concise and easy to use.

In addition to optimizing your guide for the content of the test, we've outlined our recommended steps for breaking down the preparation process into small, attainable goals so you can make sure you stay on track.

We've also analyzed the entire test-taking process, identifying the most common pitfalls and showing how you can overcome them and be ready for any curveball the test throws you.

Standardized testing is one of the biggest obstacles on your road to success, which only increases the importance of doing well in the high-pressure, high-stakes environment of test day. Your results on this test could have a significant impact on your future, and this guide provides the information and practical advice to help you achieve your full potential on test day.

Your success is our success

We would love to hear from you! If you would like to share the story of your exam success or if you have any questions or comments in regard to our products, please contact us at **800-673-8175** or **support@mometrix.com**.

Thanks again for your business and we wish you continued success!

Sincerely,
The Mometrix Test Preparation Team

Need more help? Check out our flashcards at:
http://MometrixFlashcards.com/DSST

Written and edited by the Mometrix Exam Secrets Test Prep Team
Printed in the United States of America

Table of Contents

Introduction

Thank you for purchasing this resource! You have made the choice to prepare yourself for a test that could have a huge impact on your future, and this guide is designed to help you be fully ready for test day. Obviously, it's important to have a solid understanding of the test material, but you also need to be prepared for the unique environment and stressors of the test, so that you can perform to the best of your abilities.

For this purpose, the first section that appears in this guide is the **Secret Keys**. We've devoted countless hours to meticulously researching what works and what doesn't, and we've boiled down our findings to the five most impactful steps you can take to improve your performance on the test. We start at the beginning with study planning and move through the preparation process, all the way to the testing strategies that will help you get the most out of what you know when you're finally sitting in front of the test.

We recommend that you start preparing for your test as far in advance as possible. However, if you've bought this guide as a last-minute study resource and only have a few days before your test, we recommend that you skip over the first two Secret Keys since they address a long-term study plan.

If you struggle with **test anxiety**, we strongly encourage you to check out our recommendations for how you can overcome it. Test anxiety is a formidable foe, but it can be beaten, and we want to make sure you have the tools you need to defeat it.

Secret Key #1 – Plan Big, Study Small

There's a lot riding on your performance. If you want to ace this test, you're going to need to keep your skills sharp and the material fresh in your mind. You need a plan that lets you review everything you need to know while still fitting in your schedule. We'll break this strategy down into three categories.

Information Organization

Start with the information you already have: the official test outline. From this, you can make a complete list of all the concepts you need to cover before the test. Organize these concepts into groups that can be studied together, and create a list of any related vocabulary you need to learn so you can brush up on any difficult terms. You'll want to keep this vocabulary list handy once you actually start studying since you may need to add to it along the way.

Time Management

Once you have your set of study concepts, decide how to spread them out over the time you have left before the test. Break your study plan into small, clear goals so you have a manageable task for each day and know exactly what you're doing. Then just focus on one small step at a time. When you manage your time this way, you don't need to spend hours at a time studying. Studying a small block of content for a short period each day helps you retain information better and avoid stressing over how much you have left to do. You can relax knowing that you have a plan to cover everything in time. In order for this strategy to be effective though, you have to start studying early and stick to your schedule. Avoid the exhaustion and futility that comes from last-minute cramming!

Study Environment

The environment you study in has a big impact on your learning. Studying in a coffee shop, while probably more enjoyable, is not likely to be as fruitful as studying in a quiet room. It's important to keep distractions to a minimum. You're only planning to study for a short block of time, so make the most of it. Don't pause to check your phone or get up to find a snack. It's also important to **avoid multitasking**. Research has consistently shown that multitasking will make your studying dramatically less effective. Your study area should also be comfortable and well-lit so you don't have the distraction of straining your eyes or sitting on an uncomfortable chair.

The time of day you study is also important. You want to be rested and alert. Don't wait until just before bedtime. Study when you'll be most likely to comprehend and remember. Even better, if you know what time of day your test will be, set that time aside for study. That way your brain will be used to working on that subject at that specific time and you'll have a better chance of recalling information.

Finally, it can be helpful to team up with others who are studying for the same test. Your actual studying should be done in as isolated an environment as possible, but the work of organizing the information and setting up the study plan can be divided up. In between study sessions, you can discuss with your teammates the concepts that you're all studying and quiz each other on the details. Just be sure that your teammates are as serious about the test as you are. If you find that your study time is being replaced with social time, you might need to find a new team.

Secret Key #2 – Make Your Studying Count

You're devoting a lot of time and effort to preparing for this test, so you want to be absolutely certain it will pay off. This means doing more than just reading the content and hoping you can remember it on test day. It's important to make every minute of study count. There are two main areas you can focus on to make your studying count.

Retention

It doesn't matter how much time you study if you can't remember the material. You need to make sure you are retaining the concepts. To check your retention of the information you're learning, try recalling it at later times with minimal prompting. Try carrying around flashcards and glance at one or two from time to time or ask a friend who's also studying for the test to quiz you.

To enhance your retention, look for ways to put the information into practice so that you can apply it rather than simply recalling it. If you're using the information in practical ways, it will be much easier to remember. Similarly, it helps to solidify a concept in your mind if you're not only reading it to yourself but also explaining it to someone else. Ask a friend to let you teach them about a concept you're a little shaky on (or speak aloud to an imaginary audience if necessary). As you try to summarize, define, give examples, and answer your friend's questions, you'll understand the concepts better and they will stay with you longer. Finally, step back for a big picture view and ask yourself how each piece of information fits with the whole subject. When you link the different concepts together and see them working together as a whole, it's easier to remember the individual components.

Finally, practice showing your work on any multi-step problems, even if you're just studying. Writing out each step you take to solve a problem will help solidify the process in your mind, and you'll be more likely to remember it during the test.

Modality

Modality simply refers to the means or method by which you study. Choosing a study modality that fits your own individual learning style is crucial. No two people learn best in exactly the same way, so it's important to know your strengths and use them to your advantage.

For example, if you learn best by visualization, focus on visualizing a concept in your mind and draw an image or a diagram. Try color-coding your notes, illustrating them, or creating symbols that will trigger your mind to recall a learned concept. If you learn best by hearing or discussing information, find a study partner who learns the same way or read aloud to yourself. Think about how to put the information in your own words. Imagine that you are giving a lecture on the topic and record yourself so you can listen to it later.

For any learning style, flashcards can be helpful. Organize the information so you can take advantage of spare moments to review. Underline key words or phrases. Use different colors for different categories. Mnemonic devices (such as creating a short list in which every item starts with the same letter) can also help with retention. Find what works best for you and use it to store the information in your mind most effectively and easily.

Secret Key #3 – Practice the Right Way

Your success on test day depends not only on how many hours you put into preparing, but also on whether you prepared the right way. It's good to check along the way to see if your studying is paying off. One of the most effective ways to do this is by taking practice tests to evaluate your progress. Practice tests are useful because they show exactly where you need to improve. Every time you take a practice test, pay special attention to these three groups of questions:

- The questions you got wrong
- The questions you had to guess on, even if you guessed right
- The questions you found difficult or slow to work through

This will show you exactly what your weak areas are, and where you need to devote more study time. Ask yourself why each of these questions gave you trouble. Was it because you didn't understand the material? Was it because you didn't remember the vocabulary? Do you need more repetitions on this type of question to build speed and confidence? Dig into those questions and figure out how you can strengthen your weak areas as you go back to review the material.

Additionally, many practice tests have a section explaining the answer choices. It can be tempting to read the explanation and think that you now have a good understanding of the concept. However, an explanation likely only covers part of the question's broader context. Even if the explanation makes perfect sense, **go back and investigate** every concept related to the question until you're positive you have a thorough understanding.

As you go along, keep in mind that the practice test is just that: practice. Memorizing these questions and answers will not be very helpful on the actual test because it is unlikely to have any of the same exact questions. If you only know the right answers to the sample questions, you won't be prepared for the real thing. **Study the concepts** until you understand them fully, and then you'll be able to answer any question that shows up on the test.

It's important to wait on the practice tests until you're ready. If you take a test on your first day of study, you may be overwhelmed by the amount of material covered and how much you need to learn. Work up to it gradually.

On test day, you'll need to be prepared for answering questions, managing your time, and using the test-taking strategies you've learned. It's a lot to balance, like a mental marathon that will have a big impact on your future. Like training for a marathon, you'll need to start slowly and work your way up. When test day arrives, you'll be ready.

Start with the strategies you've read in the first two Secret Keys—plan your course and study in the way that works best for you. If you have time, consider using multiple study resources to get different approaches to the same concepts. It can be helpful to see difficult concepts from more than one angle. Then find a good source for practice tests. Many times, the test website will suggest potential study resources or provide sample tests.

Practice Test Strategy

If you're able to find at least three practice tests, we recommend this strategy:

Untimed and Open-Book Practice

Take the first test with no time constraints and with your notes and study guide handy. Take your time and focus on applying the strategies you've learned.

Timed and Open-Book Practice

Take the second practice test open-book as well, but set a timer and practice pacing yourself to finish in time.

Timed and Closed-Book Practice

Take any other practice tests as if it were test day. Set a timer and put away your study materials. Sit at a table or desk in a quiet room, imagine yourself at the testing center, and answer questions as quickly and accurately as possible.

Keep repeating timed and closed-book tests on a regular basis until you run out of practice tests or it's time for the actual test. Your mind will be ready for the schedule and stress of test day, and you'll be able to focus on recalling the material you've learned.

Secret Key #4 – Pace Yourself

Once you're fully prepared for the material on the test, your biggest challenge on test day will be managing your time. Just knowing that the clock is ticking can make you panic even if you have plenty of time left. Work on pacing yourself so you can build confidence against the time constraints of the exam. Pacing is a difficult skill to master, especially in a high-pressure environment, so **practice is vital**.

Set time expectations for your pace based on how much time is available. For example, if a section has 60 questions and the time limit is 30 minutes, you know you have to average 30 seconds or less per question in order to answer them all. Although 30 seconds is the hard limit, set 25 seconds per question as your goal, so you reserve extra time to spend on harder questions. When you budget extra time for the harder questions, you no longer have any reason to stress when those questions take longer to answer.

Don't let this time expectation distract you from working through the test at a calm, steady pace, but keep it in mind so you don't spend too much time on any one question. Recognize that taking extra time on one question you don't understand may keep you from answering two that you do understand later in the test. If your time limit for a question is up and you're still not sure of the answer, mark it and move on, and come back to it later if the time and the test format allow. If the testing format doesn't allow you to return to earlier questions, just make an educated guess; then put it out of your mind and move on.

On the easier questions, be careful not to rush. It may seem wise to hurry through them so you have more time for the challenging ones, but it's not worth missing one if you know the concept and just didn't take the time to read the question fully. Work efficiently but make sure you understand the question and have looked at all of the answer choices, since more than one may seem right at first.

Even if you're paying attention to the time, you may find yourself a little behind at some point. You should speed up to get back on track, but do so wisely. Don't panic; just take a few seconds less on each question until you're caught up. Don't guess without thinking, but do look through the answer choices and eliminate any you know are wrong. If you can get down to two choices, it is often worthwhile to guess from those. Once you've chosen an answer, move on and don't dwell on any that you skipped or had to hurry through. If a question was taking too long, chances are it was one of the harder ones, so you weren't as likely to get it right anyway.

On the other hand, if you find yourself getting ahead of schedule, it may be beneficial to slow down a little. The more quickly you work, the more likely you are to make a careless mistake that will affect your score. You've budgeted time for each question, so don't be afraid to spend that time. Practice an efficient but careful pace to get the most out of the time you have.

Secret Key #5 – Have a Plan for Guessing

When you're taking the test, you may find yourself stuck on a question. Some of the answer choices seem better than others, but you don't see the one answer choice that is obviously correct. What do you do?

The scenario described above is very common, yet most test takers have not effectively prepared for it. Developing and practicing a plan for guessing may be one of the single most effective uses of your time as you get ready for the exam.

In developing your plan for guessing, there are three questions to address:

- When should you start the guessing process?
- How should you narrow down the choices?
- Which answer should you choose?

When to Start the Guessing Process

Unless your plan for guessing is to select C every time (which, despite its merits, is not what we recommend), you need to leave yourself enough time to apply your answer elimination strategies. Since you have a limited amount of time for each question, that means that if you're going to give yourself the best shot at guessing correctly, you have to decide quickly whether or not you will guess.

Of course, the best-case scenario is that you don't have to guess at all, so first, see if you can answer the question based on your knowledge of the subject and basic reasoning skills. Focus on the key words in the question and try to jog your memory of related topics. Give yourself a chance to bring the knowledge to mind, but once you realize that you don't have (or you can't access) the knowledge you need to answer the question, it's time to start the guessing process.

It's almost always better to start the guessing process too early than too late. It only takes a few seconds to remember something and answer the question from knowledge. Carefully eliminating wrong answer choices takes longer. Plus, going through the process of eliminating answer choices can actually help jog your memory.

Summary: Start the guessing process as soon as you decide that you can't answer the question based on your knowledge.

How to Narrow Down the Choices

The next chapter in this book (**Test-Taking Strategies**) includes a wide range of strategies for how to approach questions and how to look for answer choices to eliminate. You will definitely want to read those carefully, practice them, and figure out which ones work best for you. Here though, we're going to address a mindset rather than a particular strategy.

Your odds of guessing an answer correctly depend on how many options you are choosing from.

Number of options left	5	4	3	2	1
Odds of guessing correctly	20%	25%	33%	50%	100%

You can see from this chart just how valuable it is to be able to eliminate incorrect answers and make an educated guess, but there are two things that many test takers do that cause them to miss out on the benefits of guessing:

- Accidentally eliminating the correct answer
- Selecting an answer based on an impression

We'll look at the first one here, and the second one in the next section.

To avoid accidentally eliminating the correct answer, we recommend a thought exercise called **the $5 challenge**. In this challenge, you only eliminate an answer choice from contention if you are willing to bet $5 on it being wrong. Why $5? Five dollars is a small but not insignificant amount of money. It's an amount you could afford to lose but wouldn't want to throw away. And while losing $5 once might not hurt too much, doing it twenty times will set you back $100. In the same way, each small decision you make—eliminating a choice here, guessing on a question there—won't by itself impact your score very much, but when you put them all together, they can make a big difference. By holding each answer choice elimination decision to a higher standard, you can reduce the risk of accidentally eliminating the correct answer.

The $5 challenge can also be applied in a positive sense: If you are willing to bet $5 that an answer choice *is* correct, go ahead and mark it as correct.

Summary: Only eliminate an answer choice if you are willing to bet $5 that it is wrong.

Which Answer to Choose

You're taking the test. You've run into a hard question and decided you'll have to guess. You've eliminated all the answer choices you're willing to bet $5 on. Now you have to pick an answer. Why do we even need to talk about this? Why can't you just pick whichever one you feel like when the time comes?

The answer to these questions is that if you don't come into the test with a plan, you'll rely on your impression to select an answer choice, and if you do that, you risk falling into a trap. The test writers know that everyone who takes their test will be guessing on some of the questions, so they intentionally write wrong answer choices to seem plausible. You still have to pick an answer though, and if the wrong answer choices are designed to look right, how can you ever be sure that you're not falling for their trap? The best solution we've found to this dilemma is to take the decision out of your hands entirely. Here is the process we recommend:

Once you've eliminated any choices that you are confident (willing to bet $5) are wrong, select the first remaining choice as your answer.

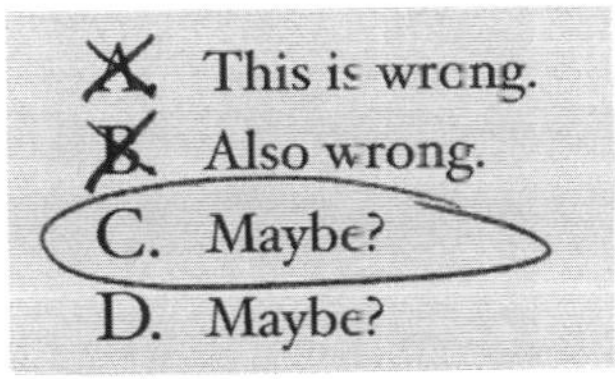

Whether you choose to select the first remaining choice, the second, or the last, the important thing is that you use some preselected standard. Using this approach guarantees that you will not be enticed into selecting an answer choice that looks right, because you are not basing your decision on how the answer choices look.

This is not meant to make you question your knowledge. Instead, it is to help you recognize the difference between your knowledge and your impressions. There's a huge difference between thinking an answer is right because of what you know, and thinking an answer is right because it looks or sounds like it should be right.

Summary: To ensure that your selection is appropriately random, make a predetermined selection from among all answer choices you have not eliminated.

Test-Taking Strategies

This section contains a list of test-taking strategies that you may find helpful as you work through the test. By taking what you know and applying logical thought, you can maximize your chances of answering any question correctly!

It is very important to realize that every question is different and every person is different: no single strategy will work on every question, and no single strategy will work for every person. That's why we've included all of them here, so you can try them out and determine which ones work best for different types of questions and which ones work best for you.

Question Strategies

☑ Read Carefully

Read the question and the answer choices carefully. Don't miss the question because you misread the terms. You have plenty of time to read each question thoroughly and make sure you understand what is being asked. Yet a happy medium must be attained, so don't waste too much time. You must read carefully and efficiently.

☑ Contextual Clues

Look for contextual clues. If the question includes a word you are not familiar with, look at the immediate context for some indication of what the word might mean. Contextual clues can often give you all the information you need to decipher the meaning of an unfamiliar word. Even if you can't determine the meaning, you may be able to narrow down the possibilities enough to make a solid guess at the answer to the question.

☑ Prefixes

If you're having trouble with a word in the question or answer choices, try dissecting it. Take advantage of every clue that the word might include. Prefixes can be a huge help. Usually, they allow you to determine a basic meaning. *Pre-* means before, *post-* means after, *pro-* is positive, *de-* is negative. From prefixes, you can get an idea of the general meaning of the word and try to put it into context.

☑ Hedge Words

Watch out for critical hedge words, such as *likely, may, can, often, almost, mostly, usually, generally, rarely*, and *sometimes*. Question writers insert these hedge phrases to cover every possibility. Often an answer choice will be wrong simply because it leaves no room for exception. Be on guard for answer choices that have definitive words such as *exactly* and *always*.

☑ Switchback Words

Stay alert for *switchbacks*. These are the words and phrases frequently used to alert you to shifts in thought. The most common switchback words are *but, although*, and *however*. Others include *nevertheless, on the other hand, even though, while, in spite of, despite*, and *regardless of*. Switchback words are important to catch because they can change the direction of the question or an answer choice.

✓ Face Value

When in doubt, use common sense. Accept the situation in the problem at face value. Don't read too much into it. These problems will not require you to make wild assumptions. If you have to go beyond creativity and warp time or space in order to have an answer choice fit the question, then you should move on and consider the other answer choices. These are normal problems rooted in reality. The applicable relationship or explanation may not be readily apparent, but it is there for you to figure out. Use your common sense to interpret anything that isn't clear.

Answer Choice Strategies

✓ Answer Selection

The most thorough way to pick an answer choice is to identify and eliminate wrong answers until only one is left, then confirm it is the correct answer. Sometimes an answer choice may immediately seem right, but be careful. The test writers will usually put more than one reasonable answer choice on each question, so take a second to read all of them and make sure that the other choices are not equally obvious. As long as you have time left, it is better to read every answer choice than to pick the first one that looks right without checking the others.

✓ Answer Choice Families

An answer choice family consists of two (in rare cases, three) answer choices that are very similar in construction and cannot all be true at the same time. If you see two answer choices that are direct opposites or parallels, one of them is usually the correct answer. For instance, if one answer choice says that quantity *x* increases and another either says that quantity *x* decreases (opposite) or says that quantity *y* increases (parallel), then those answer choices would fall into the same family. An answer choice that doesn't match the construction of the answer choice family is more likely to be incorrect. Most questions will not have answer choice families, but when they do appear, you should be prepared to recognize them.

✓ Eliminate Answers

Eliminate answer choices as soon as you realize they are wrong, but make sure you consider all possibilities. If you are eliminating answer choices and realize that the last one you are left with is also wrong, don't panic. Start over and consider each choice again. There may be something you missed the first time that you will realize on the second pass.

✓ Avoid Fact Traps

Don't be distracted by an answer choice that is factually true but doesn't answer the question. You are looking for the choice that answers the question. Stay focused on what the question is asking for so you don't accidentally pick an answer that is true but incorrect. Always go back to the question and make sure the answer choice you've selected actually answers the question and is not merely a true statement.

✓ Extreme Statements

In general, you should avoid answers that put forth extreme actions as standard practice or proclaim controversial ideas as established fact. An answer choice that states the "process should be used in certain situations, if..." is much more likely to be correct than one that states the "process should be discontinued completely." The first is a calm rational statement and doesn't even make a definitive, uncompromising stance, using a hedge word *if* to provide wiggle room, whereas the second choice is far more extreme.

⊘ Benchmark

As you read through the answer choices and you come across one that seems to answer the question well, mentally select that answer choice. This is not your final answer, but it's the one that will help you evaluate the other answer choices. The one that you selected is your benchmark or standard for judging each of the other answer choices. Every other answer choice must be compared to your benchmark. That choice is correct until proven otherwise by another answer choice beating it. If you find a better answer, then that one becomes your new benchmark. Once you've decided that no other choice answers the question as well as your benchmark, you have your final answer.

⊘ Predict the Answer

Before you even start looking at the answer choices, it is often best to try to predict the answer. When you come up with the answer on your own, it is easier to avoid distractions and traps because you will know exactly what to look for. The right answer choice is unlikely to be word-for-word what you came up with, but it should be a close match. Even if you are confident that you have the right answer, you should still take the time to read each option before moving on.

General Strategies

⊘ Tough Questions

If you are stumped on a problem or it appears too hard or too difficult, don't waste time. Move on! Remember though, if you can quickly check for obviously incorrect answer choices, your chances of guessing correctly are greatly improved. Before you completely give up, at least try to knock out a couple of possible answers. Eliminate what you can and then guess at the remaining answer choices before moving on.

⊘ Check Your Work

Since you will probably not know every term listed and the answer to every question, it is important that you get credit for the ones that you do know. Don't miss any questions through careless mistakes. If at all possible, try to take a second to look back over your answer selection and make sure you've selected the correct answer choice and haven't made a costly careless mistake (such as marking an answer choice that you didn't mean to mark). This quick double check should more than pay for itself in caught mistakes for the time it costs.

⊘ Pace Yourself

It's easy to be overwhelmed when you're looking at a page full of questions; your mind is confused and full of random thoughts, and the clock is ticking down faster than you would like. Calm down and maintain the pace that you have set for yourself. Especially as you get down to the last few minutes of the test, don't let the small numbers on the clock make you panic. As long as you are on track by monitoring your pace, you are guaranteed to have time for each question.

⊘ Don't Rush

It is very easy to make errors when you are in a hurry. Maintaining a fast pace in answering questions is pointless if it makes you miss questions that you would have gotten right otherwise. Test writers like to include distracting information and wrong answers that seem right. Taking a little extra time to avoid careless mistakes can make all the difference in your test score. Find a pace that allows you to be confident in the answers that you select.

⊘ Keep Moving

Panicking will not help you pass the test, so do your best to stay calm and keep moving. Taking deep breaths and going through the answer elimination steps you practiced can help to break through a stress barrier and keep your pace.

Final Notes

The combination of a solid foundation of content knowledge and the confidence that comes from practicing your plan for applying that knowledge is the key to maximizing your performance on test day. As your foundation of content knowledge is built up and strengthened, you'll find that the strategies included in this chapter become more and more effective in helping you quickly sift through the distractions and traps of the test to isolate the correct answer.

Now that you're preparing to move forward into the test content chapters of this book, be sure to keep your goal in mind. As you read, think about how you will be able to apply this information on the test. If you've already seen sample questions for the test and you have an idea of the question format and style, try to come up with questions of your own that you can answer based on what you're reading. This will give you valuable practice applying your knowledge in the same ways you can expect to on test day.

Good luck and good studying!

Organizational Behavior

Neglect Framework

The exit- voice- loyalty- neglect framework is one approach to understanding how job dissatisfaction impacts an organization. The exit- voice- loyalty- neglect framework is a theoretical construction designed to clarify the results of employee job dissatisfaction. The exit- voice- loyalty- neglect framework involves four responses which are compared along two continuums, delineated as constructive/ destructive and active/ passive. As the framework's name suggests, the four responses include exit, voice, loyalty and neglect. Exit refers to employee actions undertaken in the service of leaving the company, such as looking for a position in another company, being interviewed and turning in a resignation. Voice categorizes attempts to improve working conditions through communication. Examples include suggestions for improvements and making managers aware of problems. Loyalty is found when employees defend an organization in the light of criticism and believe that the organization will address and improve problematic situations. Neglect is the term used for situations that have progressively deteriorated due to passivity. Examples of neglect include tardiness and increased errors.

Research Designs

No single research design is perfect for all situations, and all must give something up to focus more deeply in another direction. Studies that result in a wealth of data are not useful in drawing generalities. Highly controlled variables result in studies with ideal rather than realistic results. Research that seeks high precision, high control, or generalizability is more costly to run.

Five Most Frequently Used Types of Research Design

Research design falls into five common types; case study, field survey, field experiment, lab experiment, and aggregate quantitative review. Case studies are in- depth narrative analyses of an individual or group, based upon information gathered most often from observation and supported by documents, records, interviews and other resources. A field survey delineates a field of focus from which standardized and easily quantifiable information is gathered via questionnaires or interviews. A field experiment is undertaken in one or more actual organizations, which results in realistic data, high validity, but a lack of control of external variables. Of all the models, it is the most costly. A laboratory experiment creates a non-natural environment where independent variables are tightly controlled and responsible for changes in the dependent variables. Aggregate quantitative reviews consider a variety of studies on a particular focus, discards those not meeting certain conditions, and applies meta-analysis to quantitatively synthesize the data.

Correlation Coefficient

Correlation coefficient is a research term that addresses the nature of the relationship between two variables or more. A correlation coefficient is represented as a number between negative 1 (-1) and positive 1 (+1); this number represents the strength of the relationship between the variables. A correlation coefficient of -1 represents a perfect negative relationship between the variables. A negative relationship is one in which a variable increases as the other decreases. Two variables whose relationship directly causes them to vary equally, is expressed as a positive number. Sometimes variables vary for reasons that have no relationship to one another. In this case, the correlation is expressed as a zero. It is important to note that the correlation coefficient demonstrates the strength of correction only; a higher number does not indicate cause.

Goal-Setting Theory

Goal- setting theory falls into the category of cognitive approaches, while reinforcement theory is behaviorist in nature. Motivational theories based in cognition begin with the premise that an individual's action is a result of thought, meaning the cause of action is internal. Motivational theories based in behaviorism begin with the premise that action is largely in reaction to environment; the cause of action is external. Goal- setting theory bases its suppositions on internal motivation by hypothesizing that the actions of an individual are the result of that individual's intended purpose or desired outcome. Goals can best be achieved when individuals see their value in terms of their own purposes. Reinforcement theory finds consequences of behavior in the past will inform similar behavior in the present. Positive consequences reinforce the likelihood a behavior will be repeated. Unadulterated reinforcement comes down to a stimulus which results in a response, bypassing thought and choice altogether; in this approach, emotion, perception, and expectations do not determine action.

Study of Organizational Behavior

The study of organizational behavior has historically taken a closed systems position. The current approach is comparatively open. Previously, the study of organizations' function was concerned with streamlining strategies to increase efficiency. This closed system approach prioritized the organization's continual development, seeing it as a machine rather than as a collection of complex, evolving relationships between its various human and nonhuman components. In fact, all organizations are impacted both by the interrelationships of human members as well as by factors external to it. Because these influences could not be absolutely measured or controlled, they were ignored; people were regarded as mechanical elements operating the organization's machine. The open system approach currently in favor regards all human and structural elements as mutually influential. Such influence can come from within, as through employees; other influences are cultural, economic or social in nature. In this model, just as the organization is influenced and changed by individuals, an individual can likewise be changed through relationship to the organization.

Closed System Viewpoint

While the closed system point of view has been superseded by a more open approach, its contributions remain. The closed system viewpoint in the study of organizational behaviors, while insufficient unto itself, has contributed important theories regarding organizational structure and design. A closed system is, by its nature, less permeable to external influences and therefore, more structurally rigid than an intrinsically more flexible open system. While rigidity can be seen as an inability to absorb change, from another perspective, because it is self contained its architecture is sounder. This permits a close examination of overall design without concern that a frail structure will collapse under scrutiny. Knowledge requires a grid or frame work within which its shape and meaning can be understood. The closed system approach was an essential first step, in that its sole focus was on formal organizational systems that have become the foundation upon which open systems strategies and viewpoints depend.

Other Disciplines

The field of organizational behavior is rooted in research and theories found in the fields of psychology, social psychology, sociology and anthropology. The field of psychology has been the source for information and strategies concerned with individual behavior. Theories concerned with learning, personality and therapeutic applications such as conflict management have provided organizational behavior with useful models. Social psychology marries psychology with sociology, and its contributions include studies about change, attitude, communication, trust, and group behavior. Sociology's focus is on groups in relationship to culture. Its major contributions to the field of organizational behavior can be found in studies about workplace culture, theories about social structures in organizations, technology, conflict behaviors, and communication. The field of anthropology studies human behavior by examining societies through time, and has made numerous contributions in clarifying how and why core values, points of view and behaviors are different in different societies or belief systems.

Types of Organizations

An organization is a group of two or more individuals working toward a set of shared goals in a manner that is coordinated, methodical and ongoing. Organizations can serve a primarily social-cultural purpose, such as schools, museums, churches; a primarily economic purpose, such as manufacturing and service industries, retailers, and banks; or exist in order to maintain order within a larger social grouping, such as military, government and police organizations. Because organizations are composed of human beings, these organizational types have considerable overlap. For example, a school adheres to schedules both within its own field of reference (staggered lunch periods and managing hallway travel are two instances), as well as outside its own needs (school holidays coincide with bank and business holidays). A hospital is both a business that schedules staff, negotiates salaries, and markets its product, as well as a community organization offering community education programs.

Managers

Without managers, most types of organizations would fall into inefficiency, confusion and ultimately, failure. One of the responsibilities of managers is to keep employees progressing toward common goals at an efficient pace. They are responsible for clarifying goals that will be assigned to an individual or a team (planning); deciding the order in which jobs must be accomplished so that goals will be reached in a timely manner, as well as for delegating these jobs to individuals (organizing); inspiring employees with their own enthusiasm for a project, smoothing rough patches and resolving significant conflicts within a team or between the team and external factors (leading); and for overseeing action, activity and efforts so that what they are accomplishing is, indeed, what they were intended to do. In this last role, the manager must also step in immediately should it become clear that an activity has devolved away from its initial purpose, and return all players back to the original goal (controlling).

Three Managerial Roles

The manager's roles can be broadly seen as consisting of three interconnected parts, which are the interpersonal, the informational and the decisional. Managers must assume distinct but interrelated roles required by the range of responsibilities the position demands. The interpersonal role might require a manager become a figurehead undertaking ceremonial, legal or social duties; a leader who inspires and guides; or a liaison who keeps track of contacts that provide information or assume necessary tasks. The Informational role consists of a monitor who is an organization 'brain' receiving all types of information; a Disseminator with the job of passing along information to the proper individuals; or a Spokesperson who carries information about the organization such as plans, activities and outcomes to people outside the organization. The Decisional role is one in which the manager can act as an Entrepreneur seeking opportunities within the organization's environment; a Disturbance handler responsible for correcting and easing negative activities; a Resource allocator making major decisions or a Negotiator who represents the organization's best interest.

Shift in Business School Focus

Prior to the late 1980s, business school focus was on technical features of management, limiting curricula to accounting, finance, quantifiable statistics and economics. The study of human behavior and teaching communication skills was not considered central. Business schools emphasized accounting, finance, quantifiable statistics and economics until the late 1980s. While these areas are important to successful organizations, they are not fully sufficient. Managers are successful to the degree their ability to communicate with, inspire and discipline employees invites employee loyalty, motivation and responsibility. Regardless of the economy, the percent of highly desirable employees is low. Attracting and retaining employees with high ethical and professional degrees of commitment bolsters the success of any organization. While offering such employees bonuses, health and other benefits might draw them to the job in the first place, it is job quality, personal satisfaction and a supportive work environment that keeps them there. The manager's job is to create and constantly nurture such an environment, attending to changes that must be made as the organizational needs and ideals evolve, and implementing those changes with clarity and shared vision.

Managerial Effectiveness and Promotion

As reported in a 1988 study by Luthans and associates, effective managers who demonstrated high quality performance and had committed employers were not promoted as quickly as those who prioritized networking over any other task. The study looked at traditional management (decisions, planning, and controlling); human resource management (inspiring, training, disciplining); communications; and networking. Managers who were considered effective but did not receive rapid promotions focused 19% of their time on traditional activities, 44% on communication, 26% on human resource management and 11% networking. In comparison, managers who climbed the professional ladder the quickest prioritized networking at 44%, deemphasized human resources management to a mere 11%, gave communication 28% of their time and allocated 13% to traditional roles. While average managers divide their time relatively evenly between the four categories, effective managers prioritize communication and limit networking and successful managers prioritize networking to nearly 50% of their efforts.

Studying Organizational Behavior

The physical sciences can be studied by applying absolute, consistent frameworks in the form of scientific laws. The study of organization behavior is a social science and lacks such a measurable, unchanging frame because human nature is constantly in flux. The study of human behavior falls under the category of a social science and, as such, cannot be approached using identical measures as those applied to physical science such as volume, weight, distance, or mathematical formulas. Still, it is possible to limit the range of variables that can complicate such a study. Human conduct is not absolutely predictable, but it is predictable to a degree that becomes more substantial when certain variables are considered and controlled. Conditions that arise in the environment—situations, relationships and so forth, are contingents that must be considered, and for this reason are called contingency variables. Contingency variables, once identified, must be considered in order to arrive at an accurate prediction or analysis. For example, the general concept employees prefer strong leadership appears to be an absolute, but given a contingent situation such as employees who are also business partners, it may not apply.

Changes in Employee Profiles

Changes in the face of workplace employees in the last two or three decades reflect social, economic and cultural changes in the country as a whole. Two of the biggest changes in employee profiles in the last 25 years are the growing number of women and people of color, together with increasing pressure from global competition. Corporate downsizing has led to less loyalty in the workers who remain (since they fear their own loss of employment) and a collateral increase in the use of temporary employees. It must be recognized that in itself, change is neither good nor bad but simply an event. While the development of the global marketplace has indeed put pressures on American industries and businesses that have caused them to share the pressure with their employees, this situation has also demonstrated the need for flexibility, creative approaches, cooperation and respect. Women and people of color have traditionally been required by their social positions to be flexible, to consider the greater good rather than the individual, and to accept necessary change with grace.

Model

A model offers a general form or ideal that can be used to consider phenomena in the shared world. One organizational behavior model that can be applied to a variety of organizational types considers three levels of focus in which the organization's systems level is dependent upon the behaviors of the organization's group, which in turn depends upon individual behaviors within the groups. In this model, the individual is the foundation, and organizational systems are the highest level. Dependent and independent variables must be taken into account at all three levels. Variables that are dependent or affected by other aspects must be identified, understood or predicted. Independent variables are those that are self- regulating (that is, outside the influence of the organization) and that suggest themselves as probable causes of alterations or adjustments in independent variables. Both dependent and independent variables are found at the individual, group and systems levels.

Collecting Data

For social scientists, the type of data that is collected is to some degree subjective, impossible to exactly measure, or somewhat obscured. The process of data collection, for a behavioral scientist, is less transparent than for a physical scientist who relies upon absolute, measurable determinants. Data can be collected in a number of ways portray the employee with relative accuracy. The most open ended strategy asks for a personal narrative that discusses the employee's positive and negative attributes, performance and ideas concerning how this employee can improve his performance. A Critical Incidents Report asks the writer for specific, delineated occurrences of efficient or unproductive behaviors. Graphic Rating Scales requires an assessor to rate specific aspects such as experience, knowledge, quality of work, and teamwork on a numeric scale. Behaviorally Anchored Rating Scales (BARS) marry a critical incident approach with a graphic rating scale; the assessor evaluates specific behaviors by rating them along a continuum. Forced Comparisons ask an evaluator to rate specific aspects of an employee's work relative to that of others.

Forced Comparison

Forced Comparisons are relative measures which attempt to locate an employee's particular performance within the whole organization. There are two distinct approaches, although both depend upon relative relationships and not absolute ones. Group Order Ranking provides a predetermined set of classifications which are ranked in terms of one another; that is, a set is either placed below or above another set along a continuum, usually in terms of a percentage. An employee might rank in the highest 10% in one type of skill, and in the bottom 70% for another. Alternatively, individual skills might be grouped into a coherent whole so that, for example, an employee might rank in the top 90% in terms of a broad overview. Individual Ranking arranges employees from most to least productive; here it is assumed that a consistent and unchanging degree of difference exists between the bottom two employees as between the top two.

Data Regarding Employees' Attitudes

Managers need to be aware of employee attitudes, because they can influence job satisfaction and the efficiency with which employees work. Supervisors need to be aware of the attitudes their employees hold concerning work because those attitudes are a strong indicator of job satisfaction and involvement, and can predict workplace efficiency. Organizations most often use attitude surveys to gather information and determine changes that need to be made to the work environment to improve the company culture. Typically, an attitude survey is composed to a number of statements regarding various aspects of the employees' work experiences. Employees indicate, using a rating scale, the degree to which they agree or disagree with statements. The statements are only useful if they are very specific. For example, asking an employee to rate the truth of the statement "I feel appreciated at my job" will not yield as much useful information as the statement "My supervisor praises my work when it is exemplary" or "the company fairly rewards my efforts with bonuses or praise."

Measuring Attitudes

At best, measuring attitudes is an imprecise business; however, some strategies have proven to more reasonable accurate. The two most widely used strategies for gathering information and measuring job satisfaction are single globe rating and a summation score that is composed of numerous aspects of the job. The single globe rating is by far the more general, and consists of posing a single general question to a group of workers and asking them to select a point on a scale that reflects the degree to which they agree or disagree. An example question is "How appreciated do you feel by your coworkers?" Employees can respond by selecting anything between "completely unappreciated" to "fully appreciated". A summation of job facets approach asks employees to rate their feelings regarding several key job elements on a standardized scale. These numbers are then averaged to determine overall job satisfaction. Interestingly, research into the two methods reveals that they are about equal in their ability to accurately demonstrate employee job satisfaction.

Summation of Job Facets Assessment

A summation of job facets assessment focuses on a number of important job characteristics to determine employee satisfaction. Among these key characteristics are the tasks employees are required to accomplish, the financial rewards for doing a satisfactory job, job promotion, the supervision an employee receives, and the employee's relationship with co- workers. Each of these facets is important to understanding job satisfaction. While both types of assessment are considered to be equally valid, the summation of job facets assessment will help a manager address specific areas where job satisfaction is not high enough in order to improve employees' overall satisfaction. The less complicated single globe rating can be completed very quickly, and is useful to managers who need to general indication of employee satisfaction. Should this indication suggest problems, the manager can turn to a summation of job facets review in order to determine what areas need correcting.

Neutral Objects Satisfaction Questionnaire

A number of instruments designed to examine an individual's job satisfaction with consideration given to personality. One, the Neutral Objects Satisfaction Questionnaire, has been widely used. The Neutral Objects Satisfaction Questionnaire is used to determine the relationship between an individual's personality satisfaction with a job. The Neutral Objects Satisfaction Questionnaire presents participants with a series of specific items and asks the participant to indicate whether he is satisfied with, neither satisfied nor dissatisfied with, or dissatisfied with the item. The items offered reflect a broad range, and are not specifically tailored to the participant's position at work.

For example, a Neutral Objects Satisfaction Questionnaire might ask if a participant is satisfied, neither satisfied nor dissatisfied, or dissatisfied with the way his neighbors maintain their properties, the quality of family television, or the layout of the local grocery store. An individual's job satisfaction is due in part to personality. Individuals who are generally positive, enjoy life and are enthusiastic are happier at work than are individuals who are negative, easily irritated by people, objects or situations or lack enthusiasm.

Organizational Behavior Research Multidisciplinary in Nature

The field of organizational behavior is a wide and varied one. It draws many of its tools from other disciplines, including both the hard and social sciences. Among the methods that are concerned with gathering information based upon specific qualities are ethnographic studies which are typically accomplished by examining case studies as well as through direct observation; linguistic studies which consider specialized language, subtextual messages, and patterns of communication; and semiotics, which is concerned with uses and meanings of signs and symbols in specific environments. Quantitative statistical methods include time dependent analysis, which looks at data that falls within a temporal boundary; non parametric statistics, in which outcomes don't require that subjects are found within particular parameters; multiple regression, which uses multiple variables to predict value in a single variable; and analysis of variance (ANOVA) models, which uses statistics to method for producing comparisons between two means or more that are coincident.

Individual Processes and Characteristics

Perception

Perception, which is how direct experience is interpreted by the perceiver, is sculpted by aspects within the perceiver, within the thing itself, and within the situation. The mental or emotional attitudes of the perceiver, motivation, specific interests, past experiences and expectations combine into one strand of influence on the total perception. The second strand is found in that which is being perceived and includes the degree to which it is unknown or unfamiliar, the background against which it is perceived, how near (physically or psychologically) to the perceiver it is, how similar it is to something known or previously perceived, the quality of movement, sounds, aromas and visual and other sensory details it exhibits. The third strand is concerned with the environment in which the perceiver and the perceived are held, and includes the work setting, the social/emotional setting, and the perceiver's relationship to time within both.

Development of Personalities

Speculation abounds about how personality forms. Some scientists believe that heredity plays the biggest part, while others attribute environmental forces as more formative. The heredity approach takes the position that personality originates in biological and psychological inheritance. Several studies focusing on identical twins (who share identical genes) separated at birth does suggest strong heredity contribution toward personality development. These studies demonstrate that two people who have never met one another (and in some cases, didn't know a twin existed) exhibit an extremely high proportion of shared personality traits with have more in common with the missing twin than they do with the siblings who shared the same family environment. Other social scientists believe personality is formed as a response to cultural, familial and social norms, expectations and values; they point to ways an individual's behaviors change depending upon the situation. Ultimately, personality is most likely the result of both.

MBTI

The Myers Briggs Type Indicator (MBTI) uses multiple choice selections to assign a place in each of four categories. The first category is Extraverted vs. Introverted. Extroverts are outwardly directed, assertive, communicative and social, while introverts are timid and reluctant to draw attention. The next category is Sensing vs. Intuitive. Individuals in the Sensing category are detail oriented, practical and comfortable with a structured routine. Intuitives forsake detail and take a broader, more inclusive view, trust their instincts, and depend upon intuition. The Thinking vs. Feeling category describes Thinkers as dependent upon logic and common sense, while those in the Feeling category work through emotional pathways and by consulting with their own ethical standards. The final category, Judging vs. Perceiving, places those who prefer to be in control in an organized, structured world in the Judging category, and those who are spontaneous and willing to bend in the Perceiving category.

Problems with the Myers Briggs Type Indicator

The Myers Briggs Type Indicator has enjoyed considerable popularity as the most used personality evaluation tool in the world. Using four categories with two possible assignments within each, the BMTI reduces the range of human personality to a total of 16 personality combinations. On one hand, this streamlining of what could be seen as a chaotic, unstructured mass of potential seems like a godsend to many managers. On the other, it can be said that the MBTI's greatest strength is also its greatest weakness. Because each category contains only positions, and because those positions are polar opposites, one well- considered criticism is that the MBTI forces conclusions that are artificial rather than natural. With the MBTI, for example, an applicant is uses either logic or personal feeling as a guide to behavior in certain situations (Thinking vs. Feeling); however, certainly there are individuals who use a combination of the two.

Big Five Model of Personality Studies

The Big Five Model of personality studies extraversion, agreeableness, conscientiousness, emotional stability and openness to experience, to appreciate distinctions in personality. Extraversion describes a degree of sociability, assertion and friendliness. Extroverts invite themselves into conversations, have a wide range of interests, and make friends easily, while introverts are far more comfortable in their own company and shy away from the limelight. Agreeableness refers to how willing to cooperate and trust a person is; a low scorer in this area is likely to be hostile, emotionally distant and won't work well with others. Conscientiousness explores a degree of responsibility, dependability, persistence and organization. Emotional stability is the spectrum between anxiety, nervousness, sadness and insecurity (negative emotional stability) and tranquility, confidence, and security. The final category of the Big Five Model of personality considers openness to experience. The category considers degree of creativity, sensitivity and curiosity exhibited by an individual.

Other Personality Tests

Personality tests that are properly administered can be a boon in terms of locating the right employee for a particular position. In addition, when managers understand the personality types with which they are working, it can help them to understand, clearly communicate with and manage individuals on their team. Three personality measures include self report surveys, observer rating surveys, and projective measures such Rorschach Inkblot Test or the Thematic Apperception Test (TAT). Self report surveys are the most commonly used type of personality measure. Because self report surveys are completed by the individual who is being assessed, a fairly wide margin of error must be considered in that the individual might attempt to manipulate results by answering to make the best impression. Observer rating surveys are completed by an outside observer Projective measures ask a participant to find meaning in abstract form or a story in a series of identifiable images.

Important Terms

Core self evaluation is a personality characteristic that affects organizational behavior, and refers to the degree to which individuals believe themselves to be responsible, able, and in control of outside elements. Individuals with low core self evaluation are judgmental about their own ability, and see themselves as pawns lacking control over outside situations. Core self evaluation involves the relationship between that individual's self esteem and locus of control.

Locus of control refers to the how much at the center of control a person feels. Internals assume that what happens to them is entirely in their control, while externals think they have no control over their own destinies.

Self esteem can be defined as the degree to which an individual feels himself to be valuable; self esteem is also concerned with self love. Low self esteem causes a person to seek approval from the outside rather than finding it in herself.

Machiavellianism

Machiavellians (Machs) are ultimately practical. They get what they desire because they will dislodge any obstacle in the way. Machs at the high end have no interest in becoming emotionally intimate at work, and often in life; feelings are useless to a Mach, and even threatening. Any action is acceptable to a high Mach as long as it produces the expected results. Mach purists are cunningly manipulative, brilliant salespeople as long as they can do their convincing face to face. They are less successful in environments that require indirect communication, such as by phone or internet. They most easily gain control in groups when emotional or ethical issues occupy the attention of low Machs, and prefer not to be saddled with too many stipulations, rules and requirements. If they feel so bound, some Machs will feel justified in breaking the rules, regardless of how clear and inflexible those rules are.

The Rorschach Inkblot Test

The Rorschach Inkblot Test and the Thematic Apperceptions Test are both projective measures tests that invite subjects to explain visual or linguistic catalysts that are cryptic, unclear, mysterious or vague. A subject's responses, evaluated by clinicians, theoretically reveal fundamental personality traits. Differences between the two are in form. The Rorschach Inkblot Test offers a series of abstract inkblots about which the subject determines meaning.

TAT

The Thematic Apperception Test, also called the TAT, was used by McClelland to assess the achievement, affiliation and power needs demonstrated by his test subjects. The Thematic Apperception Test offers test subjects a group or set of visual pictures (photographs or drawings) that can be interpreted in a wide variety of ways. Test subjects study the pictures, and then create a 'story' to explain the situations they find portrayed. It was McClelland's contention that test subjects would use the story telling scenario as a platform to display their own individual needs. Using scoring techniques that have been determined to produce consistent results, the test subjects were scored on their apparent need to achieve, to belong, and to possess power. The score offers an indication of the type of work in which a particular test subject would be most likely to find particular challenge and satisfaction. The Thematic Apperceptions Test (TAT) offers a series of realistic visual representations, such as photos or drawings. The subject writes a brief story about each visual representation, which are then read and categorized by a clinician. While in theory it seems reasonable that creating meaning from abstraction might be useful in determining personality type, in practice these types of tests are often not useful, because the clinicians, though trained, are basing their results on their own perceptions and projections and vary greatly from person to person.

Personality Trait Combinations

Possible personality trait combinations are infinite, but some individuals so fully occupy one trait to the degree they can be said to become it. Narcissists seem to be in love with themselves, and expect everyone else to feel the same way. They believe they are entitled to whatever they want, and that rules and regulations are important only for others. They arrogantly assume they have all the answers and have no interest in hearing or integrating another point of view. Interestingly, research indicates that narcissists demand extreme and constant adoration because they have no true sense of self whatsoever; without constant attention from the outside, a narcissist ceases to exist on the inside. Once attention is forthcoming, narcissists reflect and magnify it in order to project themselves into the world. Narcissistic personalities are convinced they are more capable, more efficient and better liked than supervisors report them to be.

Self Monitoring

High self monitors are well aware that every situation is, in fact, a relationship between their inner beings and external forces. They are highly adaptive, willing to adjust their expectations of both themselves and others, and can, at times, seem to be two (or more) distinct people with different value systems, different behaviors and different attitudes. This trait bases itself on practical concerns, and as such, can be desirable for certain organizational roles. High self monitor work performances tend to be better rated and the trait is common to leaders; however, high self monitors are also more committed to their own eventual success than to that of the organization. They can make excellent managers; able to adjust their strategies to fit the situation or the individual at hand without feeling they've sacrificed their personal values. Organizations that prioritize strong, unchanging ethical standards, however, are not a good fit.

Example of Proactive Personality

Eloise, 48, was laid off. Despite her age, she decided to pursue a career teaching swing dance. She offered free workshops, and enlisted her students to help her find jobs at dance camps and clubs. Within two years, Eloise was making more money doing what she loved than at her job.

Eloise exhibits a proactive personality with a high core self evaluation willing to take risks. Despite her age, Eloise saw the layoff as an opportunity. While there was no job listing for 'swing dance instructor', Eloise knew she was capable of becoming a respectable teacher. Networking her sphere of influence and asking for help from others were steps that allowed her, within the six months her previous job continued to support her, to decide that going out on her own was a realistic goal. Proactive personalities such as Eloise act rather than react. They find opportunity where others find limits, and if they don't, they create it. Eloise was willing to take a calculated risk with everything she had—six months of support. An internal with a high locus of control, Eloise was able to convince others what she already knew; her ability matched her self belief.

Value System

A person's values are the beliefs she holds to be absolute, that certain types of behavior or ways of being are essentially morally and ethically superior to any other beliefs. Values do not change over time or in response to situations. A value system ranks values by deciding where on a scale of unimportant to highly important a particular value should be placed relative to other values held by the same individual. The collective value- portrait that emerges can be a means toward understanding personality. Terminal values are those held by a person as goals she hopes to achieve before her life ends. Instrumental values are the behaviors she deems morally acceptable or superior in her pursuit of her terminal value goals. Values are abstract ideas that symbolize how an individual believes things should be, and include ideals such as freedom, respect, honesty, hard work, acceptance and justice.

Values, Attitudes and Motivation

Values and value systems typically develop when individuals are young. They reflect both what the child is taught as 'right', and what is deduced from relationships with the environment and other individuals as demonstrating moral correctness. Values reflect culture, whether it is the culture of a family, of a community or of a nation. One's value system becomes the grid through which experience is perceived, and is the ground upon which attitudes are built. Values are subjective and infused with feeling, rather than objective and dependent upon reason. We rarely question our values, because we believe them to be universally true. Therefore, the attitudes that rise from them are something we deeply identify with as well. Attitude largely determines motivation; we are motivated by what we believe an outcome will be; our attitude determines how we approach a task, and therefore contributes to our expectation of the end result.

Relationship Between Attitude and Job Satisfaction

Attitude is really an individual's point of view. It is the basis for expectation, and is largely formed by a combination of previous experience and deeply held values. Consider an employee who comes to a new job believing that working quickly is required in order to advance quickly. He holds this belief both because he learned as a child that meeting and exceeding deadlines earned praise, and because in a previous job he perceived the promotion of another employee as based upon that employee's measurable output. If the culture of his new organization is one that rewards thoughtful, high quality work over a greater quantity of lesser work, the employee will be disappointed and feel unappreciated. These feelings will not inspire the employee toward greater achievement, since doing more of what he perceives as valuable won't get him any farther. His motivation is affected by his attitude.

RVS

The Rokeach Value Survey created by Milton Rokeach is composed of two value sets, each of which contains 18 distinct value descriptions. The first set is collectively referred to as terminal values. Terminal values are those objectives an individual hopes to achieve in her lifetime. The second set of values is collectively referred to as instrumental values. Instrumental values represent actions or behaviors that the individuals believe are acceptable ways to accomplish the terminal values. The Rokeach Value Survey can be useful to managers who are looking at potential hires to determine if they will be a good fit. The Rokeach Value Survey can also be useful when two or more groups holding differing sets of ideals are negotiating toward a common goal. Exploring one another's belief systems allows insight into the degree of importance a value might be, and how much leeway to expect in negotiation that touches on that particular area.

Person Perception

Person perception refers to how people perceive one another through observation. Because people have interior, obscure reasons for many of their actions, observers project judgments in order to understand, often without realizing they are based at least as much on the observer's own assumptions. Attribution theory hypothesizes that a specific observed behavior's apparent meaning changes dependent upon what an observer has assigned to it. Assigned meaning is largely dependent upon whether the observer believes it was caused by something internal or external. When an observer assigns an internal cause to a behavior, she believes that the person under observation is in control of it. Conversely, a behavior that is believed to be externally caused is seen as not under the control of the observed person. An employee who is frequently out sick will be seen more sympathetically if the supervisor believes a serious illness, rather than frequent hangovers, is at fault.

Attribution Theory

The characteristics of distinctiveness, consensus and consistency are the touchstones upon which attribution theory is built. The first characteristic, distinctiveness, examines the degree to which someone is perceived by another as manifesting a particular negative behavior in a variety of differing situations. If the behavior is considered typical, the observer will assign it as an internal attribution and consider it a 'fault' that is within the individual's control. If it is atypical, there is a greater chance it will be seen as externally caused, and therefore as forgivable. Consensus can be described as the degree to which others in the same situation respond in the same way. If so, the cause is considered external and therefore more easily forgiven. The final category is consistency. If the individual habitually responds to the same situation with the same negative behavior, the greater the chance it will be seen as within her control to change it.

John Holland's Theory of Personality Job Fit

John Holland's theory of personality job fit describes six personality types. He suggests that job satisfaction depends to a large degree upon whether or not a specific personality type is working at what he calls a congruent job or one that correlates to that personality's qualities. His typology of personalities includes Realistic, Investigative, Social, Conventional, Enterprising and Artistic personalities. Realistic individuals enjoy physical participation that demands coordination, skill and physical exertion. Investigative personalities are happiest when thinking, comprehending and organizing ideas or information. Social individuals are at their most content when helping others, while Conventional personality types thrive in situations that prize structure, rules and clarity. Enterprising personality types enjoy verbal involvement, having influence over others and gaining control. Artistic personality types are most comfortable in situations that are not structured by rules but are, instead, open ended, even ambiguous, and that invite creative play, curiosity and interpretation.

HOLLAND'S VOCATIONAL PREFERENCE INVENTORY

Holland developed the Vocational Preference Inventory questionnaire to standardize a type of personality profile. The questionnaire consists of 160 job descriptions which are shown to participants. Participants select jobs they feel are especially interesting and those that hold no interest or are abhorrent to them. These choices are then plugged into a hexagonal model which suggests that each personality type might be satisfied with jobs assigned to adjacent categories, but would not fare well in occupations situated diagonally opposite on the hexagonal model. This research strongly indicates that when a job type is taken by a congruent personality, job satisfaction will be relatively high and turnover will be relatively low. When a job type is filled by the most incongruent personality (such as an Artistic in a conventional job) the fit will be very uncomfortable, the job satisfaction very low, the quality of work unacceptable and the turnover very high.

Among Geert Hofsteade's five values is power distance. A culture with a high rating in power distance means its members accept and tolerate exceptional inequalities of wealth and power. Individualist cultures prioritize the rights of individuals, while collectivist cultures focus on fostering the well being of groups. High masculinity cultures are those in which strictly distinct roles are played by men and women, and men have more power. High femininity cultures are ones in which there is little or no distinction between male and female roles, and power is equality distributed between men and women. Uncertainly avoidance refers to the degree of structure a people are most comfortable with; citizens of a culture with many rules, laws and regulations are typically more unsettled in unclear situations than citizens of low scoring uncertainly avoidance. Long term orientation cultures honor traditional values and frugality. Short term orientation cultures respect transformation above all else.

It is not surprising that certain of the five values cluster with others. For example, The United States ranks 38th out of 52 countries in power distance, 1st in individualism, and 27th in short term orientation. The United States is a relatively new country, built on individualism and whose citizens focus on the present. Countries with individualistic orientations are generally relatively intolerant of high power distance values and do not accept inequalities in power and wealth. Australia's power distance rank is 41st, and it places 2nd in individualistic orientations. Conversely, countries like Malaysia, Panama and the Philippines were at the top of the power distance scores and in the low- middle to bottom of individualistic orientation. Generally, wealthier countries tend toward the lower end of the power distance value; Asian cultures reflect a strong bias toward long term orientation; and Latin American countries exhibit a high tolerance for uncertainly.

Hofsteade's original statistics looked at over 100,000 employees of a single company in 40 countries. While this was the first global study of its kind, the fact that IBM employees were the only participants in a study specifically focused on work place values almost certainly contained some bias in that values of the work place are not always identical with cultural values in general. Additionally, a considerable lapse of time occurred between Hofsteade's original statistical gathering and the completion of the harvest of current statistics. In those decades, apartheid in South Africa came to an end, China has gained global power, the former USSR has fallen, and Islam has experienced considerable growth as a world religion. As well, because the social sciences lack the precision of physical science, Hofsteade was forced to make certain judgments regarding the categorization of data that another researcher might disagree with.

GLOBE

The Global Leadership and Organizational Behavior Effectiveness research program (GLOBE) was established in 1993 as an ongoing study of national cultures and leadership. 825 groups and organizations contribute data that has been gathered in 62 countries. GLOBE defines cultural differences in nine areas, a number of which incorporate Hofsteade's distinctions described in his seminal research on cultural tendencies within specific nations. GLOBE dimensions include the areas of assertiveness; future orientation; gender differentiation; uncertainly avoidance; power distance, individualism/collectivism; in group collectivism; performance orientation; and humane orientation. It is not GLOBE's intention to supersede Hofsteade but rather to expand his initial work by continuously updating the position each of the 62 ranked countries currently holds in each category. Culture, like life itself, is continuously evolving. GLOBE recognizes that as populations change through time or migration, culture redefines itself. The GLOBE survey provides a frame whereby such change can be identified and measured.

Nine distinctions GLOBE

GLOBE's areas of differentiation include assertiveness; future orientation; gender differentiation; uncertainly avoidance; power distance, individualism/collectivism; in group collectivism; performance orientation; and humane orientation. Assertiveness describes how challenging, competitive and firm a culture expects its citizens to act. Future orientation refers to cultural support of activities like future planning, postponing personal rewards, and investment of time or money. Gender differentiation is as Hofsteade described masculinity v. femininity. Uncertainly avoidance, power distance and individualism/ collectivism are also as Hofsteade delineated them. In group collectivism examines the degree to which a culture applauds membership identification in intimate groups, such as family, as well as the degree of pride its members take in family and work organizations. Performance orientation is the degree of respect a culture awards a group for improvement and excellence in its performance. Finally, humane orientation describes the degree of respect a culture shows individuals for just action, altruistic behavior, compassion, and generosity.

Organizational Cultural Profile

Some other job fit models ask respondents to rate values on a scale from not important to absolutely important. Because most people would identify most values as highly desirable (to themselves, or because they know the culture considers them such), it is more difficult to get a true picture. The Organizational Cultural Profile requires respondents to consider each of the 40 possible characteristics, and provides chart composed of 40 boxes in which to place them. Eight items can be ranked at the same level, which is 'neither characteristic nor uncharacteristic'. Seven items move toward more characteristic, and seven in the direction of less characteristic. Four items are permitted a step closer to more characteristic, and four closer to less characteristic. Three take the next step toward more or less characteristic and only two items each are permitted as most and least characteristic. Because respondents are limited, they are forced to be selective.

OCP

Among the traits listed in the Organizational Cultural Profile (OCP) are adaptability; stability; innovation; assuming individual responsibility; seeking opportunities for professional development; being willing to freely share information; being generous with praise for excellent work performance; creating and maintaining work friendships; being guided by a clear, unchanging philosophy; being competitive; being willing to take risk; willingness to follow rules; working well within a team; making or seeking decisions that reflect fairness; being tolerant of others' points of view; focusing on results; willingness to put in overtime; maintaining a good reputation; remaining calm in crisis; and able to work independently. A real estate company might prize an ability to work independently, maintaining a good reputation willing to take risks, being competitive and adaptability as highly desirable traits, but have less use for other traits, such as being generous with praise for excellent work performance; creating and maintaining work friendships; or being guided by a clear, unchanging philosophy.

LEARNING

The three most influential theories of changes in behavior brought about by learning include classical conditioning, operant conditioning, and social learning. Pavlov's famous experiments with conditioning marked the beginning of classical conditioning theories. Classical conditioning views learning as an unexpected passive reaction to a neutral stimulus that has become associated with a strong stimulus and then replaces it. Operant conditioning takes the position that behavior is a learned response to a consequence of action. Advocated by B.F. Skinner, behavior that is applauded will be most likely to reoccur, whereas behavior that is ignored or penalized is much less likely to reoccur. According to this position, emotional or intellectual responses don't contribute to a learning a behavior. Social learning theorizes that while direct experience is important, as important is observing the outcomes of other people's actions. Culture models behavior through the family, the community, and the media.

CONDITIONED AND UNCONDITIONED STIMULI AND RESPONSE

Classical conditioning theories of learning came into vogue at the turn of the last century via Ivan Pavlov's well known canine salivation experiments. Pavlov measured the amount of saliva produced when his canine subjects were shown a piece of meat, and the amount shown when he rang a bell. Initially, only the meat caused considerable salivation. Over a period of time, Pavlov combined giving the meat to the dogs directly following the ringing of a bell. Eventually, the dogs began to associate the sound of the bell with the expectation that meat would be forthcoming, and salivated as much as they previously had at the beginning of the experiment. Pavlov's experiment involved an unconditioned stimulus which consistently caused a natural unconditioned response; this was then combined with a conditioned, or artificial, stimulus which had previously held a neutral meaning to the dogs but which, through association, became a conditioned response.

SOCIAL LEARNING THEORY

Social learning theory accepts the premise of operant conditioning that learned behaviors are the result of consequences, and adds another dimension, that of behaviors learned through observing the actions or consequences of actions another person experiences. The degree to which a model is believed to be influential, according to social learning theory, is determined by attentional processes, retention processes, motor reproduction processes and reinforcement processes. Attentional processes focus on how fully the model attracts and holds attention. Consistently available models that hold considerable importance to the observer and are attractive on some level (not necessarily a physical one) are most likely to attract focused attention. Retention processes explores the depth of a model's influence based upon how well the observer retains memory of the action when the model is not present. Motor reproduction processes are the observer's imitation of observed action, and reinforcement processes are positive reinforcements that encourage similar action.

SHAPING BEHAVIOR

Shaping behavior can best be understood by imaging a manager as an artesian who is chiseling a piece of stone to fit into a stone wall. The manager mustn't chip away too much at once, because a fissure could result that would render the stone worthless. Chipping away too little, though, will result in a stone too large to be forced into the available space, and chipping away too much while avoiding a fissure will result in a stone that fits, but not tightly enough to hold. Managers must work as carefully on shaping an individual's attitudes and actions to fit the cultural 'wall', and it must be done without damaging the individual's potential worth. Positive and negative reinforcement in combination with punishment and extinction are four strategies used by successful managers in the craft of shaping employee behavior to best meet the needs of a particular organization.

MANAGERIAL TOOLS IN SHAPING BEHAVIOR

Positive reinforcement, negative reinforcement, punishment and extinction are the four most commonly used managerial tools in shaping employee behavior. Positive reinforcement is used in organizations as diverse as the military and homeless shelters, and involves reinforcing a desirable behavior by rewarding it with praise, attention, or a bonus of some sort. Negative reinforcement is responding to an unpleasant behavior by withdrawing an unpleasant response, such as ignoring a screaming child rather than screaming back. Punishment takes negative reinforcement a step further, by responding to negative behavior by creating an unpleasant situation in order to teach the negative action's source that such behavior is not acceptable. Extinction is the removal of all support, whether positive, negative or neutral, from an undesirable behavior so that it will weaken and eventually be eliminated.

REINFORCEMENT THEORY

In reinforcement theory, a behaviorist approach to learning, a continuous reinforcement schedule supports desirable behavior by rewarding it each time improvement is gained. An employee who upsets coworkers by telling others what to do and how to do it cannot be expected to abruptly cease this behavior. However, a manager who discusses the problem with the employee, then observes the employee moving toward the goal of controlling her own problems instead of others', will achieve the most rapid success by awarding the employee each time she moves closer to the ultimate goal. If she allows a team member to complete an idea without interrupting, a positive statement from the manager reinforces the behavior so that next, the employee might be willing to allow another team member to comment on the idea before she joins the conversation. Every attempt at positive change is noted and commented upon with continuous reinforcement.

INTERMITTENT REINFORCEMENT

Four types of intermittent reinforcement fall are categorized as either ratio or interval schedules. Fixed ratio schedules offer rewards (praise, bonus, advancement or another type) when a pre-established number of activities are completed. A trainer who receives a bonus every time 15 of her students pass a certification exam is inspired by a fixed ratio schedule. A variable ratio schedule offers a reward in proportion to a degree of success. A Realtor who receives 3% commission on homes sold below $200,000, and 3.5% on homes sold between $200,000 and $400,000 is responding to a variable ratio schedule. Fixed interval schedules establish rewards that are given at pre- established times, such as a paycheck every Friday. A variable interval schedule involves rewards given unpredictably through time. For example, a teacher who awards bonus points to students for reaching goals on occasion but not always is practicing a variable interval schedule.

BENEFITS AND DRAWBACKS TO REINFORCEMENT SCHEDULES

Continuous reinforcement schedules are predictable and result in rapidly learned new behaviors. However, because the learner learns not only the behavior but to rely upon the reward, when the reward ceases to be continuously offered the behavior will often vanish quickly. Fixed interval reinforcement results in rapid disappearance of the learned behavior when the reinforcement ceases, because learners regard the reward as something they've earned, not as motivation. Fixed interval reinforcement keeps employees working steadily, but not brilliantly. Variable interval reinforcement results in stable, above average performance that is slow to disappear; the employee never knows when excellence will be rewarded. Fixed ratio reinforcement results in consistent effort rapidly resulting in high quality work, but it vanishes rapidly after the reward is withdrawn. Variable ratio reinforcement results in a consistently high level of performance that is considerably slower to vanish when awards are not forthcoming.

Attitudes

Attitudes can be seen as declarations of judgments regarding other people, situations, or things. Although they are often presented as simple, direct and rational, attitudes are actually complex, multilayered and based upon feeling. Attitudes are evaluative judgments about people, situations or objects. They are complex in nature; social scientists have traditionally considered them in terms of cognitive components, affective components and behavioral components. An attitude's cognitive component is the element of opinion present in the attitude's overall constitution. It includes those absolute values the holder believes to be morally right, and becomes the foundation for the attitude's affective component. The affective component is the emotionally charged layer in an attitude. It is what the belief makes the holder feel. The behavioral component is the factor concerned with the behaviors that are manifested due to the affective element. It is nearly impossible to divorce cognitive from affective components; what one thinks about a person, situation or thing informs how one feels about it. Managers are primarily concerned with the behavioral component of an attitude, because that will have the greatest impact on the organization.

Complexity of Attitudes

Part of the complexity of attitudes is the relationship people have with their own. Most people will say that attitudes are based on values, and change very little with time. Human beings believe that their attitudes are identical with their values, and that they remain largely consistent through time. In fact, people have a strong need to behave in ways that reflect the attitudes they have espoused. Attitudes are not the same as values, although they can be affected by them. They aren't as deeply rooted, nor felt to be as inviolate. If a situation needs a change in attitude, most people will adjust to meet that change as long as it doesn't violate deeply held values, and they can justify the change as based upon new information. For example, a young woman in love with a charming, irresponsible and ultimately unfaithful man might tell her friend that marriage kills passion. When the boyfriend leaves her to marry another woman, her attitude is likely to change; she now believes passion is false love, and that true love doesn't die.

Cognitive Dissonance

While it is not always easy to change an attitude to suit new circumstances, it is easier than living with an attitude that has been exposed to the owner as false. The concept of cognitive dissonance popularized by Leon Festinger theorized that when the cognitive component of an attitude is sufficiently challenged by a behavior or when two attitudes cannot logically coexist, the incompatibility creates an uncomfortable dissonance within the individual, who responds by adjusting the belief element of his attitude so that he can maintain equilibrium. There are degrees of dissonance; all people have a personal comfort level in which they justify minor behaviors they know are wrong. Cognitive dissonance becomes problematic when the degree of importance is high, when the individual believes she has little control over the cause of dissonance or when the benefits to accepting the dissonance are high. Cognitive dissonance that develops over something unimportant doesn't create a terribly uncomfortable disproportion. A person who believes she has no control will resist changing attitude. Strong dissonance can be more easily calmed when large rewards are at stake.

Variables

It is logical to assume that behavior is by and large based upon attitudes, but research indicates that moderating variables must be considered when predicting future behaviors based on current attitudes. Moderating variables that must be taken into account in order to accurately predict future behaviors based upon current attitudes include the attitude's degree of significance, how specific it is, how accessible it is, what social or peer pressures come into play, and if the individual has personally experienced the attitude in question. Significant attitudes are those that spring from deeply held beliefs or strongly impact a group the individual feels part of; the individual is less likely to make a cognitive shift to compensate. Attitudes that are time or location specific are less easy to alter; an employee who has purchased a home near work intends to stay. Attitudes that are frequently expressed are more easily accessible, and are less likely to be sacrificed. Social pressure can cause highly uncomfortable cognitive dissonance that requires a shift in attitude. Attitudes based on abstract ideals rather than personal experiences are easier to alter.

Self Perception

Self perception theory holds that behavior influences attitude as much as attitude influences behavior. Many studies support the position that attitude influences behavior. Self perception theory holds that conversely, behavior also influences attitude. According to the precepts of self perception theory, an individual who is asked her attitude about something she doesn't have a strong opinion regarding will deduce what her attitude is based upon how she sees herself as having behaved, rather than using an attitude to direct her behavior. For example, someone who is asked if she believes everyone should vote may decide that the reason she has never voted is because there is little difference between parties, and express her conclusion as though it were a long held attitude. The fewer the individual's experiences concerning the attitude in question and the less specific that attitude is, the more likely it is that the person who is expressing that attitude will infer it based upon her actions, according to self perception theory.

Organizational Behavior

The field of organizational behavior must, of necessity, limit the number of attitudes it studies in the work environment. List and briefly define the job related attitudes that are considered of major importance. Because even a single individual can hold a vast multitude of attitudes, the field of organization behavior is forced to limit its studies of attitude to the ones most relevant to work. The three job related attitudes considered of major importance are job satisfaction, job involvement, and organizational commitment. Job satisfaction refers to the degree to which an employee values the work and the work environment's characteristics. Someone with high job satisfaction is less likely to leave and more likely to work efficiently and productively. The second major attitude, job involvement, is the degree to which employees feel themselves to be valuable to the organization, in combination with the degree to which they perceive the work they do as part of their identity. The third major attitude is organizational commitment. Organizational commitment encompasses employees' shared appreciation with the organization's goals together with their desire to remain as part of the organization.

Psychological Empowerment

Psychological empowerment is important not only to an individual's sense of self, but to contributions an empowered employee can make to an organization. Psychologically empowered employees believe their contributions to the workplace are necessary and valued; that others believe them to be competent; and that their superiors respect their work ethic as well as their professional decisions. Psychologically empowered employees make more positive contributions to the company culture, are less often absent from work, and tend to stay with job. One of the manager's key roles is to help employees feel psychologically empowered. There are a number of strategies managers utilize to increase their feeling of empowerment. For example, notifying workers about decisions that need to be made and asking for their ideas and concerns; praising or otherwise rewarding excellent work in the presence of other people; and allowing a degree of autonomy with tasks an employee is capable of undertaking without supervision, all help boost employee self confidence, lead to a sense of psychological empowerment and ultimately benefit the organization as well.

Organizational Commitment

When employees feel a sense of organizational commitment, they are proud of their association with it and share organizational goals. Organizational commitment, in which workers share the goals of an organization and want to continue being associated with it, can be reduced to three characteristics. Affective commitment is an attachment to the group's values that is based in feelings of pride, respect and worth. Continuance commitment involves an employee's perception of financial benefits of remaining with the company. These include not only salary, but health care, sick time, holidays, vacation time, and retirement. Normative commitment describes the degree to which an employee feels duty bound to stay with the company or organization for reasons that are morally or ethically based; often, this type of commitment is connected to a special project the employee feels responsible for. A strong normative commitment is achieved when an employee feels uniquely suited to some portion of her work assignment, and believes that leaving the company would negatively impact team mates or her supervisor.

POS

Perceived organizational support (POS) looks at how much value an employee feels the organization places on her efforts, as well as the amount of concern she believes it has for her over all welfare. An individual tends to ascribe appreciation and concern to an organization that, in her estimation, rewards her efforts justly, appreciates her contributions to the decision making process, and demonstrates this support through managers who reward her efforts with appreciation. Employee engagement is a relatively new term that refers to the employee's degree of participation with, satisfaction about, and enthusiasm toward her work. The concept of employee engagement has only recently begun to appear in the literature about organizational behavior. While researchers have not yet determined how employee engagement can determine job satisfaction, job involvement, or an employee's commitment to the organization, it can be assumed that an employee who is engaged with her work will bring a higher degree of dedication and greater effort.

Job Satisfaction

Job satisfaction is the most important employee attitude in terms of its impact on an organization's best interests. Most researchers agree that among employee attitudes, job satisfaction has the greatest impact upon an organization's best interests. A manager can predict employees' efficiency, or anticipate the rate of job turnover using job satisfaction data if employee attitudes have been accurately measured. Measuring employee attitude toward job satisfaction is a complex process. On the surface, a job can seem to be primarily about the tasks an employee is charged with. A waitress takes and delivers food orders. A journalist investigates and writes. A professor teaches. However, jobs are in actuality more complex, and involve numerous less obvious elements. All jobs include some degree of communication with coworkers and supervisors, fitting into company culture, achieving company expectations, following company regulations, tolerating the physical aspects of work conditions, financial rewards and other benefits. Without considering all these aspects, a manager cannot gain a true picture of employee job satisfaction.

Relationship between Job Satisfaction and Customer Satisfaction

The relationship between job satisfaction and customer satisfaction in service industries is an important one. While it may seem obvious that an employee who deals with customers all day long can affect those customers' sense of satisfaction, the relationship works in reverse, as well. Happy customer service representatives create happier customers; happier customers encourage customer service representatives to enjoy their work. Service industries depend upon customer loyalty. The greatest investment in terms of both time and money is in attracting those customers in the first place. Retaining them is the payoff. An employee with low job satisfaction is less likely to respond to a customer's needs, particularly when those needs seem unreasonable or excessive. A happy employee will be more willing to go the distance. Customers respond with loyalty when they feel their needs are being taken seriously. Happy employees stay in jobs longer, as well, giving more experienced service.

Job Satisfaction and Employees' Timely Presence at Work

On the surface, a clear relationship between job dissatisfaction and employee absenteeism can be seen. Employees who don't get along well with co- workers, who feel unappreciated by a supervisor, or who are simply not happy because the personality/ job fit is wrong, will obviously be more likely to decide a minor cold is really the flu. It must be noted, however, that a number of other situations contribute to employee absenteeism. For example, employees for a company that offers a generous number of sick days typically take more sick days off than employees who are docked pay beyond a limited number of absences. Where the relationship between job satisfaction and absenteeism comes into play is narrow, but very clear. Less satisfied employees will take advantage of situations that can be perceived as beyond their control such as bad weather or a sick child, and miss work. More satisfied employees will not.

Job Satisfaction to Self- Employment

Many workers dream of the day they own their own business. Not having to answer to a supervisor, not being forced to follow rules and regulations set forth by a company, and not having to deal with company culture that rubs the wrong way are all motivating factors. Some people like the idea of working from home, either because it's comfortable or because it makes child care easier. Others like the idea of establishing and owning a business outside the home. Not surprisingly, a study of self- employed and business employed people in 23 countries (Benz and Frey) indicates that self-employed people do, indeed, exhibit higher job satisfaction across the board. However, their degree of job satisfaction is only slightly greater; while self- employment alleviates certain stresses, it produces other ones. Budget concerns, daily decisions with major impact, and the weight of responsibility means self- employed job satisfaction is only slightly greater.

Selective Perception

In the work place, as in life, people must consciously or unconsciously decide what stimuli to pay attention to. Selective perception is a necessary response to a world brimming with infinite stimuli. Nobody can process the vast amount of detail in even a single experience. Instead, people select certain stimuli to pay attention to and ignore or push the rest to the background where its contributions are diminished. People tend to pay greater attention to things, people or situations they identify with. This attention is unconscious, but nonetheless selective. A mother with young children will notice how another parent at the park disciplines an unruly child; a teenager with a new car will notice similar cars on the highway. Halo effect is the term given to the human tendency to take a single personality feature and base a complex (and not very accurate) impression of the whole person upon it. Contrast effect means the tendency to assess someone's characteristics by comparing where they rank in that characteristic against others.

Perceptual Short Cuts

Because people must repress or ignore considerable information contained in any experience in order to concentrate on that which is most useful to their purposes, they rely upon several types of perceptual short cuts. One of these is projection. When supervisors or employees, are in situations where decisions must be made quickly, based upon little more than an impression, perceptual short cuts step in. In projection, one person judges another based upon psychologically perceived similarities. A team leader who sees himself as down to earth and serious might misidentify a new volunteer as being very much like him, when in fact the volunteer simply feels intimidated by the new situation and is responding to his insecurity with solemnity. Projection becomes problematic when it replaces reality with a misconceived idea. Another problem with projection is when its use fails to recognize the vastness of personal and cultural difference.

Stereotyping

Stereotyping begins with mentally assigning an individual to a group. While all individuals are individual, unique, and distinct, it is also true that all individuals are also members of many groups. We belong to families, friendship groups, work groups, interest groups, religious groups, historical groups. Decisions are really problems that must be resolved within a framed time period. When a manager must resolve a problem within a team or department, he will include certain shortcuts in his process because he must. One shortcut is to decide what group an individual belongs to, and proceed toward a solution based, in part, upon a perception of that group's characteristics. This practice becomes troublesome when the decision maker's perception of the group is either inaccurate, or when his perception is accurate but this particular individual represents an exception. In either of these cases, the decision is based on false information.

Interviewer Perception

A job interview is, by necessity, brief. The interviewer must rapidly form an impression based on a gathering of facts overlaid with the interviewer's perceptions. It is reasonable to say that all interviews result in faulty impressions, in that it simply isn't possible to get to know another person in a few short minutes. First impressions are the strongest, and studies have shown that once a first impression is made, it becomes embedded and often times over shadows later, equally valid pieces of information. This causes particular distortion when the interviewee reveals information that is taken in a negative light early in the interview, and is made even more complicated when the interviewee then meets with a number of people in succession, or with a panel of interviewers. What one interviewer perceives through projection, stereotyping, expectations or through other distortions won't always be what another perceives.

Performance Expectations

Considerable research supports the idea that we accomplish what we believe others expect us to accomplish. Interestingly, what we are told to expect of others also influences perception to the degree that we base our impressions of them more upon inherited expectations than upon our own immediate and direct experiences. A fourth grade teacher who tells her fifth grade counterpart that she will have particular difficulties with a certain student, will arrive the first day of class with a set of preconceived notions that bias her expectations. Consequently, the child she is predisposed to expect trouble from will find himself in trouble sooner than he otherwise would; her expectations cause her to be more highly sensitive to it. The child learns that his teacher expects trouble from him, and with this as <u>his</u> inherited performance expectation, he fulfills her expectations and in the process, makes them his own.

Fundamental Attribution Error and Self-Serving Bias

Fundamental attribution error is a type of preconception that distorts attribution. A supervisor in a position that requires her to pass judgment on an employee will more readily assume a failure to perform was caused by internal (and therefore controllable) rather than external causes. Even when a supervisor is told that an employee's failure to fulfill expectations was due to circumstances beyond control, a fundamental attribution error in perception could make doubtful. In contrast, a self- serving bias is a distortion which is used by individuals or groups to assert that certain accomplishments were purely the result of internal factors over which they had complete control, and to take credit for the success to a greater degree than is actually deserved. Self- serving bias can also refer to the tendency of individuals or groups to excuse their own failures by ascribing them to external factors outside their control.

Decision Making

Everyone is forced to make many small and large decisions during the course of a lifetime. Some decisions are based wholly upon pleasure or desire, such as what restaurant to visit or what movie to see. Others are arrived at more thoughtfully, with numerous factors given consideration. The first thing to consider is that situations that require a decision contain a problem. The problem is the incongruity between a desired outcome and the way things currently stand. Making a decision that will resolve the problem requires considering possible alternative options, and selecting the best from among them. For those who have made many similar decisions in the past, the process typically becomes streamlined through practice. Others, however, must deliberate, considering all available information, rejecting what doesn't need to be addressed, processing the information that does and interpreting the results. Motivations that contribute toward decision making include recognition, reward, expectations, or punishment.

Creative People

Creative people are less likely to pattern themselves after other people. Creatives are open to a wide array of experiences, are independently minded, and feel certain of their abilities. Creative individuals perceive frustrating situations in the positive light of a challenge, and respond to any difficulties in arriving at goals with dogged determination. Independence and a determination to see frustrating circumstances as opportunities are enhanced by a creative individual's higher than average willingness to tolerate ambiguity and to take risks. Creative people believe themselves to be masters of most situations, and this internal locus of control results in useful self- perception. Creative individuals are often of higher intelligence than the norm; it is plausible to assume this is the case both because highly intelligent people are curious and deeply interested in ideas, and because creative people delight in looking at things or situations in the freshest, newest light possible.

Creativity in Problem Solving

The three component model of creativity is based on the hypothesis that creativity depends upon relationships between proficiency, creative thought, and intrinsic task motivation. Creativity is profoundly enhanced when an individual has a high degree of proficiency based upon depth of knowledge, experience, and capability. For example, it's unlikely someone who has never studied music could write a brilliant opera. Thinking creatively is both a habit and a talent. Creative thinkers use metaphor and analogy, finding something familiar within something very unfamiliar, as a means of problem solving. Creative thinkers are also playful, mentally if not physically so. Borrowing an idea from one field and playing with it to make it accommodate another can turn simply seeing a problem into envisioning a solution. Intrinsic task motivation is what compels and excites someone enough to delve into a project with full creative spirit, turning what is potential into something real and new.

MOTIVATION

It can be said that motivation is the most important characteristic of any organization.

Any organization, whether a volunteer, social, educational, governmental or business organization, needs to be constantly aware of the role motivation plays in the achievement of its goals. When employees hold values that are in line with organizational goals, morale is higher, resulting in increased productivity, better product quality and enhanced financial increase. Without motivation there is little chance employees will hold positive attitudes. Employees who approach tasks positively see workplaces problems as challenges with a solution, rather than obstacles too large to deal with. When turnover is high, productivity is on the downslide and goals out of reach, motivation is most likely the hero. Unmotivated workers waste time, allow redundancy in their work process, don't hold themselves accountable for inferior work, create discord with other employees and resign more readily than do workers impelled by motivation, costing the organization the time and expense required to locate and train a new hire.

PROCESS THEORIES

The three most important process theories of motivation are the expectancy theory, the equity theory, and the theory of goal setting. The foundation of expectancy theory is that an outcome must be perceived as both meaningful and highly likely to occur in order for an individual to feel motivated regarding a task. Equity theory finds motivation in fair treatment. When employees perceive that the rewards for their work, skills, talents and workplace attitude are in line with rewards others receive, they are satisfied that resources have been justly distributed and they are motivated to continue this relationship. The goal setting theory of motivation considers that higher performance levels are achieved when workers are motivated by specific and attainable goals. The more challenging the goal, the more important it is to include workers in setting it. Such participation amplifies a worker's degree of commitment, and commitment is highly motivating.

RESEARCH ASPECTS OF THE REINFORCEMENT THEORY OF MOTIVATION

According to the reinforcement theory of motivation, goals alone are not an adequate source of motivation, but need to be supported with reinforcers in the work place environment. Reinforcers can be looked at as positive outcomes of particular behaviors, and are most effective when they are immediately available, the clear consequence of a particular behavior, and authentic. Reinforcing steady goal- oriented progression by maintaining a high expectation of performance will efficiently lead to attaining the goal and rising above it. Reinforces are a type of behavior modification that utilizes rewards and punishments to reinforce certain desirable or undesirable actions. According to reinforcement theory, there are multiple ways to react to a situation; individuals typically choose a response that was successful in the past. This is known as the law of effect, which states that in the absence of contingencies, satisfactory responses to stimuli are strengthened, and responses that result in discomfort will be abandoned.

VROOM'S MODEL OF THREE VARIANTS WITHIN THE EXPECTANCY THEORY

Expectancy theory has become widely accepted as a motivational theory; nearly all the field research supports its hypotheses. According to expectancy theory, the outcomes of behaviors must be perceived by the actor as both meaningful and probable to effect an individual's motivation in regards to a specific task. The model Vroom developed presents three primary ideas; valence, instrumentality and expectancy. Valence refers to the degree of intensity with which an individual desires a specific outcome to occur. To be sufficiently motivating, the valence must be positive, meaning the individual has a high desire for that specific outcome. Instrumentality refers to how well the first level result will gain the desired second level result, which is reward. Vroom's third variant is expectancy. Expectancy here describes the degree to which the individual is convinced a specific behavior will lead to a specific outcome at the first level.

Popularity of Vroom's Expectancy Theory

The three variants model holds that the concepts of valence, instrumentality and expectancy can be variably combined to result in enhanced motivation. Vroom hypothesizes that the relationship of these three parts will also determine the degree of motivation. The performance- outcome expectancy links positive incentives directly and immediately to the degree of performance success. These incentives can be recognition, monetary bonuses, or other types of reward; it is important that the manager in certain that the particular reward being offered is one that is highly desired. Managers can depend upon the effort- performance expectancy to increase motivation as well. Providing training designed to improve workers skills, abilities or understanding will at the same time enhance workers' belief that increased effort on their parts will result in higher quality performance; and higher quality performance as described by the performance- outcome expectancy, is motivating because it will be rewarded.

Equity Theory

The first of the interconnected propositions of equity theory is Proposition 1. Briefly described, proposition one states that individuals will characteristically attempt to take full advantage of their outcomes. Outcome in this case as described as what remains after cost (which may or may not be financial) is deducted from rewards. Proposition 2 states that (1) groups that develop an acceptable system for equitably distributing resources to its members, will maximize their collective reward. (2) groups praise members who are fair in their treatment of others and penalize those who are not. Proposition 3 holds that individuals involved in unfair relationships will feel distress in direct proportion to the degree of inequality. The fourth proposition claims that individuals who find themselves involved in an imbalanced association will try to eradicate their discomfort by re-establishing equality with determination in direct proportion to the degree in which they feel uncomfortable.

Proposition 1 of the Equity Theory of Motivation

Proposition 1 of the equity theory of motivation assumes that people put their own interests ahead of those of others. Assuming this to be true, they will take any opportunity to enhance their own personal gains. One argument against this hypothesis is that people in intimate relationships, such as a parent and a child or a couple who are in love do not behave in a manner that could be called self- interested. In these cases, according to the argument, relationships must be seen as based upon mutual concern. This contradiction can be defended against by considering that there are differences in 'exchange orientation', and that keeping a cost/ benefits score is highly subjective. Individuals who carefully monitor output and intake are more likely to see themselves as slighted. Another argument is that people in a highly intimate relationship see themselves as one unit; in this case, what benefits one, benefits both.

Maslow's Highly Influential Hierarchy of Needs

Maslow's Hierarchy of Needs describes five levels of basic human needs. Once basic needs are satisfied, a second, higher level of needs emerges. Beyond this second tier of needs is yet another level which does not reveal itself until the needs of the second tier are satisfied, and so on. The needs on the bottom level of Maslow's Hierarchy are physical in nature; the higher one climbs, the closer to self-actualization the needs become. Once an individual has satisfied a lower level of need and ascended to a higher one, the lower level needs lose priority. If these lower needs aren't being met, a temporary reversal will occur only as long as necessary to permit the individual to return to the higher level. The bottom level, or 'deficiency needs' are physiological needs, followed by security needs, friendship/ love needs, and esteem. Only when these needs are satisfied do self-actualization needs become apparent.

First Four Levels of Needs

According to Maslow, physiological needs are the foundation of the hierarchy, those most basic to life. They include air, food and sexuality. The next level involves safety. Safety includes individual security, financial security, national safety, future security, insurance against risks, and wellness. Social needs at the third level is composed of emotional relationships, including romantic, parent-child, sibling –sibling, friend, community and other intimate bonding. Relationships offered by religious groups, shared interest groups, work, sports teams, and even gangs are considered in this layer. Lacking sufficient social satisfaction causes anxiety and depression. The layer Maslow refers to as esteem includes both how the individual sees herself and how others see her. An individual who is satisfied in regard to this layer feels accepted and worthy. She feels she contributes to her groups, and that her contributions are appreciated. Only when these levels are achieved can the final level, self- actualization, be realized.

Herzberg's Motivation-Hygiene Theory or Two- Factor Theory

Herzberg's model, like Maslow's, requires the satisfaction of basic needs as well as of higher level psychological needs, such as praise for accomplishment, being promoted, and doing work that is fulfilling. Herzberg's Two- Factor Theory goes on to suggest job satisfaction and dissatisfaction result from unrelated sets of causes. An increase in one does not therefore cause a decrease in the other. Individuals are satisfied when the kind of work being undertaken satisfies status, achievement, self- worth, and competency needs. When these psychological supports are missing, however, it does not necessarily follow that job dissatisfaction will result. The characteristics the lead to job dissatisfaction include critical assessments, technical difficulties, unhappy work place relationships, and an unsatisfactory working environment. This means successful managers must look at the nature of a job to increase worker satisfaction, and must also concentrate on the environment in terms of work policy, procedures, and supervision.

Two- Factor Theory is Concerned with the Relationship Between Job Satisfaction and Motivators Intrinsic to the Job

The Two- Factor theory hypothesizes that job satisfaction is the result of motivators that are inherently found within the job itself. Work that requires creative thinking and personal responsibility while simultaneously challenging an employee to reach beyond her comfort zone is highly motivating. When that work is rewarded with praise, incentives, or recognition, or when that employee realizes a degree of personal growth that has developed out of it, she will feel job satisfaction. On the other hand, the satisfaction of hygiene factors do not add to job satisfaction, but merely keep employees from experiencing job dissatisfaction. Hygiene factors are found in the work environment and include such things as future security, benefits, the work place culture, and company policies. Job satisfaction must be continuously nurtured. Increased ability must receive increased responsibility; employees are most motivated when the job requires their top level of skill and respond with their greatest effort.

McClelland's Acquired Needs Theory

McClelland's acquired needs theory suggests that the needs of an individual develop through a period of time and are honed by that individual's experiences. These needs fall under the categories of achievement, affiliation or power needs, and they influence both an individual's motivation regarding a task and how effective that person will be. For those whose achievement needs are higher, situations in which they will be challenged to do extremely well but that lack a high degree of risk, are motivating. Achievers work well in autonomous situations, as well as with people who likewise want to achieve. People who register an increased need for affiliation seek relationships that are tranquil and peaceful. They are comfortable following policy and fitting into the workplace culture. They thrive when a task involves close interaction. An individual can need personal power, or control others; or institutional power in which they organize and lead, and are often managers.

CONTENT-BASED THEORIES OF MOTIVATION

While Maslow proposed five levels in his Hierarchy of Needs, Alderfer believed the middle levels of Maslow's model had overlapping characteristics. Alderfer described three levels of needs instead, specifically Existence, at which level individuals are focused on and motivated by basic needs; Relatedness, at which level individuals are focused on and motivated by intimate personal relationships; and Growth, at which level individuals develop a impelling need for personal development. Both Maslow's Hierarchy of Needs and Alderfer's ERG models are organized as hierarchies and visually represented as pyramids, and both begin with base survival needs, progress through relationship needs, and find self- actualization at the highest level. Alderfer, however, suggests that multiple needs can simultaneously motivate, and that movement to a higher level is not absolutely dependent upon full satisfaction at the lower level. Alderfer's ERG model is more easily applied to account for cultural differences in motivation, by permitting the needs order flexibility.

ALDERFER'S ERG THEORY

Alderfer's Existence, Relatedness and Growth model demonstrates that employees are likely to experience the need to fulfill numerous motivators at the same time. A manager can most efficiently inspire employee motivation by focusing on the right combination of motivating factors. Alderfer's Existence, Relatedness and Growth theory also describes situations in which higher-order needs become frustrated, resulting in an individual retreating to an earlier, baser level in order to amplify a satisfaction that may come from a lower need, but can more easily be satisfied. This frustration- regression principle has implications in terms of work place motivation; an employee who is not inspired and challenged (motivated) is unlikely to remain in place, treading water. According to Alderfer's model, the employee is more likely to regress to an earlier, lower level, substituting increased satisfaction at that level for the frustrated satisfaction he was denied at a higher level.

GOALS

Goal acceptance refers to the degree an individual is willing to embrace an organizational goal as her own. When an employee identifies with an organizational goal, her commitment to achieving the goal is greatly enhanced. Conversely, an employee who strongly dislikes or disagrees with a particular goal will not be convinced to take ownership of it, and will (most likely unconsciously), be likely to attempt to sabotage it to some degree. Goal commitment refers to the degree to which an employee has a personal, vested interest in a collective goal being reached. If the collective goal is achieved, her personal interest is also satisfied. Goal difficulty means the degree to which a goal offers challenge and demands additional or extraordinary effort. Goal specificity refers to how clearly and accurately a goal is presented, so that it can be pursued. Goals that are precisely delineated have a considerably greater chance of being accomplished.

EMPLOYEE COMPENSATION

While a compensation package, a reward system, a flexible reward system and an incentive system are all means of compensating employees, they are also distinctly different. A compensation package is the sum total of every benefit that an organization gives to an employee. It can include the employee's salary, bonuses, incentives, health care, life insurance, vacation days, sick leave, awards and other real or ideal benefits the employee is given. A reward system is composed of individuals, organizational procedures, rules and regulations, decision making efforts and other organizational elements that are part of the allocation process by which employees receive goods in exchange for their efforts. A flexible reward system permits individuals to select a blend of compensations from a pool of possibilities. An incentive system is one which encourages exemplary performance from employees by offering a specific additional bonus for a particular level of achievement.

Cognitive Evaluation Theory

A job can have multiple intrinsic rewards. An employee might feel proud of her work, believe she contributes a great deal, knows she is deeply appreciated, or perform work at a level she knows is beyond expectation. Early motivational theories took the position that motivators that come from within such as a sense of responsibility, accomplishment, and competence operated separately from externally given motivators, such as an increase in salary, a promotion, recognition, or a working environment that is enjoyable. Cognitive evaluation theory suggests that when rewards are externally given in recognition of excellence in work, it diminishes the intensity of the previously felt intrinsic reward, and results in an employee who feels less satisfied rather than more satisfied. Some theorists suggest this is because previously, the employee felt an inner sense of control, but when the reward was moved to an external source, the control shifted as well.

Self-Concordance

The term self-concordance grew out of cognitive evaluation theory. It is concerned with the relationship between an individual's personal interests and core values, and his reasons for striving to achieve a particular goal. According to the principle of self-concordance, a person who is intrinsically attracted by the content of the goal or has core values that are in alignment with it, has a greater chance of achieving the goal because pursuing it produces a sense of challenge and pleasure that is satisfying. In fact, goals that are aligned with intrinsic values needn't even be achieved for the individual to feel satisfaction; just the process of attempting to reach the goal is enjoyable. At the same time, individuals asked to pursue goals who are driven by extrinsic motivators will be less satisfied than those driven by intrinsic motivators. This is true even when the individual reached the goal.

Cognitive Evaluation Theory

Cognitive evaluation theory does in fact consider extrinsic motivators to be less effective than intrinsic motivators. Not only are extrinsic motivators less motivating, but when intrinsic motivators are removed from the equation and replaced with extrinsic ones, the previous commitment to achieving the goal is undermined to some degree. A closer look yields a clearer understanding, however. When an employee is told what the reward will be for achieving the goal, she feels that it is already hers, as she intends to achieve the goal. She expects the reward as promised when the goal is achieved, but it ceases to be motivating since subconsciously, it already belongs to her. She begins to focus on the reward instead of on the goal. However, verbal rather than tangible rewards coming from an extrinsic source are, in fact, also intrinsically motivating and result in the employee continuing to focus on the task with renewed

Implications of Cognitive Evaluation Theory on Managers and on Employees

Cognitive evaluation theory's supporters point to research studies indicating the theory is a valid one. Detractors, however, believe the methodology used to gather data is flawed, and the theory is further compromised by inaccurate analysis of the findings. If cognitive evaluation theory is valid, it suggests that employees who want a job that is fully satisfying need to look beyond salary, benefits and company culture. They need to know themselves, understand their core values, appreciate their character traits and consider not only what the company can provide for them in terms of tangibles, but what they will derive in terms of intrinsic satisfaction and growth. To managers, cognitive evaluation theory suggests that goals will be best achieved when employees are intrinsically motivated. By creating goals that match an employee's interests, praising outstanding work, and offering opportunity for personal development and growth, greater commitment to the goals will be the likely result.

VARIABLES IN SETTING GOALS

According to Locke, a more developed sense of motivation and commitment result from establishing goals that are useful. However, goals that are implied, suggested or imprecisely stated do not inspire a similar peak performance. Instructing someone to do the best work they can, might seem like encouragement, but more often than not it leads only to frustration. Goals that clearly define what is expected, the time it should take, and what degree of effort should be spent give employees a clear sense of what they must do. Goals that are specific will enhance performance. Challenging goals inspire more effort from employees than do easily accomplished goals. Feedback is an essential piece of the goal- setting equation. Remaining silent and allowing an employee to proceed without being told how he is doing along the way has been demonstrated to result in a lower quality performance than offering feedback instead.

CONTRIBUTION OF EMPLOYEES TO GOAL SETTING

Some research shows that a superior quality of work is accomplished when employees help to shape goals. Other research suggests that employees reach a higher performance level when assigned explicit goals by their supervisor. It has been posited that involving employees in goal setting results in a sense of ownership and willingness to more readily accept the goal's requirements. Supervisors who assign goals without eliciting employee contribution get the best response when the goal's value and purpose are clearly stated. The lowest level of performance occurs when no sincere commitment has been made. Employees who don't understand the goal's purpose or importance, who haven't had it explained clearly, who did not help shape the goal, or who have a moral or ethical objection to it will lack passion for it. When employees simply don't care about the expected results of a task, they lack the desire to accomplish to the best of their abilities.

HIGH COMMITMENT TO GOAL SETTING

Commitment to a goal can be found in individuals who are unwavering in their desire to achieve, who are unwilling to lower their standards and who will persevere rather than abandon the goal if it proves difficult, because they have forged a personal relationship with it. Commitment to a goal is more likely when the individual knows she is capable of reaching it. More than ability is required; if she knows she is capable but doesn't personally care if she does or does not succeed, commitment is not in place. If she believes she is capable and also has a personal reason for wanting the goal to be achieved, the chances are much greater that she will succeed. Other elements that enhance a commitment to a goal include the goal being made public, the participant's locus of control being an internal one, and self- set goals in place of assigned ones.

STRESS

In recent years, psychologists and medical doctors have paid closer attention to the nature, causes and implications of stress, as well as to ways in which it can be alleviated. Stress has many possible causes. Too much pressure at work brought on by unrealistic goals or expectations, a single strongly negative event, financial and emotional personal problems, as well as physiological causes such as diagnosed or undiagnosed illness, depression or anxiety caused by chemical imbalance are all common sources of stress. Stress can manifest in a number of ways. For some, stress can not only be caused by physical anxiety, but can trigger high anxiety as well. Such an individual may experience a racing heart, sweating, nervousness, distracting thoughts, and unprovoked anger. For others, stress brings on a general feeling of malaise, robbing the individual of enthusiasm and interest compounded by a lessened sense of worth.

STRESS IN ORGANIZATIONAL SETTING

Distress is a response to a difficult event or situation that causes some degree of emotional suffering. Distress can manifest as sorrow or grief, leaving the sufferer to feel as though something important has been lost or died; as anguish, in which the sufferer feels overwhelmed by torment and fearful of what else might happen; or even as physical pain, in which the sufferer may experience headaches, nausea, aching muscles or bones, or anxiety attacks. Eustress is the opposite of distress. It refers to the type of stress that energizes rather than depletes energy. For example, an individual who is rushing to meet a deadline on a project that holds profound personal interest will experience the stress that accompanies the approaching deadline as a sort of energizing charge. Rather than producing the feeling that meeting the deadline is impossible, it creates a sense of excitement and even pleasure.

LIFE CHANGE AND LIFE TRAUMA

Both life change and life trauma develop as a result of major changes in the life of an individual. Both life change and life trauma result are linked to changes that are of a permanent or long lasting nature. Life changes can be defined as any profound change in an individual's private or work-related life. These changes can be either positive or negative transformations, and they result in some degree of stress. Life trauma is any kind of disturbance in a person's life that results in a significant, long- lasting adjustment in attitudes, emotion, or behaviors. Differences in the two can be noted in the fact that the adaptations that result from life changes are external; they are changes within the individual's environment, while the changes a life trauma brings to bear are internal, in that they are alterations within the individual but not necessarily with the individual's environment.

CHANGES IN PERSONAL LIFE

Life changes are any significant transformation in the private or professional arena. Life changes are profound, and either permanent or long lasting. Life changes can be the types of adjustments generally seen in a positive or negative light For example, marriage and divorce are both types of life changes, as are the birth of a child and the death of a spouse. When too many life changes occur in a limited time frame, the stress they collectively cause can be considerable. This is true even when the life changes are exclusively positive ones. For example, an individual who marries, purchasing a home, receiving a job promotion, has a baby, and inherits a great deal of money in the course of a year will no doubt be nearly overwhelmed with happiness. That happiness, however, almost certainly comes with stress created by the necessary adjustments in behavior and habit that each change has brought.

TWO CHARACTERISTICS THAT CAN EITHER HELP OR HURT A PERSON WHO IS EXPERIENCING A LIFE CHANGE OR A LIFE TRAUMA ARE AS FOLLOWS:

Social scientists are well aware that personality traits and the attitudes that individuals bring into situations can have tremendous influence over how well the person copes. People have different degrees of hardiness. Someone in possession of a great deal of hardiness remains strong in the face of difficulty. This is oftentimes a person who has withstood much in the past, and has learned that strength can be summoned from a sturdy inner core. Conversely, a person with little hardiness will not have the determination to face down adversity. This type of person often has a limited sense of self- worth, and depends upon others to resolve problematic situations. A second characteristic that will be helpful to someone experiencing a life change or life trauma is optimism. The more optimistic an individual, the more positive and forward looking he is. Optimists know the proper attitude can make changes more manageable.

GAS

Responses to stress can manifest through emotion, physical illness, an inability to think clearly, or through behaviors like aggression or withdrawal. Stressors that produce short term effects are called acute stressors, while those whose effect is longer are chronic stressors. General adaptation syndrome (GAS), described by Selye in rat studies, finds three stages of response. The first, alarm, triggers a flight- or- flight response when the presence of the stress stimulus is first sensed. Resistance follows, during which time the body quickly adjusts in order to deal with the source of the stress. This phase requires a great deal of energy and cannot be sustained indefinitely, resulting in the third stage of general adaptation syndrome, which is exhaustion. In this stage, panting, raised heart beat and sweating may occur, with possible long- term physical auto- immune or glandular damage may occur if the source of stress is not alleviated.

Affects of Job Requirements

Employees are affected by the requirements of their jobs. Fulfilling demands they perceive as expected, as well as those that are actually expected helps shape on the job behavior.

- Task demands are stress causing factors related to the specific job an individual does. An employee required to juggle several projects at various stages of completion at once is stressed by task demands.
- Role demands are stress causing factors connected to the role an individual is expected to play. For example, an employee who is told to mislead staff members about problems with a product will experience role demand.
- Interpersonal demands are stress causing factors related to pressures from a team or group, from someone in a leadership role, or as the result of clashes in personality. An example of interpersonal demands is a co- worker who constantly undermines an employee's presentations.
- Physical demands refer to stress causing factors that arise from the organization's physical environment. Examples of physical demands might include a work area that is excessively hot, inadequate soundproofing, or equipment that frequently fails to operate.

Role of Behavior

The term 'role' can be defined as a group of behaviors connected to an individual's specific relationship within an organization, which all members of the organization expect the individual to embody. These behaviors are as follows:

- Role conflict is the result of role cues and role messages that are individually clear but contradictory when considered together.
- Role ambiguity results when the role that has been assigned to an individual is either unclear, or contains expectations that change or transform for reasons that are unclear.
- Role overload is the natural result of a situation in which an individual's expected role behaviors surpass the abilities of the individual for any number of reasons.
- Role demands are aspects of a role that create stress to the individual. For example, an employee who is working with highly sensitive information that must be guarded at all times is likely to experience stress related to that particular role demand.

WORK-RELATED STRESS

Strategies to reduce or eliminate workplace stress include developing a more effective approach to time management; place a greater focus on physical exercise; learn and employ relaxation techniques such as yoga or biofeedback, and seeking support through social network opportunities. Numerous studies have shown that employees who learn to better manage time are able to greatly reduce time- related stressors. Physical exercise that is not competitive in nature, for example, or walking or running, swimming, or bike riding lowers the resting heart rate, and shifts focus from work stressors to enjoyable physical exertion Relaxation techniques like yoga, biofeedback, meditation or hypnosis teaches how to achieve a state of deep mind and body relaxation where tension can release and tranquility replace feeling stress. Sharing with colleagues or friends is a form of talk therapy, and can discharge stress and provide a more objective perspective in which the stressor can be considered.

SYMPTOMS OF STRESS

A person who is experiencing unmanageable levels of stress feels a host of symptoms that manifest physically and psychologically, and can result in behavioral changes. Stress leaves employees feeling discontented and frustrated, a primary cause of job dissatisfaction. Behaviors that result include procrastinating; feeling bored; feeling overwhelmed; feeling highly anxious; becoming teary; or becoming unreasonably irritable. Employees who feel an internal locus of control, who is given meaningful work and is autonomous, and who feels valued will experience less stress and manifest fewer stress-related psychological behaviors. Physically, stress contributes to a lowered autoimmune system; increased susceptibility to illness; headache, higher blood pressure; and has been linked to heart attacks. Behavioral changes that can be attributed to a high level of stress include lowered productivity; appetite that is either severely decreased or increased; an increase in alcohol consumption; problems with sleeping; tardiness or work absences, and a higher work turnover.

TIME MANAGEMENT

The importance of time management cannot be overstated. When employees mismanage time by focusing on the wrong things, failing to prioritize tasks, or determine the most efficient order in which to accomplish them, they find themselves unable to meet deadlines. An employee who is taught to become better organized can radically increase both the level and quality of her production, and do so with less stress. A few basic steps in effective time management include creating and following a daily list of tasks that need to be completed; determining which tasks have the highest importance or greatest urgency, a middle range of importance, and those that are of lesser importance or less urgent, and prioritize the tasks accordingly; create a schedule of action based upon the priorities that have been established; assume the most difficult tasks during the part of the day in which greatest mental energy and productiveness cycles in.

LOOP LEARNING

Both single loop and double loop learning are designed to correct miscalculations or faulty results, but they do so in different ways. Single loop learning is destined to repeat itself, changing only a little from one learning attempt to another. It identifies an error and looks to earlier practices for models of how to proceed, but enacts the procedure within the framework of current policies, resulting in a disconnect between the practices of the past and policies of the present. Double loop learning is more sophisticated in its approach, and is the style used by learning organizations. In this model, once an error is recognized, its correction involves a review of the organizational objectives, routine behaviors and policies, and necessary modifications made to these areas where necessary. Double loop learning strives to infuse vitality by considering each new problem by questioning what in the organization's prior thinking and behavior could have caused it.

JOB SATISFACTION

An employee who participates in the creation of a product from start to finish, such as an instrument maker, experiences two psychological effects; the employee feels proud of the work because he identifies with it, and this raises his job satisfaction level. He also more clearly understands the importance of each step along the way, which contributes to his productivity as well as to the overall quality of his work. This type of work typically gives the employee greater autonomy to make decisions, and also increases his sense of responsibility, because he knows he will be evaluated on the quality of the finished product. Jobs high in task significance are those that strongly contribute to improving the work or lives of others, such as teaching. A high degree of task significance produces a sense of meaningful purpose in the worker, which results in a greater sense of satisfaction.

IMPACT OF WORK ON OTHERS

The traits of skill variety, task identity and task significance lead to a worker's heightened awareness of the ways in which her efforts contribute to important and meaningful products that positively influence the lives of others. As a result, her internal motivation regarding work becomes clearer and stronger. The trait of autonomy results in an employee's heightened sense of responsibility concerning the results of her work. This heightened sensitivity leads to work performance of higher quality, as well as to an increased level of job satisfaction. Receiving direct feedback provides the employee with an increased awareness of the success of her efforts, or, if the results are not successful, an understanding of which areas need to be corrected. In practical terms, an employee who understands how her efforts contribute and how to improve them tends to remain with a job longer, and avoids being absent as often.

MOTIVATIONAL THEORIES AND CONCEPTS

Motivational theories and concepts are being increasingly applied to real world situations. Changes to job designs are often based upon theories that job productivity and job satisfaction are directly linked to the manner in which the various components of a specific job interrelate. The job characteristics model (JCM) created by Richard Hackman and Greg Oldham, describes five essential areas common to all jobs. The characteristics include skill variety; task identity; task significance; autonomy; and feedback. Briefly, skill variety suggests that jobs which demand a range of different abilities or skills are more satisfying to a worker than jobs requiring only one or two. Jobs high in task identity are likewise more satisfying because they engage a worker from the beginning to end of a complete task. Jobs high in task significance provide meaningful improvements to the work or lives of individuals. Positions in which an employee is given a high degree of autonomy are those that allow independence in terms of scheduling, approach, and project design; these individuals are typically more productive than those whose jobs are low in autonomy. Employees who receive immediate, clear feedback on their work also exhibit better work performance.

AUTONOMY AND FEEDBACK

To the casual observer, the roles of autonomy and feedback might seem to be exclusive. Autonomy permits independence, while feedback requires some type of meaningful relationship. A job with a high degree of autonomy allows for more employee independence. A job with a high feedback score provides information that clearly and promptly lets workers know their success. Employees given a high level of autonomy do work independently and probably don't receive feedback from supervisors on a daily basis, but they nonetheless do have opportunities to gain understanding from feedback. Forms of feedback other than verbal feedback from another person include how well a product functions, its physical appearance, and nonverbal cues from others. For example, an artist who designs fabric dolls might create a mock-up with a head slightly too large for the body. The doll flops over when placed in a seated position, and the oversized head gives it an odd appearance. A child sees the doll, frowns and turns away. The artist has received sufficient feedback to understand she needs to redesign the doll.

MPS

The motivating potential score (MPS) is an equation which combines the five essential traits into a single score, predictive in purpose. The motivating potential score is calculated based on a formula that states that in order for a job to be high in motivating potential it must be high in skill variety, task identity, task significance, a combination of two, or all three characteristics. Furthermore, jobs with high motivating potential must also be high in both the areas of autonomy and feedback. According to the theory, high MPS jobs result in employees with high motivation, performance, and job satisfaction, who are rarely absent and who tend not to leave the position. A tremendous amount of research on the jobs characteristics model has been undertaken; while nearly all of it points to the validity of the theoretical framework, almost none of it supports the validity of the motivating potential score.

SKILL VARIETY

Skill variety is one of the five core elements the job characteristics model describes as essential. Jobs in which workers repeat the same task over and over are both low motivator jobs and result in a low degree of job satisfaction. Job rotation can be used to alleviate the boredom of repetitive tasks. Employees with jobs that are repetitive quickly become bored, pay less attention to the quality of their work, and do not identify with their work. One way to alleviate these negative responses to a job that is nothing but repeated routine is by redesigning it to include job rotation. Job rotation, also called cross training, involves moving employees from one assignment to another from time to time. When the employee has been at one task for a long enough period of time that it is no longer challenging enough to hold his attention or motivate him, he is shifted to another assignment at the same work level that takes advantage of the same skill set. The idea is that doing similar but different work re-involves the employee, and also serves the best interests of the organization by increasing structural flexibility as well as by providing an alternative to layoffs.

PLUSES TO JOB ROTATION

Potential pluses to job rotation include re-involving bored employees and providing managers with greater scheduling flexibility; they can also postpone layoffs. Discuss how job rotation might be detrimental to an organization. Job rotation can be seen in a positive light in that it re-involves bored employees and provides a deeper understanding of their contributions; allows greater flexibility for managers in terms of scheduling, and can reduce or postpone layoffs. However, these advantages require certain organizational sacrifices. One important point is that job rotation requires additional training for employees who will only apply the training periodically. A worker who is moved from a job before he becomes bored is working at peak efficiency. He will be replaced by a worker more experienced in another task, and he will be moved into that worker's position; in both cases, productivity suffers. Supervisors will need to assign a greater portion of their time to overseeing the work to make sure the new position is understood. Other workers in the same area will also have to adjust to a new personality, which can affect group dynamic.

TELECOMMUTING

While at first glance, many employees would respond positively to the idea of telecommuting, there are also a number of potential disadvantages. While working in one's pajamas might seem ideal, an employee needs to consider disadvantages to telecommuting before deciding if it is right. A strong work ethic, sense of responsibility and time management skills are requirements. Telecommuting means greater difficulty obtaining supervisory support when necessary. It isn't possible to simply show a supervisor the nature of a problem, it must be explained. When office equipment such as computers, printers, scanners and the like go out, it is up to the employee to figure out how to stay on task while necessary repairs are made. It might be more difficult for a supervisor to accept a legitimate reason why a project is late from a telecommuter. While a telecommuter knows she's at work, to her family, it looks like she's home. Demands can be made on her work time from children, pets, spouses, neighbors and friends that distract and drain energy.

Advantages to Telecommuting

With the development of personal computers and the internet, many types of employees can now work from home either several days a week, or full time. An employee who works in a metropolitan area can save several hours a week commuting, which can be put toward higher work productivity or greater personal satisfaction. Without the expense of gas, tolls, car maintenance, public transportation, higher auto insurance, lunches, dry cleaning, office appropriate clothing and the like, working out of the home can save considerable money. Working from home allows an employee to set her own schedule, and for the most part, to decide how she prefers to organize her work tasks. Time can be taken in the middle of the day for personal reasons, and hours made up later or the following day. Water cooler distractions will be absent, allowing work at peak productivity. Many employees consider telemarketing's many advantages a real plus.

Employee Involvement

Currently, a great deal of attention is being given to the concept of employee involvement.

The concept of employee involvement is based upon a simple hypothesis: employees who are invited and encouraged to offer their input toward informing the decisions that will directly affect them will respond with greater willingness to accept the decision and to make a greater commitment to it. By extension, employees more committed to their own projects become more committed to the organization as a whole, because they see themselves as active, vital members of it. Some programs that utilize greater employee involvement include participative management; quality circles; and representative participation. Participative management programs involve collective decision making, with little regard given to the power position of the participants. Representative participation involves a set of employees who participate in decision making as representatives of all employees. Quality circles are typically composed of fewer than ten employees and supervisors who meet at scheduled times to study problems with quality and consider cures.

Salary Distribution Options

One option for salary distribution is offering employee compensation through a skill based pay plan. Skill based pay plans offer employees the opportunity to increase salary by acquiring new skills. Employees with a great number of skills can perform a greater number of jobs, and are therefore more valuable to the company both now and in the future. Should such an employee decide to leave the company for another job, replacing that individual with another who has a similar set of skills would be more difficult. Skill based pay is also known as competency based or knowledge based pay, and it is not an augmentation of an established salary but is an alternative to a salary that pays a flat salary based upon job description rather than upon quality of work. Employees with multiple skills are a boon to managers, giving them flexibility in scheduling and greater control when layoffs are necessary. Workers with few advancement opportunities can increase pay by learning new skills.

Variable Pay Plans

Individual employees can be paid through variable pay plans. A variable pay plan is one in which part of an employee's salary is based upon the degree to which she has achieved specific performance measures. There are a number of different ways a company can structure this type of salary program. Piece rate pay rewards employees a set amount for every production unit they complete. Merit based pay evaluates employees' performance in order to determine the variable portion of their salaries. Bonuses are a common incentive, one that most employees rely upon but don't consider to be part of their salary, although they differ from merit pay only in that they are reward incentives for recent production increases rather than for longer term performance. Profit sharing plans reward all their employees for increased profit using a predetermined formula. Gainsharing offers similarities to profit sharing, but looks at productivity gains instead of profits. Employee stock ownership plans offer stock at prices below market.

Recently, variable pay programs have grown in popularity over the more traditional salary programs that increase employees' pay based upon seniority only. Variable pay programs link part of employee pay to achieving or surpassing a standard of performance established in advance. Traditionally, an employee joined a company at a certain salary, which increased the longer the employee remained with the company. Many businesses and organizations still operate this way, and in many cases, employees without job seniority who are capable of excellence feel frustrated and underappreciated. Variable pay programs offer a number of advantages to both organization and employees. Salary is, in general, an organization's greatest expense. Then a company fails to perform, it loses income. When salary is, in part, linked to performance, companies that have experienced a decline are better equipped to quickly lesson lesser labor expenses. Employees and managers alike see variable pay as award for exemplary performance, rather than (to employees) as entitlement. High performing employees receive more rapid financial gains.

Success of Variable Pay Plans

Many studies have been done to determine the degree of success that variable pay plans have in terms of employee motivation and enhanced production. mResults of studies concerning variable pay plans agree that this type of compensation program, properly handled, does enhance production and inspire greater employee motivation. Profit sharing is designed to increase profitability and it does; gainsharing is designed to enhance productivity and it, too, is generally successful. Both types of variable pay programs also are frequently found to result in employees with greater job satisfaction. However, variable pay plans do have one unknown that, from the worker's point of view, can be damning: they aren't predictable, and they aren't under an employee's control. Should a recession cause a loss in company profit, employees will share that loss. Should a team fail to perform regardless of one individual's exemplary efforts that variable pay will drop. As well, when employees begin to depend upon a healthy incentive after receiving one several times in a row, and it fails to materialize, their dissatisfaction will be felt.

ESOPs

Employee stock ownership plans (ESOPs) can be an important piece to a benefits package.

A range of possibilities exist for how employee stock ownership plans are designed and operated. ESOPs might be as simple as employees receiving a set amount of company stock, to employees holding most or all of the shares themselves. ESOPs are created by companies as part of benefits packages that give employees a specific number of stock shares in the company; some companies discount the shares, so employees can see immediate gains. Most ESOPs are found in relatively small companies that don't offer public shares. They are established by a company that creates a stock ownership trust. The company contributes stock, which is then allocated to employees.

Employees are 'given' a certain number of shares at various points in time, but can only sell the stock after leaving the company. Employees who see themselves as company owners are more motivated, more interested and involved in company business, and happier.

Motivation Theories

Because motivating employees is core to any organization's success, many theories have been postulated and studies undertaken to test them. Theories can be grouped into a handful of categories concerned with specific outcome variables. The first category is Needs Theories, and includes Maslow's hierarchy; McClelland's needs; Existence, Relatedness and Growth; and Herzberg's motivation-hygiene theory. Current research indicates that while well known, they are not predictable indicators of motivation. Goal-setting theory postulates clearly defined, challenging goals result in higher productivity. While it doesn't address turnover, job satisfaction or absenteeism, this theory is predictive for productivity. Reinforcement Theory is a reliable predictor of work quality and quantity, absenteeism, and accident rates but rates low on turnover or satisfaction prediction. Equity Theory is not a reliable predictor for productivity, absenteeism, job satisfaction, and turnover. Expectancy theory looks at variables in performance and is valid regarding important decisions (leaving a job) but less so for daily decisions.

Personal Development

Many theories of motivation touch upon how a continuing sense of personal development contributes to job motivation. Skill based pay plan programs manifest a number of factors that a number of motivation theories point to as important motivators. When employees' learning and personal growth are supported, according to Existence, Relatedness and Growth theory, increased motivation is the result. Ambitious employees who gain new skills will encounter new challenges, which motivation theories indicate is fundamental to ongoing motivation. Because skill based pay encourages a generalist mentality, supports collaboration, and cross trains —all skills highly prized by managers —skill based pay reinforces motivation. Finally, employees who are able to see a clear correlation between how their pay, sense of self- worth and job satisfaction increases in direct relationship to their output, feel they are being given fair treatment that is not based on seniority or a college degree. When employees perceive equity in the work place, their motivation is undoubtedly likewise enhanced.

Skill-Based Pay

Recent studies indicate that in spite of potential drawbacks, skill based pay programs are increasing in popularity and use. These studies further indicate that a higher quality of employee performance is realized, greater job satisfaction achieved, and that employees feel they are being treated more equitably. Skill based pay plans were originally successful in industries which needed an increasing menu of skills and abilities but that could offer little in terms of advancement, just as factories and other industrial operations. Interestingly, the trend has expanded to include companies who are nose to nose with aggressive, determined global competitors, as well as those whose product lifecycles are short, and those who must attend to the speed at which their product reaches the market. Although skill based pay plan programs were once used primarily by factory and shop employees, the concept is currently being applied at a white collar level in many cases. Changes in the marketplace and in the world are causing organizations to redesign themselves into entities that are willing to recognize, highly prize, and pay for those skills for which they have an immediate and strong need in order to remain competitive.

Benefits Packages

Benefits packages are important to attracting new hires and retaining current employees. The last several decades have resulted in tremendous changes to the types of employees organizations are hiring. As a result, benefits packages must tailor themselves accordingly. Three popular kinds of benefit plans include modular plans, flexible spending accounts and core plus options. Modular plans are benefits packages that variably combine units that have been designed with an eye toward a specific group of employee. For example, unmarried employees without dependents will prefer benefits packages that contain only the basics, while one created for single parents will include family health insurance, life insurance, and disability insurance. Flexible spending plans are especially attractive to individuals with specific needs. A flexible spending plan assigns a specific dollar figure which can be set aside by the employee for particular benefits, such as dental insurance, life or health insurance that she deems important. Flexible spending plans are effectively increase take home pay because taxes aren't paid for dollars set aside for this type of account. Core-plus plans include crucial core benefits along with a list of other possibilities from which the employee can pick and choose until the 'benefit credits' she has been given are used up.

Recognition and Applause

Having efforts recognized and applauded is important to most employees. Workers who believe their contributions are recognized are more likely to commit themselves more fully. Rewards for a job well done can be extrinsic, such as bonuses, shares of stock, or all expenses paid trips. They can also be intrinsic, for example, employee recognition opportunities. Hard work deserves to be applauded. Recognition for outstanding effort is a powerful motivator, and the lack of a special thank you can dishearten employees. Considerable research has gone into studying bonuses, paid vacations and other material motivators, but in many cases a public thank you will mean as much; in fact, employee recognition doesn't even need to be public to be effective. A manager who sees an employee handle a difficult customer, re-think a strategic problem, or supply the extra effort her team needs in order to succeed can take the opportunity to offer a private and heartfelt 'good job'. More structured intrinsic employee recognition programs can include certificates, awards or plaques presented monthly or annually in front of one's peers. While these programs are good for employees, they're also good for the organization not only because they boost morale, but because they do it so effectively at almost no expense.

Unfairness in Employee Recognition Programs

In addition to the objection that employee recognition programs manipulate lower paid employees, a second concern is directed toward the criteria used to determine who is to be recognized. Employee recognition programs are popular with managers because they are both effective motivators and extremely inexpensive to operate. It is important, however, that managers remain highly conscientious of how they use such programs; they hold the potential to demoralize rather than motivate if unrecognized employees feel they've been unfairly passed over. These programs work best when public recognition and praise is based upon objective, measurable criteria. An employee who sold a greater number of units in a particular time period deserves such recognition than one whose sales remained static. However, often public recognition is based on criteria that aren't measurable. A consistently cheerful waitress may not sell more breakfasts than a dour one, but her customers are more likely to return. While such an employee deserves appreciation, charges of favoritism can undermine the boost such recognition is designed to give and infect a workplace with negativity and petty jealousy.

Criticism of Employee Recognition Programs

Employee recognition programs have grown by leaps and bounds. However, objections have been raised, such as that these programs are often aimed at low paid workers at the bottom of the job ladder who are hungry for and respond very well to respect. Critics of these programs charge that these employees deserve the same kind of material reward as do their higher ups. Critics of employee recognition programs say that those at the bottom of the pay scale are subtly and unfairly manipulated by employee recognition programs. These workers are typically less educated, less worldly and more naïve. While a fry cook might swell with pride at the plaque that bears his name, protestors suggest that he deserves the same degree of intrinsic and extrinsic recognition his superiors receive. When managers, supervisors and team leaders are publicly congratulated, that praise often includes something of monetary value as well, be it a check, stock shares, or other goods. Critics of employee recognition programs point out that offering the same degree of material reward to a low paid workers would go a very long way in terms of motivation, cost the company much less than similar rewards that are regularly dispensed to and expected by those higher on the ladder, and demonstrate the organization's commitment to equality.

Cultural Differences in Employee Recognition Programs

International research studies have concluded that extrinsic characteristics such as comfortable work environments and salaries that employees feel are competitive contribute strongly to job satisfaction regardless of culture. However, the degree to which intrinsic characteristics contributed to overall job satisfaction appears to be culturally bound. While studies indicate that, regardless of cultural differences, all employees equally prize extrinsic factors such as fair salary and comfortable work environment in regards to job satisfaction, the degree to which intrinsic factors contribute to job satisfaction isn't as predictable. While in some countries employees saw jobs that complement their specific skills and interests or being publicly recognized for outstanding work as important to satisfaction, those in other countries did not. Countries with both wealth and organizational power distributed more equitably, and that prioritized individuals over groups had a stronger relationship between intrinsic factors and job satisfaction than countries where wealth and power are assigned to higher castes, and collectivism is favored. A possible explanation for this is that people whose cultural norms favor individualism are more finely attuned to intrinsically satisfying aspects of work, and require those aspects to be present in order to be truly satisfied.

Keeping Employees Motivated

Keeping employees motivated is both essential to achieving organizational goals efficiently and effectively, as well as to job satisfaction. One of the most important jobs a manager does is to find new ways to inspire and motivate her employees. A handful of concepts are fundamental. First, most research on the importance of goals and feedback agree that very clear goals that are also challenging are essential, as is feedback so that an employee knows what is working and what is not. Second, involving employees in decisions has been proven to increase their commitment and job satisfaction along with motivation. Third, she must be sensitive to cultural and individual difference. What motivates one employee could upset another. Fourth, excellence must be rewarded, and the reward must be clearly connected to specific work of outstanding quality. Finally, a manager must frequently examine her criteria to be certain she is rewarding employees fairly, based upon their skills, effort, and output rather than on criteria others might judge as favoritism.

Emotions

Some psychologists believe that emotions can be universally categorized. There are some problems contemporary researchers have encountered when trying to identify a universal 'language' of emotions manifested through facial expression. Descartes, the father of modern philosophy, described all emotions as mixtures of love, hate, desire, wonder, joy and sorrow. Much contemporary research has focused upon trying to identify consistent facial expressions that manifest particular emotions. While the results are fascinating, the studies are not conclusive for a number of reasons. First is the degree to which cultural norms inhibit clear expression of certain emotions. Linked to this likelihood is the problem of the researcher's cultural perspective, which is either shared with the subjects or distinct; either way, interpreting the results of the research will be tinged. Another problem is that researchers must make some assumptions about their subjects that amount to projection on the researcher's part. A researcher who finds a particular stimulus disgusting will likely interpret the subject's facial expression in response to the stimulus as that, even if the subject actually found the photograph disturbing, but not disgusting.

Emotionally Expressive People

The consensus among many is that people who are emotional are weaker and more fragile than those who feel little emotion. Emotionally expressive people have been considered a detriment in the workplace for two reasons. First, strong emotions are seen as distracting to others; secondly, individuals who express frustration, anger, disappointment and even joy are looked upon as weaker and more fragile than those who demonstrate little emotion. Recent studies suggest that in many cases, this belief may be erroneous; strong emotions actually make essential contributions to reasoning. Brain injured people who are left with limited or absent emotion make erratic and irrational decisions, suggesting that emotion contributes information to thought processes that reason alone cannot. For example, an actor who previously chose emotionally rich roles that spoke to him but now bases selection solely on pay and marketing potential is acting with complete rationality. While this might seem like a smart business decision, it is almost certain that his acting will suffer, and his career along with it.

Differences Between Mood and Emotion

A casual look at mood and emotion might lead one to believe they are simply two words for the same thing. There's no doubt that they are interrelated, and that a change in one can cause a change in the other, but they are, in fact distinct states. Mood and emotion are interchangeable terms in casual conversation but in fact, they are not the same. Emotion is both more immediate and mercurial than is mood. Emotion rises in immediate response to an event or situation, but as quickly as it arrives it vanishes, often leaving a shadow behind that contributes to the development of a mood. A mood arrives more slowly than an emotion; where an emotion flashes, a mood builds. Moods aren't reactions, as are emotions, and can be oddly detached from their source. For example, an employee irritated by a teammate begins to feel depleted long after the irritation has passed. She awakes in the morning overwhelmed by a feeling of incompetence and sorrow that seem to have come from nowhere. Just as emotion influences mood, mood affects emotion by shaping a negative or positive perspective about an experience and the emotional response to it.

Mercurial and Reactive Feelings

The point has been made that feelings are mercurial and reactive rather than conceived and chosen. Human beings place so much confidence is our ability to conceive of ideas, to intellectualize experience, to deduce, assume and predict, that we have forgotten we are as much animals as every other species. Emotions are immediate strongly felt reactions to a specific person, event or situation. There is nothing thoughtful or rational about an emotion but they are not frivolous, self indulgent or 'thoughtless'; rather, they are composed of pure truth. Emotions arise in response to limbic activity. The limbic system, situated at the top of the spine, is the brain's most primitive area. An active limbic system produces strong negative emotions such as hostility or shame. A peacefully resting limbic system produces feelings of happiness, tranquility or joy. Biologically, women's limbic systems demonstrate more activity than men, possibly to give them an edge in bonding with children. This may explain the reason women are more vulnerable to depression.

Emotions Involved in Threats to Survival

In The Expression of the Emotions in Man and Animals, Charles Darwin postulates that emotions provide information required to resolve threats to survival. According to Darwin, the evolutionary role of emotions is to create immediate reaction to both positive and negative stimuli. For example, if ancient man stumbled upon a sleeping bear, he would feel alarm and fear great enough to make him want to flee. Seeing a group of men not of his tribe who were carrying spears and running toward his village would quickly bring feelings of rage, fear and excitement to the fore to incite him to fight. Evolutionary psychologists claim that even today, both positive and negative emotions serve the same evolutionary purpose of survival as before, although the environment has changed. Today, an employee who feels nervous before a presentation can channel that excess energy into reviewing her information and practicing what she will say. An envious team mate may try to steal her thunder (which serves his survival instincts), causing her to pay careful attention and defend her property (her ideas).

MBP

Management by objectives (MBO) programs are designed to take goal setting from the theoretical arena and putting it to work. Management by objectives programs are real- life applications that take their inspiration from motivational theories. Practice indicates that these programs work best when the situation contains a number of conditions. First, employees must participate in goal-setting for those objectives that will affect them or their work in order to be willing to fully commit to the goals to the degree necessary to make them their own. Goals cannot be conjectural, vague, nor subjectively measured. They must be concrete, demonstrable and measurable by objective standards. The goals exist in time, meaning there is a defined beginning and end; this helps participants gauge where they need to be at a given point in time in terms of reaching the goal. Participants are kept on- track through feedback, either coming from the outside, from team mates, from supervisors or from non living sources, such as the functionality of a product.

Confident Employees

Confident employees are more willing to assume challenging tasks, push past obstacles, and achieve goals efficiently and effectively. Social cognitive theory (also known as self- efficacy theory) holds that confident individuals will increase their efforts in order to accomplish challenging tasks, while those lacking in confidence are more likely to believe the task is beyond their abilities and give up. Efficient and effective employee performance requires a high degree of personal faith that tasks and goals that have been assigned can, indeed, be accomplished with the right amount of effort. It follows that it is essential for managers to find ways to build authentic confidence in their employees. One strategy to accomplish this is found in the marriage of goal- setting and social cognitive theories. According to goal- setting theory, raising the bar by assigning a challenging objective telegraphs the manager's confidence in the employee. External confidence leads to internal confidence. Internal confidence, according to social cognitive theory, raises the inner bar, inspiring greater effort. The two approaches in tandem are likely to succeed.

Self- Efficacy Theory

It is often said that the body will do what the mind tells it to do. The fields of sports, medicine and business abound with stories in which a high degree of success was achieved simply because of a person's determination. Self- efficacy theory hypothesizes that performance depends in part upon what an individual believes her ability to be. Also known as social cognitive theory, as well as social learning theory, self- efficacy theory proposes that greater challenges inspire greater effort in high self- efficacy individuals. This suggests that individuals with low self- confidence commit less effort to completing a task the more difficult it is. In short, highly confident people increase effort in response to difficult challenges, while those with low self- esteem reduce effort in response to difficult challenges. Another part of the equation is that highly confident people use negative feedback to fuel their efforts, while insecure individuals respond to negative feedback by giving up. Obviously, employees with a healthy sense of self- worth will achieve goals more frequently than those with little confidence to give up in the face of greater challenge or negative feedback.

Albert Bandura's self- efficacy theory proposes that an individual's confidence can be enhanced through enactive mastery, vicarious modeling, verbal persuasion, and arousal. Enactive mastery occurs when someone has successful past experience in a particular task. Because she was successful in the past, she sees her success in the present as a given. Vicarious modeling takes place when an employee observes someone else accomplishing a task. The effectiveness of vicarious modeling is increased when the observer sees similarities between herself and the model. Verbal persuasion is what enables motivational presenters to inspire audiences to greater success. Telling employees they will be successful leads to success. Verbal persuasion is successful insofar as the motivator authentically believes and expresses conviction in the employee's skills and talents. Arousal, as described by Bandura, can be seen as positive, electric energy. An employee who is charged up and excited about a task will be more successful.

Moods

According to structure of moods models, moods can be categorized as having positive and negative effect, and within those categories, as residing in a low or high position. Positive affect includes a range of moods that involve emotional energy or movement which can be described as optimistic or affirmative in the high position, and unresponsive in the low position. High positive affect moods are constructive, while low positive affect moods are destructive. For example, high positive affect moods include excitement, alertness, joy, elation. The presence of these moods charge the individual experiencing them with increased energy which can be productively channeled. Low positive affect moods include boredom, emotional exhaustion, sorrow and depression. In this quadrant, the moods drain energy, leaving the individual with lessened energy and without the desire to be productive. Negative affect includes a range of mood states that in the high position are distressing and in the low position are soothing. High negative affect moods include anxiety, stress, tension and distress, while low negative affect moods include serenity, tranquility, relaxation and contentment.

Jobs

Job characteristics theory considers how employees experience a task's meaningfulness, assume task outcome responsibility, and understand the results. Job characteristics approach examines the motivating characteristics of a job. Job design refers to the way an organization structures employment positions, and how their responsibilities are defined. Job enrichment is the practice of assigning a larger number of tasks to complete together with greater control over how they are to be accomplished. Job enlargement is similar to job enrichment, but does not assign a greater degree of autonomy to the employee in terms of decisions about how to complete the increased number of tasks. Job rotation is designed to alleviate on the job boredom by periodically reassigning employees to a different task that uses the same skills as a previous task. Job sharing is the practice of permitting two employees to split a single full time position with work time, structured as employees see fit.

Loyal Shoppers

While many items are, indeed, cheaper at these stores than others, it is interesting to note that some items may actually be more costly, or less convenient in the long run. Shoppers remain loyal to a business as long as they perceive their needs are being met in a superior manner. Skillful marketing which convinces consumers that both convenience and price are unparalleled keeps those customers from shopping elsewhere. However, convenience and price can be illusory. A single parent with one child must repackage meats, cereals and other foods purchased in bulk at a small discount. This takes time and requires purchasing freezer bags or plastic storage cartons, which may sell for more than elsewhere. Superstores convince buyers of incredible savings by advertising prices on popular items in each department that are either loss leaders or close. The impression consumers come away with is, if prices are this low on that product, they must be equally low on all products. In fact, prices on mundane but oft-purchased goods (like those freezer bags) can be higher than the competition and escape the notice of most purchasers.

PROCESS CONSULTATION

When a manager feels there is a problem or issue within the team or department that is affecting productivity but cannot determine what it is, a process consultant is often brought in. Process consultation is an organizational development tool designed to help managers identify snags in the work process, ascertain the cause for the snags, and consider options in correcting them. Process consultation is based upon the premise that the efficiency of an organization is affected by the interpersonal relationships of its members. Problems can be based in the self's relationship to itself; in relationships among two or more individuals, or externally, within the organization or other connected environment. A second, and equally important, tenet of process consultation is that the process must involve the manager as much as the consultant. The manager learns lifelong skills in diagnosing interpersonal problems and handling them.

POLITICS OF CHANGE

The nature of change is to disrupt the status quo, which by definition indicates political activity. Change of any sort means some degree of disruption within a previously established system. When change agents come from within, they are often times individuals who currently hold little power, function at a relatively low level of influence, and have little invested in the organization in terms of time or finances; they have little to lose and much to gain. When a low-level internal change agent is successful, the change that is implemented is accomplished quickly and effectively. To the change agent, it means a rapid increase in power, influence and respect. Managers with many years invested and who have earned their way to the top and find change unsettling, are sometimes forced to implement it to demonstrate to customers, clients, shareholders or other interested outsiders that they are acting in the organization's best interests. Higher level change agents with more to lose typically bring about change incrementally.

CONFLICT BETWEEN EMPLOYEES

Because an organization is composed of people with different personalities, needs and goals, and because the organization itself often has tasks or goals that can work in opposition for a period of time, if is inevitable that conflict will arise. At its most basic and stripped of emotion, conflict is nothing more than two or more positions that do not agree. But the more strongly people feel about their position, the more emotionally involved they become about protecting it. Conflict can quickly reach a level where it is unproductive, resulting in negative stress that taints the working environment. People respond to conflict and the resulting stress in a variety of ways, dependent upon their personalities, their relative position in the organization, the degree of importance they ascribe to the issue, what they perceive their own influence and power to be within the organization, and a number of other factors. In general, the less an employee identifies with a position, the more likely he will be to try to 'erase' the conflict. The more strongly an employee believes in the position he supports, the more willing he will be to enter into conflict.

CONFLICT WITHIN ORGANIZATIONS

While early schools of thought regarding conflict described it as damaging to an organization in that it negatively affected efficient and effective production, post WWII through the 1970s saw a major shift in thinking. The human relations school of thought considered that conflict was both natural and healthy. The best response to conflict, in this viewpoint, was to accept it and work with its presence as one of many components informing a situation. The human relations view even went so far as to suggest that conflict could, at times, inspire greater job performance by forcing individuals involved to deeply examine their positions, consider other possibilities and try to negotiate an agreement.

The Grapevine

The term 'the grapevine' has become pervasive. Much information arrives through the grapevine long before it arrives through authorized channels, whether it's about a neighborhood robbery that doesn't make it to the news for days, or rumors of layoffs that management is trying to control. The grapevine is an informal communications network; much of what it carries is rumor. Although by its nature, the authenticity of the information it delivers is questionable, the grapevine can be a source of vital information. Among the grapevine's primary characteristics is the fact that management might utilize it, but cannot control it. Smart managers slip information in from time to time, knowing it will disperse itself, and managers can also slip false information into the grapevine in an effort to manipulate employees. However, management does not control who participates in the grapevine, nor how important it is to company culture. Because the grapevine isn't under corporate ownership, employees are more likely to believe information it brings to them. This is ironic, since the true purpose of the grapevine appears to be to serve the interests of those who are using it to spread innuendo.

Models of Learning

In order to grow and develop, both organizations and the people who compose them must be open to learning. Learning occurs in an infinite number of ways. Some information is best learned through hands- on experience, such as how to operate a piece of machinery or bake a pie. Some material is best absorbed when a number of learners work through it collaboratively and experimentally, trying different approaches and combinations in an effort toward discovery. Some things, such as mathematical formulas, can be learned through repetition and memorization. Problem- based learning occurs when a problem must be resolved. Some learning is accomplished as a response to stimuli, as in behaviorist models. Some learning involves reference to previous experiences, while some requires creative juxtapositions, overlaps and insights that are unique and original. There are people who learn best by observing a master execute a process, and others who learn best by doing.

Reinforcement Theory

In reinforcement theory, two types of reinforcement are noted. Positive reinforcement increases the chances of a particular desired behavior being repeated by rewarding it. Negative reinforcement operates by increasing the chances of a particular behavior by withholding negative consequences. In reinforcement theory, both positive and negative reinforcers are used to increase the chances of a particular behavior being repeated. Positive reinforcers encourage a repetition of the preferred behavior by providing a pleasurable or desired consequence; in order to obtain the same desired consequence in the future, the preferred behavior will be repeated. For example, a real estate broker wants his agents to increase sales. She offers a family cruise to the individual who shows the greatest increase in sales in the next 60 days. This incentive is positive, and will increase the possibility that sales will increase considerably. Negative reinforcers are also used to encourage desired behavior. It is important to note that negative reinforcers are not the same as punishments. Like positive reinforcers, negative reinforcers are designed to increase the chances of a desired behavior being repeated; this is done by withholding consequences that are perceived as undesirable.

Basic Tenets of Reinforcement Theory

Reinforcement theory takes a behavior modification (behavioral contingency modification) approach, based upon the premise that behavior is reinforced by the results of past behaviors, both negative and positive; however, positive behavior results are stronger reinforcers, according to the law of effect. Most behavior modification programs take a four step approach. The first is to objectively determine the intended outcome or behavior. Next, review how often that intended outcome or behavior currently occurs. Thirdly, attach a behavioral corollary to reinforce that outcome or behavior. Finally, establish a systematic framework to evaluate the change in outcome or behavior in order to gauge how effective the approach has been. Reinforcement theory combines both rewards and punishments for operant behavior, which is behavior to which a consequence is assigned. Operant conditioning is the correlation between the operant behavior and the corollary consequences, and is the focus of reinforcement theory.

Differences in Negative Reinforcement and Punishment; Extinction

Negative reinforcement seeks to increase the chances of preferred behaviors being repeated, while punishment is designed to decrease the chances of unwanted behaviors. Negative reinforcement puts undesirable consequences at bay, while punishment delivers them in an effort to lessen the operant behavior. Research suggests that punishment should be applied only when positive and negative reinforcement have failed to work because it can, on occasion, backfire. Failing a student who plagiarizes is an example of punishment. Allowing the student to redo the assignment is negative reinforcement. A combination of the two—allowing the student to redo the assignment, but subtracting a full grade point from the results, or making the assignment twice as complex—can also be effective. Like punishment, extinction can be used to decrease the incidence of undesirable behaviors. Rather than assigning a punishment, however, extinction withholds a consequence; this eventually results in the undesirable behavior dying out.

Reinforcement Schedules

Behavioral consequences can follow an operant behavior in a couple of distinct ways, continuous reinforcement and intermittent reinforcement. Two types of reinforcement schedules are used in reinforcement theory. Consistently supporting a wanted behavior is a continuous reinforcement schedule. Research suggests that continuous reinforcement is the fastest way to ground desirable behaviors, as well as to eradicate unwanted ones. While this type of reinforcement is efficient, there are two main problems with it. The first is that people who consistently receive positive reinforcement grow to expect it, even after the new behavior is firmly in place. Withdrawing positive reinforcement can eventually result in extinction. Secondly, while efficient, continuous reinforcement schedules are time- intensive, which lessens their usefulness to organizations. Intermittent reinforcement schedules are often substituted for continuous ones, in which desirable behaviors are reinforced occasionally and unpredictably. Because it is harder for an individual to determine that reinforcement is no longer attached, he is therefore be more likely to continue that behavior even after reinforcement has been withdrawn.

Fixed Ratio Reinforcement and Variable Ratio Reinforcement Schedules

Both fix ratio and variable ratio intermittent reinforcement schedules are activated after a pre-established number of desirable behaviors occur. For example, a factory worker who is given a bonus every time she completes 10,000 production units is operating within a fixed ratio reinforcement schedule. Because the worker knows at what point the bonus will arrive, it is not a consistent motivator and any changes in work habits or other desired behaviors it affects are vulnerable to extinction. In contrast, the variable ratio schedule creates changes to behavior that are long lasting, steady, and considerably better able to resist extinction. Variable ratio schedules accomplish this by offering reinforcers following a predetermined (but unknown to the worker) number of behavior events; the number of behavior events are inconsistent, unpredictable and vary depending upon a number of contingencies.

Intermittent Reinforcement Schedules

Fixed interval schedules of reinforcement are used to intermittently reinforce specific behaviors at pre- established and predictable periods of time. A salary check that arrives on the first and 15th of the month is an example of a fixed interval schedule. Because it is predictable, should it be withdrawn as a reinforcer, its absence is rapidly recognized and extinction is likely to occur just as it does when a continuous reinforcement is removed. Variable interval reinforcement schedules are used to encourage desirable behavior. An example of a variable interval reinforcement schedule is an annual organizational awards ceremony where top producing teams are recognized, presented with plaques and bonus checks. While variable interval reinforcement schedules may be pre-established and therefore predicable, these types of intermittent reinforcement schedules occur infrequently enough that withholding them doesn't typically result in extinction of the desired behavior.

IM

Impression management (IM) refers to strategies employed by people trying to manage how they appear to others. Impression management isn't something low self monitors engage in. Because low self monitors don't adapt behavior to suit situations, they present themselves as they are, and are often oblivious that it may hurt their own self- interests. High self monitors, however, are exceptionally sensitive to social cues, and are highly capable of adapting behaviors to manipulate the perceptions of others for their own benefit. From a manager's perspective, a degree of adaptability is useful, in that employees who are capable of and willing to be flexible as needed can help increase production, adapt to minor changes, and are generally pleasanter to work with than employees who are entrenched and rigid. However, self monitors who are overly focused on impression management can be dishonest, manipulative and ultimately disliked by peers.

IM Strategies When Applying for a Job

Two types of IM strategies that are likely to surface during a job interview as well as a performance review are self- promotion and ingratiation. A number of studies agree that there is a high degree of IM strategy use during job interviews. This is understandable, given that a candidate has limited time to impress the interviewers with his exceptional competencies, agreeable personality and willingness to work. Research studies agree that symbolically demonstrating these desirable characteristics through self promotion is effective. Emphasizing accomplishments and successes while minimizing and justifying areas of lesser success left interviewers with the impression that interviewees were more competent than others, even when their resumes showed less training and fewer skills. However, once the job is secured, the candidate who continues to self promote will quickly irritate both co- workers and superiors, leading to lower performance reviews.

High Self Monitors Management Strategies

Impression management can be looked at as a form of personal advertising. Just as ads can be completely truthful and merely promoting a product, or entirely misleading, so, too, can IM strategies be used honestly or dishonestly. Some IM strategies that are common include offering compliments designed to increase trust or likability, and to forge a connection with someone in power. Doing an unasked favor is another popular strategy, both because it gets favorable notice, and because it subtly suggests a debt is owed. IM employees are eager to assume blame for minor infractions that are easily forgivable, because it makes them appear humble and responsible, and allows them to ask a favor of a superior, which results in a connection. However, if the infraction is major, an IMer will offer an excuse that is outside of her control, or point blame at someone she knows her superior already distrusts.

TERMINAL VALUES

Terminal values as described by Rokeach in his Value Survey are abstract ideals, while instrumental values describe specific actions. For example, Rokeach includes self respect, freedom, familial security, a sense of accomplishment, social recognition, true friendship, happiness, mature love, a comfortable life and world peace as terminal values. The set of instrumental values counts honesty, obedience, behaving responsibly, behaving with self control, being independent, being forgiving, being cheerful, being ambitious, being open minded, and being courageous, among its values. Freedom, a terminal value, is an abstract ideal with many possible real world applications but no absolute real world manifestation.

Freedom is, in reality, relative; in that a world where everyone is given utter freedom would be a world of chaos. However, as a terminal value, it is an absolute ideal, inviting those who hold it high to employ practices that will bring them as close as possible to realizing that goal.

HOLLAND'S PERSONALITY TYPES

Realistic personalities are stable and sensible, willing to conform. They can be timid and sincere and are happiest building, repairing, or farming. Investigative personalities are inquisitive; enjoy analyzing information and demonstrating self- reliance. They make good detectives, journalists or scientists. Social people enjoy teamwork, and excel as teachers, therapists and social workers. Conventional types carry their willingness to conform a step further than do Realists, are practical, highly efficient, and inflexibly adhere to rules. They do best as accountants, bank employees, and clerks. Enterprising personalities exude self confidence to the point where they can become overbearing. They make excellent public relations personnel, attorneys, or Realtors. Artistic individuals are idealists who feel deeply about things. They aren't always practical, and enjoy a bit of chaos they can organize in their own creative way. They will be happy in an interior decorator position, working as a musician, writer, or in the theater.

PROFESSIONAL'S MOTIVATION

Professionals such as doctors, dentists, attorneys, engineers, architects and doctors have demonstrated their long term commitment to their jobs by finishing their education. Pay is ultimately less a motivating factor for professionals than for nonprofessionals. Professionals know that they will receive a high salary regardless of where they work, and they leave unsatisfactory jobs for ones more likely to please more readily than do nonprofessionals because their loyalty is to the ideals they see as typifying their field, not to any particular organization. Most professionals work hard to keep their education current by attending workshops and seminars, reading professional journals and meeting with colleagues, which means they are desirable to other employers, and they know it. What does motivate professionals are challenges that call forth the best they've got. They want the skills they've spent years developing to be used, and they have a strong desire to be appreciated and admired.

Interpersonal and Group Processes and Characteristics

360 DEGREE EVALUATIONS

A 360 degree evaluation seeks commentary from the range of employee 'customers' in regards to performance; 'customers' are internal and external individuals the employee deals with daily. The value of a 260 degree evaluation lies in the fact that the data, which come from a multitude of sources, are well- rounded and offer a relatively accurate portrait. Additionally, soliciting the opinions and experiences of others involves them proactively and makes the evaluation process more meaningful to all involved. Individuals participating in this type of evaluation must be properly trained in order for it to be useful. Untrained evaluators are less likely to provide constructive feedback in which they not only describe a problem but suggest possible methods of approach. If the employee to be evaluated is permitted to select other group members or outside group members to complete that portion of the evaluation, the results will be skewered.

TYPE A PERSONALITIES

Type A personalities are likely to succeed in positions that demand more time, more energy and more determination than most. Type A's thrive on challenge; if they don't find it in their environment, they impose it upon themselves by setting artificial deadlines or by competing with the best in the field. Type A's are ambitious and acquisitive, seeing possessions as representative of their outstanding value. They are multitaskers, and keep detailed mental or actual records that measure their successes. While Type A's work quickly, their concern is with quantity over quality. They will work overtime even when they don't need to, but some of the decisions they make in the wee hours may not be the best. Their style is fairly predictable, because new decisions are based upon previous experience and not upon creative, thoughtful responses to specific needs. They can be excellent project managers, but are not a good choice for research positions.

RISK IN ORGANIZATIONAL BEHAVIOR

The role of risk in organizational behavior has been explored through research, reports, statistics and even through reality TV programs. As a culture, Americans applaud it, glorifying the individual who reaches for greater and greater heights by putting everything on the line. Risk takers are gamblers, and the best among them will gamble with everything they've got—but the risks they take will be specifically selected to reach a particular goal. Sometimes they lose, but loss, for a risk taker, is just another opportunity to start over again. Managers who are seen by others as risk takers make fast, sometimes instantaneous decisions that sometimes are based on gut feeling rather than information. Risk takers trust their instincts because they feel they know themselves. Certain organizational positions require a risk taking personality, such as a loan broker; others might be damaged by it, such as a loan underwriter.

GENERATIONAL DIFFERENCES IN CULTURE

Culture, a major contributor in shaping value systems, attitudes and motivation, transforms when looked at through the lens of time. Culture is creating by large numbers of individuals who change within themselves through experience, or leave through death and are replaced by new individuals with other values. Specific time periods, such as generations or centuries, can be studied to discover commonly held attributes. Different generations face different social, economic and spiritual challenges, which partially determine the values that form attitudes which inform motivation typical to that generation. For example, post WW II Baby Boomers grew up in intact families during a period of economic growth. They developed a strongly spiritual attitude influenced by the music and flower child ethics of the 60s. Their children, members of Generation X, experienced single parent households, an explosion of material goods, and a world community both online and off, and cherish relationships, choices and independence.

Multicultural Perspectives

The study of organization behavior was originally an American one. American social scientists studied American professional, social, religious and community groups in an effort to understand the dynamics at play. The United States is, indeed, a melting pot, with a strong cultural bias toward equality. Civil rights, the counterculture movement and the women's movement brought the perspectives of women, seniors, and people of color front and center, and social scientists broadened their research to include these groups. With worldwide industrialization, the internet and global economy, it has been essential to broaden the focus even more. The work force is no longer primarily white middle- class men, but contains a vibrant mix of peoples from many cultures. Culture helps shape beliefs and values. Managers need at least a basic understanding of specific cultural differences in order to understand the expectations and limits of their employees, and to predict future behavior.

Traits

Traits strongly suggest personal values. Because human beings are multifaceted and unique, personalities are motivated by a complex mixture of values. Studying personality in terms of values requires three steps. The first is to determine which behaviors demonstrate what values. The next step is determining the values an individual has internalized, or is motivated by, and which values remain external to his own personal value system. Third, it's important to determine where, in that value system, each value belongs. Some values are core, intensely felt and inform every decision. The traits that they manifest are called cardinal traits. Primary traits are nearly as important and are fairly consistently exhibited, but special situations permit them to be temporarily set aside. Secondary traits demonstrate values that are part of an individual's value system but not absolutely essential to it. They manifest during specific situations. In general, traits are consistent over time.

Trait Theorists

Trait theorists take the position that personality characteristics remain consistent and unchanging over time, and are therefore a clear predictor of how a person will act in a given situation. While it is true that many traits remain stable over time, they can and do evolve in 'strong' situations where maintaining that trait would be counterproductive. It is obviously easiest to let go of a secondary trait and hold onto a cardinal trait as long as possible. However, if forced, people will adapt or transform a value to the degree necessary for survival. They may do so by changing a definition or basic belief about the cardinal value's meaning so that they can continue to exist in that particular environment. Work environments are generally strong ones; an employee who defies rules or insists upon behavior not sanctioned by the workplace culture is risking losing his job. Acceptable actions are clearly defined in a workplace environment, and unacceptable actions are punished. In addition, there are informal, unstated constraints in the form of behavioral norms manifested by the majority of employees.

Teams

A team can be defined as a group of individuals with skills, training and ability that is complementary who have identified a common goal and purpose, and see themselves as equally accountable. A number of types of formal and informal teams contribute to the accomplishment of organizational goals. For example, a management team is a collection of managers from several departments tasked with organizing work teams. A work team is a long term group of employees in a single area or department who are responsible for daily work. Quality circles are a few people from one department that meet on a regular basis to consider, discuss and suggest resolutions to issues that arise in the work environment. A virtual team communicates using the internet, office networks, or the like. Virtual teams are relatively fluid, and gain or lose members as each situation requires. A product development team is often composed of both work and problem- solving teams who are charged with developing new product designs or services. A problem solving team is a short term group created to aggressively address specific workplace issues.

High Level Managers

Employees who have achieved a high degree of influence, control or power in an organization are very likely to be resistant to change of any kind. High- level managers assume positions diametrically opposed to change less because of what the change might potentially mean to the organization than because of what it might potentially mean to them. For this reason, change agents (other than those who have been established from within the organization by the board of directors) usually have little influence within the organization, are new hires, or come from outside in the form of consultants. Employees who have been with a company for years and have worked themselves into positions of authority are threatened by any. If the status quo is unsettled, if tradition isn't observed, not only is their personal power at risk, but the safest way for them to proceed in order to protect their worth unknowable and unpredictable. Furthermore, disruption of the status quo can mean a coup in which their own power is dissipated or reduced in order to benefit a new competitor.

Work Groups and Work Teams

Most organizations are composed of both work groups and work teams, with some individuals participating in both simultaneously or sequentially. Groups and teams are both composed of individuals who interact in order to achieve one or more goals. A work group is generally considered to be smaller and less structured than a work team. In a work group, two people or more join forces and interact interdependently by sharing information and suggestions in order to satisfy certain established aims. Though members are part of a group, they function and see themselves as independent agents. The work group's output is equal to the sum total of the output of its individual members. Work teams, however, exist for a collective purpose, are both individually accountable and accountable as a group entity, and function efficiently by making the best use of complementary abilities and training. Teams, unlike groups, are able to realize enhanced production through synergy; the work team's output is greater than the sum total of the output of its individual members.

Groupthink

'Groupthink' has been used to describe a potentially dangerous process that can distort decision making, planning and other activities that require making choices. 'Groupthink' is a psychological event that can occur when a group of individuals prioritize solidarity within the group above all other matters. 'Groupthink' can be described as each member of a group suspending any individual idea or concern that would potentially unsettle the group's camaraderie or cause another type of disruption. Individuals may be fully aware that they have an objection or concern about the way the group has decided to orchestrate some part of a project, but push the concern aside, believing the group knows best or that to speak up will isolate the doubter. It is the very lack of conflict that becomes a self fulfilling prophesy; no one speaks up because no one speaks up. While the first person to voice questions or hesitation may meet with a wall of denial, should that person gain an advocate, the house of straw will likely come down.

Brainstorming

Brainstorming is a no-holds-barred idea gathering technique that has gained wide popularity and application in nearly every corner. Elementary teachers lead brainstorming sessions, as do gang members and CEOs. In contrast, the nominal group technique limits conversation, written correspondence and all other forms of communication during the procedure of making a decision. The nominal group technique is at the opposite end of the spectrum from brainstorming, which is inclusive, nonjudgmental and invites tremendous, intimate, charged dialogue. Using the nominal group technique requires that participants meet together in one location. Prior to any discussion whatsoever, each participant notes her concerns and ideas about the issue under study. Next, each participant must present only one idea to the gathering. Again, except for each speaker in turn, these presentations are done in silence. Following presentations, the group discusses each idea. Following this is another period of silence, during which time each participant puts each idea that was presented in order of what she considers more useful to least useful. Finally, the ideas are once again examined, this time in order to determine the idea that received the highest 'vote'. This is the idea that the group accepts as their final decision.

Cultural Norms and Differences

The American work place has changed considerably in a few short decades. Where it was once the stronghold of men, it is now populated as much with women. Where before managers, supervisors and others in positions of power were almost exclusively of Western European descent, now such positions are frequently held by people from many different cultures. Cultural norms are just that—normal to those who were raised in that culture. A profoundly belief in one culture may be simply baffling to members of another. While it is important for all people to be aware of and respectful toward cultural difference, it is especially so for managers. An innocent remark or action can bring an employee embarrassment or rage. A manager who loudly praises a female Korean employee and asks his staff to model themselves after her, for example, has inadvertently shamed her deeply by singling her out.

Channels of Communication

Organizations are filled with thousands of channels of communication, some formal, and many that are informal in nature. Formal channels of communication are intentionally created to communicate specific types of information to specific individuals. In formal communication, information travels from the managerial level down to departments, teams and individuals. Changes in organizational policy, notices, office manuals and announcements are typically handled via formal communication, so that information can be tracked in the future, and in order to adhere to organizational formulas or guidelines. Informal channels of communication, unlike formal channels, are unprompted, unstructured and are frequently reactions to formal communication. Informal communication typically contains a greater degree of opinion and emotion, and is often not as concerned with the accuracy of the information being shared as with the desire to express it. Informal communication can include gossip and rumors, as well as verbal communication between team mates, from managers to employees, or from employees to managers. Written communications such as emails or memos are typically informal in nature.

Efficiency

Organizations that are running at a high level of efficiency are those in which management, teams and individual employees are working in concert. Communication is shared both through formal and informal channels, problems are dealt with swiftly and fully, and strategies are implemented according to plan. Larger organizations, because they contain more levels of administration, are structurally more prone to errors that affect overall efficiency than are smaller organizations that have fewer top administrators and managers, and often times fewer levels and fewer departments. However, small organizations are only relatively more efficient if their goals are clear, their strategies for achieving them logical, and their communication and other systems well structures and complete. Lacking these things, small organizations can quickly fall into a greater degree of inefficiency.

Mintzberg's Organizational Model

Organizational power is both extremely rigid and extremely fluid. It is rigid, in that individuals who possess a greater portion of power at any given moment in time are not interested in sharing it unless there is a specific benefit to them in doing so. It is fluid, in that events can suddenly and radically shift power from one area to another. When power is vertically and horizontally centralized, the strategic apex (top managers) holds all the power. Limited horizontal decentralization occurs when these managers allocate a portion to techno structure employees who standardize work. Limited vertical decentralization occurs when market-based units' managers gain enough power to control decisions concerning their units. Vertical and horizontal decentralization occurs when a greater portion of power is under ownership of the operating core at the base of the model. Selective vertical and horizontal decentralization is what happens when decision making power is spread throughout the organization.

The Garbage Can Model of Organizational Theory

The Garbage Can model of organizational theory addresses ambiguous behaviors within an organization that on the surface, cannot be rationally explained. The Garbage Can theory was designed to explain how irrational behaviors within an organization are caused by a disconnect in the decision making processes. Illogical behaviors or those that don't follow prediction can be the result. The model hypothesizes that when decision making is riddled with an intense degree of uncertainty, individuals within that environment begin to behave in ways that don't seem reasonable and a kind of organizational anarchy takes hold. The problem that the decision is supposed to resolve, the solution that the decision suggests, and the individuals charged with making the decision, effectively disengage to the point at which any decisions that are ultimately made are arbitrarily based upon a collection of event streams that do not necessarily have any association with one another. The four event streams that decision making in this case has failed to unify can be categorized as problems; solutions; choice opportunities and participants. The four event streams the Garbage Can model finds as the source of irrational behavior within an organization are described as belonging to the areas of problems, solutions, choice opportunities and participants.

Problems result from gaps in performance or inadequate information. Often, the decision making process is not used to address them. A solution that may not fit the problem is applied so that work can continue. Solutions in this model have little to do with the problems they are expected to resolve. They exist as ideals, and are applied to existing problems regardless of how inappropriate the fit may be. While decision makers are able to create possible solutions, without thoroughly understanding the problem, it's impossible to create an adequate solution. Choice opportunities are those moments when an organization believes it must make a decision for public reasons that have no relationship to the problem, as a way of demonstrating or signaling that the problem has been addressed. It has been addressed, but inappropriately so. Participants are those involved in the decision making; being human, their decisions are not always well considered.

Groups

Groups are everywhere in human society, as small as two individuals that come together to achieve a common goal, or as large as a nation. In organizations, groups can be informal or formal; the latter are called work teams. The relationship between a group or team as a whole and the individuals comprising it is complex. While it is obvious that individuals shape and influence the groups to which they belong, it is equally true that a group can profoundly influence the actions and even perceptions of individuals who compose it; an example of this is found in groupthink, when individuals suppress their own ideas to stay in sync with the group. Managers need to protect against the deadening effects of groupthink while remaining focused on organizational goals. Often the most efficient way to do so is to ensure the various members are getting their own needs met. Managers must remember that individuals within a work team are there because of their own agendas; they hope to meet a personal goal, satisfy a desire, or exert influence upon something inside or outside the team.

A GROUP CAN BE TEMPORARY OR RELATIVELY PERMANENT, FORMAL OR INFORMAL.

Formal groups are created to meet goals decided prior to the group's formation. They fall under the headings task groups, affinity groups and command groups. Of these, command groups are more permanent. Command groups, usually part of the organizational chart, establish chain of command for the reporting of information. Task groups are organizationally established as well but are temporary in nature, created to fulfill a single or related group of tasks and dissolve when goals are achieved. Affinity groups, also created by the organization, are composed of same- level employees who meet at scheduled times to examine issues or share important facts. Informal groups are most often specified as friendship groups or interest groups. Informal groups are formed casually, without outside intention. Friendship groups are formed by social interactions and relationships. Interest groups are more temporary, and are formed around a shared activity or unique interest members have in common.

GROUPS CAN PERFORM WITH VARYING DEGREES OF EFFICIENCY AND EFFECTIVENESS.

A number of factors can influence the group's performance. While the purpose of any group is to achieve at the highest level, many influences factor into how well the group succeeds. Four important characteristics that contribute toward the outcome are the group's size, composition, norms, and ability to cohere. An increased group size affects performance positively when there are a greater number of tasks or more complex ones, and negatively when the work to be done is simple. Relative uniformity in group composition influences how individual members interface with one another as well as how productive the group is able to become. Group norms can contribute to the group's longevity, predict group and individual behaviors, curtail unacceptable behaviors, and organize the group's purpose in terms of vision and values. A group's ability to cohere greatly influences both the speed at which it functions and how successful it is. A group that is coherent communicates with a fluency that wastes nothing.

THE STAGES A GROUP MOVES THROUGH DURING THE COURSE OF ITS DEVELOPMENT.

There are four distinct stages groups pass through from inception to successful conclusion. The first is mutual acceptance, when members identify themselves with others and with the group's purpose as a whole. Without this initial bonding, the next stage, which focuses on the twin roles of decision making and communication, would not succeed. The second stage is when group members reflect upon goals, share ideas, and decide how to decide. The third stage, motivation and productivity, occurs when the group's energy becomes purposeful and driven. Ideas have been contemplated, decisions made concerning how to resolve an issue, and the group as a whole directs itself forcefully toward accomplishment. The fourth stage is control and organization. By this stage, the group has generated considerable information which needs to be categorized, prioritized and managed. In order for a group to perform with a high degree of success, the stages must be fully engaged.

Within an Organization, the Manners in Which Various Work Groups Relate Are Complex and Intertwined.

How and how well groups function within an organization is largely dependent upon a handful of facets. The first is physical proximity. Groups working near one another are likely to interact, share information and resources. Groups that need access to the same resources such as information, materials, technology and tools will be more likely to interact, particularly if one group has control over materials needed by the other. Groups whose individual tasks are related to tasks another group has been assigned will be likely to interrelate more often and more fluently than groups whose tasks are distinct. Groups that are on schedules with similar deadlines will become more interconnected than those working under greater or lesser pressure. The greater the number of these elements—nearness, the need to share resources, relatedness of tasks, and similar deadlines—that two groups share, the more interconnected will be their relationship.

Productivity

A high level of productivity is important to all organizations. Many factors can affect productivity, some of which are under a manager's control and others which are not. Managers who are skillful in dealing with conflicts have a higher level of productivity in the employees they manage. Employees who perceive themselves as holding little power are likely to avoid conflict. At the first sign of disagreement, if it isn't possible to physically leave, they will mentally withdraw. Employees who perceive themselves as having a small amount of influence tend to deal with conflict by making themselves as accommodating as possible. When an employee is in conflict with someone of equal power, and when that employee feels either threatened or that future power is at stake, she will often respond to conflict with overtly challenging or competitive behavior. Colleagues who feel their position in the organization isn't challenged, or those who are able to emotionally detach, will approach conflict as an opportunity to collaborate. Collaborating employees arrive at a unified position in which compromise has been made. The most productive response to conflict is collaboration; managers can teach employees skills to handle conflict productively.

Leadership

Early research concerned with leadership roles sought to create a universal definition of leadership qualities. The goal of early research in the area of leadership was to locate and describe characteristics and behaviors successful leaders tended to share in order to create a universal definition of essential leadership qualities. The conclusions these studies came to were that leaders exhibited two types of behavior. The first type of behavior that studies identified was concerned with elements found within jobs. The second type of leadership behavior was concerned with characteristics found within people. A study done at the University of Michigan placed both types of leadership values as distinct points along a single continuum. Another study undertaken at Ohio State viewed the two types as separate and unrelated, and found that the most successful leaders took a holistic approach in combining a high degree of concentration directed at both human and job- related elements, seeing them as influences upon one another.

Initial Trait Theory

Initial trait theory models led later researchers to examine the intersections where less successful leaders were most likely to become entangled, and ultimately fail. Early studies of highly successful leaders quite naturally led to later research on leaders who failed. Four characteristics were found to represent the most common areas of weakness. Unsuccessful leaders often lacked composure under stress. Rather than behaving confidently and with unruffled assurance when the environment became unstable, unsuccessful leaders exhibited confusion, anger or anxiety. Unsuccessful leaders were reluctant to admit fault or being in the wrong, channeling energy into trying to conceal their errors instead. Ineffective leaders too often resorted to manipulation, coercion or hostility when their persuasive skills were not enough to convince others of the rightness of their point of view; this alienated rather than convinced followers. The final characteristic where leaders fail is in intelligence. While unsuccessful leaders were quite often highly intelligent, their brilliance remained focused upon a narrow range of ideas and ideals rather than widening to take in the big picture.

CRT

Cognitive Resource Theory (CRT) is based on the assumption that successful leadership is enhanced by cognitive assets such as intelligence, creativity, and conceptual understanding during periods of low stress; however, cognitive resources alone are insufficient because of the role high stress plays in a leader's decision- making abilities. In Cognitive Resource Theory, cognitive resources contribute to successful leadership but are insufficient on their own. The presence of stress and how a leader responds to it is an equally important variable. According to Cognitive Resource Theory, a leader's advanced cognitive resources are useful only when the leader is operating in an instructional or commanding role. Plans and decisions can most effectively be enabled under firm guidance. Situations low in stress permit intelligence full flower. High stress situations, however, often require a non- rational 'gut' intelligence to take over. Leaders with past experience in similar high stress situations permit successful leaders to respond appropriately while bypassing rational thought. Cognitive Resource Theory finds one other area where a leader's developed cognitive assets may not be important. Tasks that are simple in nature don't require instruction or guidance; therefore, a leader's ability to make wise decisions contributes nothing to the success of the task.

Trait Theory of Leadership

According to the trait theory of leadership, traits are inherited and unchanging. Leaders are born, not made, and by discovering traits and skills found in highly successful leaders, others with similar qualities could become equally successful. Trait theory operates on the assumption that true leaders are those born with a certain combination of qualities that allow them to excel. The research that grew out of trait theory was designed to determine which traits and skills were the most desirable by studying highly successful leaders; others with similar trait combinations were likely to be equally successful leaders in this model. According to Stogdill's 1974 model, great leaders were adaptable to circumstances, aware of social environment, ambitious, assertive and decisive, reliable, and energetic. In addition, great leaders were capable of and willing to cooperate, while at the same time possessed a strong need to be influential. Great leaders exhibit a high degree of confidence, persist until goals are met, are untroubled by stress, and are highly responsible. Their skills include cleverness, creativity, diplomacy, and intuitive understanding of group dynamics. They are socially skilled and use their highly developed eloquence to persuade others.

Contingency Theories of Leadership

Contingency theories of leadership find that leadership ability is contingent upon circumstances. According to contingency theories of leadership, changing circumstances can directly affect a previously successful leader's ability to continue to lead. Followers may change their behaviors, goals or values due to outside influences. The leader's previously successful personal style might become socially or politically unacceptable. New information about the leader's personal or professional life can change the public's opinion. A leader with a history of being highly competent with one type of population or in one particular area may discover upon trying to widen his base that those previously outside his sphere of influence are not willing to follow him because their ideals, needs, or cultural environments differ in essential ways. According to contingency theories, leaders are not born with inherited traits; in fact, effective leadership depends almost entirely upon outside influences to the degree that no one style or approach can be considered best in all cases.

LEAST PREFERRED COWORKER THEORY

The least preferred coworker theory developed by Fiedler hypothesizes that the success of a leader depends upon the leader's traits, the particulars of the situation and a number of other contributing factors. In least preferred coworker theory (LPC), a leader's success is dependent upon a number of contributing factors, among them the degree of correlation between the leader's traits and a favorable situation. The leader's actions are seen as reflective of his personality characteristics and, as a result, constant and unlikely to change. In turn, the favorability of a situation is shaped by the form the task takes in combination with the shared relationship between the leader and the followers, and where the leader ranks in terms of power. High least preferred coworker leaders typically develop personal, positive rapport with others, behave supportively, and rank the importance of the relationship above the importance of the task. Low least preferred coworker leaders place the importance of the task above that of relationships; indeed, low LPC leaders tend to completely ignore relationships unless they are completely satisfied with employee efforts toward task achievement.

PATH- GOAL THEORY

Path- goal theory, one of the contingency theories of the 1970's contends that followers' willingness to accept and follow a leader is contingent upon a number of factors.

FOLLOWERS' ACCEPTANCE

Path- goal theory holds that a leader's success is dependent upon followers' acceptance and willingness to be guided toward their goals. A successful leader must satisfy followers in three areas. The first is in clarifying the task, so that followers have a clear understanding of what they are expected to do. Secondly, a successful leader whom followers will support must be able to either remove obstacles along the path toward success, or must establish an efficient detour around such obstacles. Leaders who enjoy the acceptance of their followers must also reward them as they move in the direction of achievement; the closer followers get to success, the greater the incentives must be. In goal- path theory, the emphasis is upon how leaders serve followers. Should a leader fail in any of these areas to meet followers' expectations, they will remove their support and the leadership will fail to be effective.

CHANGING LEADERSHIP STYLE

One premise of path-goal theory is that leaders are capable of changing leadership style when the situation demands. The relationship between the leader's behavior and outcomes are contingent upon variable combinations. These variable combinations can be found in the environment or be a characteristic of followers. Path- goal theory contends that successful leaders must adapt leadership style to meet needs of various situations. According to the theory, combinations of two contingency variables determine the relationship between the leader and the outcome of the situation. Elements in the environment are outside the follower- task structure, the leader's authority, or the workgroup's control. Environmental components are deciding factors in which leadership behaviors are required in order to enhance follower outcomes. Follower characteristics are found in the intersection of control, experience, and how ability is perceived. It is followers' individual traits that interpret the relationship between environment and leader. A leader's ability to make up for deficiencies in the environment or within followers contributes to followers' acceptance of the leader, and therefore, to the leader's ultimate success or failure. While LPC presumes leaders cannot adapt leadership style, path- goal theory assumes leadership adaptability is contingent upon the situation.

Types of Headership Behavior

Path-goal theory describes four types of leadership behaviors as achievement-oriented, directive, participative, and supportive.

- Achievement- oriented leader behavior is demonstrated when a leader establishes challenging goals, and displays faith in followers' abilities.
- Directive leadership behavior is found in task clarification together with specific steps followers will adhere to in order to accomplish it. This leadership type is especially important in cases where a task is somewhat ambiguous and there are a number of possible ways to accomplish it.
- Participative leader behavior is demonstrated in situations where a leader discusses the tasks and goals with followers, and asks for their input. Followers who feel that their input helps inform the leader's decisions are especially willing to follow this leader when they have a strong sense of identification with the work.
- Supportive leadership is demonstrated in situations where a leader's behavior guides followers in the direction of satisfaction of their own goals and needs. This type of behavior is especially effective in stressful situations.

T-Groups

One model based in organizational development theory is variously called T- groups (training groups), laboratory groups, encounter groups or sensitivity training. T- groups, encounter groups and sensitivity training are all terms for the same activity. These groups encourage healthy behavioral changes, and so via group interaction that is not specifically prescribed. In a T- group, members gather in an environment that is 'free'; that is, an environment that is not seen as 'belonging' to a group or individual, nor one with negative associations. Three constants only are in place; the rest of what happens in a T- group is spontaneous and unscripted. The three constants are a scheduled time for meetings, a specific location where meetings take place, and a 'guide', generally someone with appropriate training, who will lead the sessions. T- groups focus on process, and members develop and change through their experiences and through observing the experiences of others. Individuals develop enhanced awareness of how their actions affect others, develop conflict resolution skills, and gain greater empathy.

Informal Organizations

Informal organizations can, at times, be disadvantageous to a formal organization. For this reason, it is important for managers to carefully monitor them and address situations that could become dangerous. While informal organizations can be very useful to a formal organization, because they are difficult to control there are times when they can threaten the status quo. For example, informal organizations are remarkably resistant to change, given that their very makeup requires it. Be that as it may, once informal organizations come into existence, they understand the value of continuity and demonstrate it by protecting their unique culture; this can lead an informal organization to confronting a formal one when it is threatened. Informal groups are largely focused on their own satisfaction; when it conflicts with formal objectives, an informal organization can be a real threat to the organization as a whole. It is important that managers attend to this possibility by integrating interests, needs and strategies found in both informal groups and the organization as a whole within a single vision.

Rumor

The role of rumor in informal organizations, and how managers can both eradicate the dangers inherent in it as well as employ them to further the goals of the organization.

Formal organizations need informal organizations for a number of reasons. Informal organizations can be an under the radar method to disperse real information, or to manipulate employees by spreading information that isn't true. However, if informal organizations are not carefully managed, they can become dangerous to the organization as a whole. Rumor and conformity are both the results of informal organizations operating on levels that are less concerned with authenticity than they are with power. Rumor isn't concerned about what is communicated, only that communication is made; its ultimate purpose is to forge a connection between the speaker and listeners, and to give the speaker an edge in terms of power in suggesting that he has inside information. Rumor can negatively affect morale, cause insecurity or depression, and even ruin careers. Managers must watch for the negative effects of rumor and address them immediately to protect the work environment.

CONFORMITY

Informal organizations are primarily social in nature. One of their characteristics is a tendency to encourage conformity because it contributes to group cohesion; additionally, conformity discourages aberrant behavior that could lead to criticism of the group. While oftentimes a formal organization benefits from conformity within informal organizations because they tend to stabilize and protect company norms, there is also a more dangerous side to conformity. Informal groups tend to be highly critical of anyone whose behavior is 'other'; this means an individual with uniquely creative or innovative ideas, or one whose performance is at a higher level than that of other group members, are either ostracized from the group or pressured into conforming. Individuals who have much to contribute to the organization as a whole, but who feel unappreciated or disliked by the employees she spends the most time with, is very likely to feel dissatisfied and leave the company.

CONFLICT

As anyone who has ever had a friend, been part of a family, or been in a romantic relationship knows, conflict is an inevitable fact of life. Conflict is a matter of perception to those involved. If the people drawn into what appears to be a conflict see it as an interesting discussion on opposing points, , no conflict exists. Conflict is not simply a heated exchange of words, but involves action. At its most basic, conflict can be defined as one side that believes another side has inflicted harm to something they feel is important. In organizations, conflict can take many forms. Teammates who disagree on how to accomplish goals; department heads who are convinced another department has been given an unfair advantage in some way; one person who is conflicted about their own personal desires and the best interests of the team, all exemplify conflict. Because conflict is inevitable, it's important that managers know the best ways to resolve it in certain situations and to use it to organizational advantage in others.

AVOIDING CONFLICT

The traditional organizational view of conflict has been that it must avoided if it cannot be easily resolved or managed. In this view, conflict is always negative, unreasonable, unpredictable and destructive. While contemporary views of conflict are not necessarily negative, historically organizations considered conflict as a source of danger that grew out of a malfunction in personal interaction caused by an individual or group within the organization. Conflict is to be avoided, because of the negative affect it has upon production. The cause of conflict in the traditional view was a failure to communicate or to be open and trusting or trustworthy, and was seen as inherently dysfunctional. When conflict could not be avoided, the best course of action was thought to be to compartmentalize and defuse it by attending to the communication breakdown that caused it. The primary reason conflict needs to be handled, from this perspective, is because it has a negative effect on performance at both the individual and organizational levels.

POSITIVE CONFLICT

The most current position on conflict in organizations argues that not only can conflict be a positive force, but that there are situations in which it is required for the most successful possible performance. In the interactionist view, there are times when the presence of conflict is not only useful, it is essential in driving a team to the highest possible level of accomplishment. This school of thought considers a highly tranquil environment is in danger of becoming static. In stasis, things at rest tend to stay at rest. Organizational situations that are overly relaxed are also lacking in energy; without the sense of urgency, excitement or even anxiety that conflict provides, a collaborative group will only grow more placid, fail to recognize issues that require changes in behavior, and will lack an innovative perspective. Interactionists argue that managers should infuse the group with a low level of conflict in order to literally stir things up. When members begin to disagree, to challenge one another and even their own ideas, creativity enters into the process, and results in innovative ideas and increased energy.

DESTRUCTIVE CONFLICT

The interactionist view of conflict finds that conflict is both healthy and necessary for groups within an organization to achieve the highest possible level of performance. However, the interactionist position also finds that conflict can also be highly destructive.

The interactionist school of thought concerning conflict within an organization raised the earlier human relations view to another level. While human relationists found that conflict could be a positive force in certain situations, the interactionist position is that conflict is an essential ingredient to the highest possible level of achievement a group can reach. However, this is not the same as postulating all conflict is always constructive. The interactionist model organizes conflict into functional and dysfunctional forms, which are dependent upon whether the conflict arises in relation to personal relationship, the task at hand, or the process undertaken. Interactionist research suggests that in almost all cases, personal conflict is destructive to group performance for the simple reason that it diminishes mutual respect and understanding and hampers efficient task completion. Process conflict at low levels enhance productivity, while task conflicts about work goals encourage communication about ideas from which the group benefits.

ESSENTIALS TO THE CONFLICT PROCESS

The first phase generally recognized as essential to the conflict process is called incompatibility, or potential opposition, and is manifested by the presence of one or more necessary conditions. For conflict to arise, certain conditions must be present in order to provide opportunity. Contemporary research finds three primary conditions are communicative, structural or personal in nature. It is certainly possible for situations to contain one or more of these conditions without becoming full blown conflict; at any stage along the way the potential can become defused or derailed. However, without one of these three conditions, conflict lacks opportunity and cannot, therefore, develop. Problems in communication are rampant; a lack of shared information, differences in what words or expressions mean, even regional accents can contribute to conflict. Structural conditions in this context are the differing expectations between jobs; a loan officer and underwriter working on the same loan have very different roles that can conflict. Personal conditions are those in which at least one of the parties involved perceives a conflict, and has an emotional response to that perception.

POWER, INFLUENCE AND AUTHORITY

Although power, influence and authority contain substantial areas of overlap, they are, in fact, not identical. A powerful individual is capable of causing some kind of transformation in groups or individuals. This transformation is deeply felt; it is not simply a change on the surface, but in some way, a shift on the structural level. Not all power is justifiable; while it is often dynamically balanced with an individual's position in the company, there are certainly times when power manifests from unexpected quarters. Influence comes from a different source than does power; influence isn't the result of control but of persuasion. Influence can be broadly interpreted and is broadly applied. Authority and power bear much in common, but while power can belong to individuals without the blessing of the organization, authority cannot. Authority can be defined as power endorsed by the organization and invested in an individual.

Contemporary Theories

Contemporary theories break the conflict process into five phases. Five phases in the conflict process have been identified as incompatibility, cognition and personalization, intentions, behavior, and outcomes. The first of these, incompatibility, is also called potential opposition by some research studies. This phase presents one or more conditions that could be opportunities for conflict to take hold. These conditions are typically communicative, structural or personal in nature. The next phase, cognition and personalization, is typified by conflict that is perceived or felt by the parties involved. Phase 3, intentions, is characterized by how the conflict is handled. This can be done collaboratively, competitively, through avoidance, compromise or accommodation. The fourth phase, behavior, is the stage at which the conflict blossoms into action through the behavior of one participant and the reaction of the other. The final phase is the conflict outcome. Either the conflict results in an enhanced group performance, or it diminishes the performance.

Definition of Power

Power exists only in so far as it is interconnected with other elements within an organization. While the most common image that power carries is that of a monolithic force that bends all else to its will, in practice, power requires a relationship. One definition of power is the capacity to sway opinion or action in order to control the outcome. Should a manager want a particular outcome and works covertly or overtly upon his employees to exact it, his power is demonstrated only to the degree they behave as he desires and the behaviors are not ones they would otherwise have chosen. If, instead, their behavior was predictable and of their own volition, it might demonstrate respect or compliance on the parts of the employees toward their manager, but it is not necessarily indicative of the degree of power the manager possesses.

Five Types of Power

The five basic types of power include those that can be seen as positive in nature, those that can be positive or negative, and those that are negative or hostile in nature. Coercive power is always negative because it is based upon threats and fear. Coercive power seizes control rather than negotiating it and cares nothing for what it costs others. Legitimate power, or that bestowed upon an individual by the organization, and referent power which rises out of others' identification with and imitation of a powerful person, can be either positive or negative, depending upon the degree of intentional manipulation, force or rewards used to secure power. Reward power, based upon an individual's capacity to grant rewards, and expert power, which comes as a result of specialized knowledge, are both considered to be positive types of power in that they are the result of dynamic, earned action.

Dependency and Contingency

The concept of dependency is central to determining the degree of power an individual is in possession of. A manager, leader or coworker who is attempting to exert power over an employee, follower or coworker will be successful to the degree the target is dependent upon the negotiator. In this case, dependence is demonstrated by the degree to which the target believes the negotiator uniquely controls limited resources that are of considerable importance to the target. Recently, contingency theories of power are becoming more accepted. This approach suggests that possession of power is the result of the processes of compliance, identification and internalization. Power is contingent to some degree upon both how willing the target is to being influenced, as well as to how well the negotiator is situated to be seen as a source of power by the target.

Areas of Essential Communicative Function

Communication serves four organizational purposes: sharing information; expressing emotion; inspiring motivation; and control.

- Sharing information is essential to decision making, to guiding work, to following instructions and ultimately, to satisfactory job performance.
- Communication permits emotional expression. Satisfaction, frustration, happiness and anger are natural responses to any interaction. They need healthy expression or they can contaminate a task or environment. Informal avenues of communication via office relationships allow the expression of positive feelings that inspire the group as a whole, and negative expressions which can then be considered and resolved, or isolated.
- Third, communication nurtures motivation when it clearly delineates tasks, provides feedback, and rewards success with praise.
- Finally communication enables control. For example, formal guidelines describe communication avenues based upon job descriptions in accordance with company policies. This allows controls of both top down and bottom up communications; creates a trail that can be followed; and formalizes complaints.

Communication

Communication, the conveyance of meaning, is successful to the degree that the receiver understands what the communicator intended. Ideally, intended meaning is perfectly transferred , but realistically, absolute communication is impossible for three reasons. First, speakers are always eccentric to some degree. They assume listeners share linguistic and contextual beliefs. They may compress parts of messages, inflating them to a greater degree that the overall meaning warrants, or neglect to codify them at all. Secondly, all communication is encoded into a medium. Whether spoken, written, signed, or otherwise codified, the medium is not identical to the message; it represents it. All codes have limits in what they can express, as well as potential areas where confusion is possible. Writing 'fed' instead of 'led' can transform a meeting. Third, recipients accept messages through cultural and personal frameworks of understanding with many areas where meaning can be distorted, erased, or otherwise misunderstood. A communication begins when a communicator encodes a concept in order to transmit it to a receiver. The concept becomes the message, and encoding formalizes it. Encoding is both an objective and subjective act; it removes extraneous elements and forms the communication into an artifact with shared attributes. At the same time, a communicator subjectively decides that to leave out. The medium is the channel through which the message is sent. It might be written, spoken, signed, or otherwise delivered. The receiver must 'open' the message by decoding it. Successful transmission is determined in part by the degree to which the principles for encoding are the same as for decoding. It is impossible for a receiver to decode a message sans environment, and all environments are to some degree, contaminated by previous information, perception, cultural and linguistic differences. When the communicator receives feedback, the message's successful transmission can be determined.

Communication Directions

Downward and upward flowing communication are both vertical. Downward communication begins at higher managerial. Formal in nature, it is useful in assigning tasks, providing goals, giving instructions, and offering organizational information.

Upward flowing information is often in response to specific downward flowing communication, and often, though not always, flows through the same channels. Upward communication provides supervisors with feedback regarding projects, issues or problems within a team or department, and possible ways to improve a specific area, task, or issue within the organization. Suggestion box contributions, surveys, grievances, performance reports and manager reviews are all examples of upward flowing communication.

Lateral communication flows between individuals who are functioning at the same level, and is often, although not always, informal in nature. They can be sources of information regarding employee satisfaction, used to control organizational norms, and can potentially create dysfunction within the working environment through misinformation or personal conflict.

Messages

Messages are communicated verbally, in writing, and nonverbally. Human beings constantly use orality for self expression and to share ideas. Formal oral communications include speeches, theatrical productions, interviews and presentations, while informal communication is spontaneous and includes personal conversation, communication between salesperson and customer, and gossip. Verbal communication is instantaneous, and feedback nearly instantaneous; errors in communication are often spotted and corrected during the initial conversational stream. Written communication such as emails, faxes, memos, and industry publications involve symbolizing meaning into a standardized scripted code. They can be verified, referenced at a later date, and tend to be more cautiously expressed. Written communication takes longer, and feedback is not instantaneous, allowing for misunderstanding. Nonverbal communication accompanies verbal communication and provides substantial information that is context or subtext related. Body language, tone of voice, and spatial relationship all contribute meaning, although often the speaker isn't conscious of it. Perceived status and personal interest contribute strongly in nonverbal communication.

Small group networks

Formal small group organizational networks can be defined as those containing fewer than half a dozen members. It is important to note that there are hundreds of variations within these three configurations that can be reduced to fit one of these categories. Chain networks are rigid in structure. All task related information must pass through an approved hierarchy of command. Communication is initiated by a previously determined individual, who passes it to other predetermined individuals, and so on. Communication in this model flows from the top down or bottom up, by only through the appropriate stops. Wheel networks establish a 'spoke' who communicates directly and individually with all other members. The person occupying the 'spoke' position must be strong and respected by members of the team. All channel networks, featuring no team leader, are the most complex of these models and permits communication from any member to any other.

KM

Knowledge management (KM) is the gathering of an organization's cooperative insights so that it is readily available to appropriate individuals within the organization. With knowledge management, organizations can increase productivity and gain a lead position in terms of the competition. Knowledge management has become vitally important to large organizations with a variety of information types, who need to enhance productivity or take a position at the forefront of the industry. Organizations populated by innovative employees who have gathered and organized their original ideas so they can be immediately accessed and understood, even by organization members unfamiliar with them, has a tremendous advantage in the marketplace. Additionally, the generation that is currently reaching retirement age was the first to experience the advent of the computer age as it transformed working conditions. They carry a wealth of information that must either be recorded for future use, or lost. Furthermore, a good KM system streamlines procedures, making the organization less redundant and more efficient overall.

CHANNELS OF COMMUNICATION

The richest channels of communication offer instantaneous feedback, provide a sense of personal connection, and can process informational cues on a number of levels at once. The richest conduits, such as face to face communication, videoconferences and phone calls are best used for dispersing complex information that isn't part of the daily pattern. Conduits with low channel richness, such as memos, email and recorded announcements, offer no immediate feedback, no sense of personal connection and do not process multiple informational cues, and are most appropriate for unambiguous, habitually dispersed information. The more complex the message, the greater the opportunities for misunderstanding; the more out of the ordinary a message is, the greater the opportunities for misunderstanding, as well. Complex, non- habitual messages should always be conveyed using the highest channel of richness available. In recent years, more and more highly successful managers demonstrate greater sensitivity to the variety of mediums.

CONNECTION VIA THE INTERNET

Computers have reshaped every aspect of business. Office workers sit in front of a computer all day with access to the internet for professional reasons; undoubtedly many abuse the easy availability, wasting company time and resources. Nonetheless, the internet offers advantages to companies. Emails are quick to write, easy to save and can be blasted to a lot of recipients. There's no limit to the number that can be sent, no paper and no postage costs; an advantage which leads to its biggest disadvantage. Because emails are easy and inexpensive, their rise in popularity as a marketing took coupled with the tendency to be fairly indiscriminate in who received personal email means inboxes can be stuffed to the point where work-related messages cannot get through. If the recipient is online, text and instant messages are instantly delivered. However, they cannot be saved for long periods of time.

CHANNELS OF COMMUNICATION

As technology develops, more and more potential channels of communication become available. Email, instant and text messages, twitter, Facebook, and other social networking systems have joined telephone calls and faxes as well as interoffice memos, publications and other forms of paper communications. Managers need to understand how to use newer technology appropriately, or risk serious consequence. For example, email should never be used to convey upsetting or unexpected information because it is a relatively cold medium. The more complex or disturbing the message, the more likely the recipient will be to misread it, assign it some subtextual interpretation that was not intended, or feel personally offended. On the other hand, using the telephone to contact each member of a team to relay information such as a minor schedule change is not only a tremendous waste of a manager's time, it will strike team members as inappropriate or even too intimate.

OBSTACLES TO CLEAR COMMUNICATION

A message's sender might manipulatively leave out information to trick the receiver into a particular position; emphasize information for the same reason; or filter a message to make it more palatable. Filtering can also involve outright lying. Message recipients always perceive the meaning that makes greatest sense given their previous experiences, level of education, personalities, needs, and motivations. Managers who recognize that all communication takes place within environments that can be highly personal, can tailor messages accordingly. Clear communication can also stumble as a result of too much information coming in without sufficient time or resources to process it.

Receiving a message is often a matter of attending to it; a recipient who is emotionally upset, distracted or excited can easily miss or misinterpret part of the message. Managers who are alert to these common areas of snag and address them accordingly will likely increase efficiency.

MODEL OF GROUP DEVELOPMENT

A common sequence to group development has been seen in a wide variety of situations. The resulting model locates five distinct points along the developmental continuum. The stages are forming, storming, norming, performing and adjourning, and most group behaviors can be explained by this sequential model. The forming stage is liquid; lacking leadership, individuals seek purpose, and ultimately settle into a loosely defined group. The storming stage is reactive with conflict over leadership and norms, and stage finishes when hierarchy is established. In the norming stage members connect with a deeper sense of identity. The group develops structure through acceptable norms. By the time the group reaches the performing stage, it has streamlined itself into a heightened state of efficiency. It knows what it is about, and everyone works together to achieve it. The final stage, adjourning, occurs when the task has been accomplished and the group disbands.

SHAPING GROUP BEHAVIOR

Philip Zimbardo's famous Stanford University prison experiment demonstrated that even emotionally healthy, well adjusted individuals will readily assume roles they initially have no commonality with, and allow behaviors to emerge to fit the role, even if it means violating their own personal codes of ethics. In the experiment, 24 students who had passed a battery of personality tests and were carefully examined to insure they were 'normal average' were assigned roles as prison guards, or as prisoners. Violence was prohibited, but other forms of manipulation, intimidation and coercion were not. Very rapidly, the prisoners began to see themselves as lacking in power and importance, and to behave accordingly. Guards readily assumed the role of increased authority, and behaved in ways they later deplored. The experiment, originally designed to last two weeks, was ended after a mere six days because participants' role responses had become psychotic.

NORMS

Norms, behavioral expectations used by a group to coerce members in conforming behaviors, fall into a number of types. One of the most common norm types is performance norms. Performance norms control individual output, approved work practices, absenteeism and the like. The purpose of performance norms is to protect the group from an overzealous worker whose output might make management raise that of the group's, or a lazy worker who is not doing her share. Appearance norms cover everything from clothing and accessories to giving the appearance of organizational loyalty. Social arrangement norms control group dynamics and social behaviors among group members, such as lunches, who reports gossip and who merely listens, after work activities, and friendships both within and outside of the work environment.

PUNCTUATED EQUILIBRIUM MODEL OF GROUP DEVELOPMENT

Punctuated equilibrium describes the operation of temporary groups established for a specific purpose. It begins with an initial meeting at which goals and timeline are created. Group members willingly cooperate in the establishment of regulations regarding work- related behavior early in the meeting; these regulations are not challenged until beyond the halfway point of the project's lifetime. Until that halfway point, the remainder of the group's time is spent doing nothing, or locked in unproductive, but fixed, action. At the midway point, the group collectively awakens to the realization their time is drawing to an end. Ineffective patterns are replaced, innovative perspectives take over, new plans are adopted, work begins, and nearly as rapidly, falls into a second state of inertia. Finally, as the group approaches deadline, the task is completed in a major burst of effort and energy. This model explicitly describes temporary work- groups with time limitations.

Western Company's Hawthorne Works Chicago Studies

The Western Company's Hawthorne studies, undertaking between the mid-1920s and mid-1930s, came to the conclusion that while an employee's individual behavior was closely tied to her feelings, that behavior could easily be influenced by group expectations; additionally, secure membership in the group was a greater influence on productivity than salary. In one of the studies, the presence of a research assistant who tracked output, working environment, product rejects, and kept a daily log was sufficient to steadily increase output and reduce absenteeism by 30%; the conclusion was that it made workers feel special and therefore, happy. Another study examined actual weekly output against daily reported output. Workers reported a uniform level of daily output that did not tally with weekly output. Investigation proved workers were acting to protect the group by slowing production; they believe this would avoid having the per unit incentive cut or group output expectation increased.

Deviant Workplace Behavior

Deviant workplace behavior, sometimes called work place incivility or antisocial workplace behavior, is behavior that radically deviates from an organizational norm. Employees who slow down work production, are wasteful with office materials, or frequently leave early are affecting norms in the area of production. Those who take office supplies or equipment or intentionally sabotage a project are demonstrating deviant workplace property behavior. Deviant political behavior is found in a manager who rewards her favorites at the expense of others, a coworker who spreads malicious gossip to put herself in the spotlight, or a teammate who blames others for her own mistakes. Sexual harassment and insults demonstrate deviant personal aggression. Managers must be constantly aware of deviant workplace behavior both because it is outside the limits of more organizational ethical standards, and because if allowed to continue, it wounds workplace morale and ultimately leads to greater turnover.

Nonverbal Communication

Most of the time, speakers aren't consciously aware that their bodies are adding to a message nonverbally. When a speaker is impassioned, she nods, leans forward, raises her eyebrows and waves her hands; the listener understands the message is important. When a speaker isn't in full agreement with the message, however, body language tells another story. Arms crossed on the chest say, 'I don't believe you', while hands on the hips communicate, 'Don't push me'. Listeners use body language, too. A coworker won't stop jabbering to a new teammate who is afraid of not getting her work done. She listens politely, but her steady nodding and disengaged gaze are dead giveaways. Nonverbal communication can involve both communicators. After a fight, a husband brings home a huge bouquet. "Aren't you sweet", she says, turning her back and burying her face in the flowers so he understands her feelings are still hurt.

Problems with Nonverbal Communication

Nonverbal communication is both intentional (in that it is intended for another to receive it) and at the same time, largely unconscious. Nonverbal communication is largely socio- emotional. People's values and beliefs are laid bare via body language; it's nearly impossible to lie in this area of communication, and therefore, its meanings are, on some felt level, sacred. What an American may see as haughty arrogance might, for a Parisian, simply suggest confidence. The Parisian (or his European cousins) might stand a tad too close to an American business associate for the latter's comfort, who feels his space is being invaded by an aggressive individual. The European would be surprised by this, since professional space, like all space, is at more of a premium. Any organization that either employs or serves a cultural mix of individuals needs to educate its members about what is considered insulting, rude or aggressive in terms of body language within those cultures.

Likability and Perceived Status

It is relatively to tell a lie; you simply choose words to express something you don't believe or that you know didn't happen. It is far less easy to express a lie, though, in face to face communication. Body language doesn't lie; it reveals. Body language nearly always expresses how much communicators like, trust or respect one another. The closer people feel to one another, the closer they physically draw together, sometimes reaching out to touch with a hand or nudge with a foot to create an even closer bond. However, if some is annoyed by or distrustful of another, the body space will be dramatically widened. Perceived status is another type of information that is revealed in virtually all nonverbal communications. Higher status individuals will slouch or sprawl to help an underling relax. The underling, in the meantime, is sitting ramrod straight with eyes slightly down subordinately.

Speaker's Inflection of Words and Phrases

A statement is more than just the meanings of the individual words it contains. Intonation, or the way the speaker emphasizes certain of these words, provides subtextual information that completely changes the statement's neutral meaning, or the one that would be assumed if the words appeared on a page instead of on the stage of face to face communication. For example, a manager might say, "Why don't you take over the project?" The employee is confused—what was the manager really saying? If the emphasis was on why, the manager is frustrated and has previously urged the employee to do so, and is asking for reasons why this has not occurred. Emphasizing don't suggests the manager is getting short- tempered about the situation, or is tired of hearing complaints about it. Emphasizing you implies the manager is telling the employee to take more responsibility if there are problems.

Written Documentation

Within an organization, written documentation should be kept regarding policy, announcements, memos and the like. There are three potential drawbacks to written interpersonal communication, however. The first is that written communication, unlike face to face communication, offers no nonverbal subtext. Neither phrasal intonation nor body language is available to help make meaning clear. Any message that is more than a simple statement of fact with a single interpretation is in danger of misinterpretation if it is committed to writing. Secondly, it is not conducive to immediate feedback. Any misunderstanding has time to solidify, making it harder to root out in the future. Finally, communications that are highly charged with emotion should never be initially committed to writing. It is too difficult to control the message when one is angry, hurt or frightened. These missives, if they must be communicated, should be done face to face whenever possible.

Hierarchy in Channels of Communication

Within an organization, it is not always convenient or appropriate to put all communications into written form. Some pieces of information are passed along orally for the sake of convenience or speed, or because the message is spontaneous. Organizations of any substantial size have channels of communication in place to insure that messages are received by the people who need to know them. The problem with oral communications is that, regardless of how careful their carriers may be to maintain their integrity, their meaning decays further with each telling. If an oral communication is made between a manager and a team leader, and the communication began with the manager and not one of her supervisors, it will probably arrive fairly intact. However, if the message came from upper management through middle management, to team leaders who disseminated it to their teams, it is likely to be riddled with misinterpretation or misinformation.

WORKPLACE POLITICAL BEHAVIOR

Political behavior uses influence to gain a degree of control and increase personal power. Political behavior is not publicly sanctioned by the organization, nor formally addressed within a job description. Political behavior wants to sway decision making through legitimate and illegitimate means. An informal group or a single individual can try to gain power through political behaviors such as withholding or disguising information to lead decision makers in a particular direction; creating and spreading gossip; sharing information with groups or individuals it isn't intended for; leaking sensitive information outside the organization, particularly to the media; joining forces with others with similar goals, and actively and publicly standing in favor of a particular position. Legitimate political behavior can behave in a slightly underhanded way; going past a supervisor to get to his manager, for example. Illegitimate behaviors include outright sabotage, organization-wide slowdowns, and other acts intended to cause real harm.

POLITICAL JOCKEYING

Organizations contain differing values and goals, simply because they are composed of a variety of individuals with different task assignments. Disagreements over budgets, equipment, bonuses, office space and so forth are inevitable. The more limited the resources, the greater the competition. Individuals and coalitions able to secure a greater portion are looked upon as heroes by their peers and with resentment by others. Some decisions regarding who gets what are made according to relatively objective standards, such as an increase in cost savings over a specific time period, or a specific number of units manufactured. But many decisions are based on data that is subjective or too close to fairly call; it is here that office politics is most apparent, as individuals and loosely defined groups vie to sway decision makers, gain a greater portion of resources, and, in the process, also gain personal power, respect and control.

BEHAVIORS THAT COULD BE SEEN AS POLITICAL SCHEMING BY COMPETITIVE COWORKERS

There will always be those who cast a negative light on behavior that is essentially pure, and those who cast a positive light on behavior that, upon examination, seems to be self- serving. A manager might see a favorite employee's habit of stirring up unnecessary conflict as an attempt to infuse the organization with creative, innovative thinking, while his teammates recognize it as an attempt to cause trouble just for fun. There may be no lack of employees in another department to call an employee who insists upon documenting all conversations as out to cover his own behind, while his supporters will find his actions merely good business practice. One manager's overachiever is another manager's highly proficient and dependable assistant. One skill area's tendency to create alliances to strengthen their platforms is threatening to another skill area, but seen as effective teamwork by the manager who handles both.

CHARACTERISTICS THAT CONTRIBUTE TO POLITICAL BEHAVIOR.

High self- monitors, socially sensitive and able to adjust their behaviors to conform, have an increased likelihood of displaying political behavior, as do those with an internal locus of control who believe themselves able to manipulate people and events. The greater the desire for power, the greater the chances employees will politick to increase it. High Machiavellians are almost guaranteed to politick because they are driven to obtain power; to them, manipulation is practical rather than distasteful. Interestingly, the more an employee identifies with company values, is invested in the organization, and believes his future in it is secure, the less likely he will be to pursue illegitimate political behavior because too much is at stake. However, in an environment where jobs are plentiful or the employee possesses unusual abilities, the more willing he will be to engage in such behaviors because his ultimate bottom line is his own advancement.

Defensive Behaviors

Co- workers are likely to respond to political behavior with defensiveness in an attempt to protect themselves. For example, a group of co- workers who are threatened by one employee who is aggressively seeking a promotion may refuse to participate in her attempts to increase production by slowing down work on team tasks because 'it needs to be done better, not faster.' Assignments might be dodged by co- workers who claim not to have the necessary skill or training, or refused on the grounds that this particular task is supposed to be done by someone else. Co- workers might protect themselves by documenting every action and conversation, which simultaneously gives the appearance of diligent hard work. Avoiding any risky tasks, blaming failures on other employees or external situations, and obscuring information by minimizing, dramatizing, or lying are common self- defenses in response to political behavior.

Politically Charged Organizational Culture

Considerable organizational change, limited resources and the prospect of advancement are three organizational situations which typically result in an increase in political behavior among lower level employees. Organizations that could be described as unhealthy or undirected are even more likely to experience greater than average political behavior. If professional roles and performance evaluation standards are not clear and consistent, if top management displays self- serving behaviors with little regard for either the organization or their charges, if there is a low degree of trust organization- wide, and if employees feel pressure to perform at a high level, political behavior is likely as employees scramble to carve out a foothold for themselves in what they feel to be an uncertain professional landscape. The less clear the means by which an employee will be recognized, rewarded and advanced, the more likely the chance that the culture will become riddled with politicking.

Politicking Can Reduce Office Place Morale

Office politicking is, ultimately, an attempt to promote oneself above others in order to secure a more stable position at better pay and gain greater respect and power in the process While some organizational environments practically ensure political behavior will occur as employees who believe they are underappreciated scramble to be recognized, more stable environments can be hurt by overly political employees who appear to be out for their own advancement. Overall, surveys indicate that the more predominate political behavior is in an organization, the lower employees rate job satisfaction. Many valuable workers with satisfactory production, developed skills and a solid work ethic are uncomfortable with politicking, and will step back in its presence. Some end up feeling they are jeopardizing their own positions by not being more outspoken, and the resulting stress can affect their work. In a worst case scenario, employees are more likely to leave an organization they feel has become riddled with political behavior, rather than adopt that behavior. In a best case scenario, those same employees simply become unmotivated.

Workplace Politicking in the United States Follows Certain Patterns and Calls Forth Certain Responses in Co- Workers

Most research studies on effects of political organizational behavior have been done in the United States, and indicate low tolerance among co- workers, leading to reduced job satisfaction and greater turnover. While fewer studies have been done in other countries, the results are worth studying. Nations that are politically stable follow the model suggested by studies done on organizations in the United States. Interestingly, however, nations that are less stable have work forces that are more tolerant of political behavior within organizations. Two possible reasons suggest themselves here. The first is that power struggles, sudden reversals and other changes and other political turbulence is more familiar; workers have learned strategies for dealing with the stress they create. Secondly, workers are less likely to leave a job because of political behavior, both because they are likely to find it elsewhere, and because less national political security means less workplace security.

Backstabbing

Backstabbing is the devious, intentional and illegitimate devaluing of co-workers for personal gain. Backstabbers justify themselves by claiming a co- worker isn't efficient, knowledgeable or capable enough, but these justifications don't address the fact that backstabbers aren't concerned about the organization, but themselves. They are manipulating decisions that aren't theirs to make. Backstabbing is a deliberate act, in which seeds of doubt are planted in a supervisor's mind or gossip spread among peers. The backstabber wants what his victim has; a particular position, respect, responsibility, the corner office; it doesn't matter. Backstabbers are true Machiavellians, willing to do whatever it takes to get whatever they want. Managers should be suspicious of employees who 'reluctantly' bring attention to a co- worker friend's failure to perform; claiming friendship, stabbers believe, deflects suspicion. Managers should also be careful to confirm information with other sources; the more objective, the better.

What an Individual Should Consider Before Engaging in Political Behavior for Her Own Best Interest

Most people will agree that a gentle fib offered to avoid hurting someone's feelings (and remain well- liked) isn't a 'real' lie, but before resorting to manipulation, consider if personal benefits outweigh personal risks. Stretching a minor truth likely to lead to an promotion is less risky than a complex lie crafted to impress an acquaintance—especially if the lie gets repeated. Consider, too, whether personal benefits outweigh potential harm to others. For example, covering for a normally reliable peer who has momentarily dropped the ball will produce both gratitude and a debt without inflicting much damage. Covering for a chronically late co- worker who also takes home office supplies hurts the organization. Covering for a co- worker who is passing information to a rival company by blaming someone who is uninvolved hurts not only the organization, but the one who shoulders the blame.

Interest Group or Friendship Group at Work

Informal groups within an organization can form with relative spontaneity, to meet the shared needs of a group of individuals. Because individuals are a complex blend of personality traits, history, emotions and goals, there are an infinite number of possible reasons someone might join a group. However, most of these complex reasons can be gathered into a few categories. The first and probably most common reason is for connection and interaction. Informal groups satisfy social needs and the desire to feel part of something larger than the self. Secondly, informal friendship groups provide a sense of security; perceived threats are less frightening when they are directed at a group of people. A third category is status; being seen as part of a popular crowd confers recognition. Another reason is an increased sense of self- worth. Informal friendship groups can also offer a strong power- base that employs group action to gain a desired result.

Joining

The five stage model that explores the stages of group development suggests 'adjourning' as the final stage. The five stage model of group development includes stages named forming (coming together), storming (struggle for power), norming (reaching common goals), performing (addressing the task), and adjourning. The final stage, adjourning, is essentially a debriefing period. The assigned task has been completed, so the group's attention can now shift to a review of the work accomplished and the steps taken to complete it, and then to wrapping up any loose ends. This is an emotional stage for many; some are energized by the success of the work and the bonding of the group, while others are saddened that the work has come to an end. This stage represents an opportunity for the team leader or supervisor to 'package' the group's development so that it can be used either with future group, or with individuals from the current group in the future when they are struggling with new group dynamics.

Concerns of the Five Stage Model of Group Development

The five stage model of group development suggests that the stages of forming, storming, norming, performing and adjourning are distinct and unique. Each appears to be a necessary step which must be completed in order to arrive at the next stage. In fact, groups rarely work so neatly. Two or more stages might overlap. For example, while three group members are struggling over strategies or control of the group, a fourth member might have already entered the performing stage, and be well on his way in terms of addressing the tasks that must be completed. Another criticism is that groups do, on occasion, reverse direction and return to an earlier stage. Another criticism is that the model suggests stage four, performing, is where work is accomplished with greatest efficiency and highest quality, but in fact, conflict (stage two) can result in effective work accomplished efficiently.

Role conflict

When an individual joins an organization or other group, a number of possible roles comes along with it. In addition to a role an employee might think is expected of him (and which may or may not be truly expected), are roles that are explicitly expected by other group or organizational members or supervisors. Role conflict comes about when two or more of an employee's roles can be seen as mutually exclusive. For example, an employee has been given a promotion that carries additional job responsibilities, including some travel. He can refuse the promotion, but fears doing so will label him as not a team player and might even lead to eventual job loss. His wife is in the first trimester of a risky pregnancy. The roles he identifies with—responsible husband and responsible employee—are in conflict. From his perspective, he can only fulfill one role by abandoning another.

Psychological contract

While there are many written documents that are part and parcel of working within an organization, there are also many unwritten agreements, as well. Employees need to clearly understand the expectations of their employer, including goals, tasks to accomplish those goals, steps to be taken in the completion of tasks, types of rewards, what rewards are based upon, and so forth. At the same time, it is equally useful for employers to understand the expectations their employees hold, such as the type of work they have been hired to do, what constitutes acceptable, above average and subpar work, how quickly they expect to be advanced, how often incentives will be offered, how they are offered and the types of incentives, and so forth. When all parties clearly understand one another, basic respect is in place; managers are expected to be fair with employees, employees are expected to be loyal in return.

Length of time a group remains in the various stages

Because groups are composed of individuals who are complex combinations of personality, knowledge and need, every group proceeds through a task at its own pace. Situational conditions that can affect how quickly a group comes together to complete a task include urgency of need, possible reward, and deadlines. For example, an emergency room team that is unexpectedly overwhelmed by dozens of victims of a bombing must rapidly assess what needs to be done and how to do it. A group of reality show contestants who have been joined into a new group and assigned a task which must be successfully completed before another group accomplishes it has very little time to spend discussing advantages and disadvantages of particular approaches. A group of journalists who are investigating a national story that has just broken, must simultaneously make their own deadline and also provide more and better information than competing journalists from other papers.

EASING OR RESOLVING ROLE CONFLICT

Any organizational relationship that creates conflict resulting in crippling inertia is problematic for a manager. This is no less true when the relationship involves only a single individual. A conflicted employee cannot easily make decisions, work productively or otherwise contribute. The best resolution may involve re-examining the employee's perceived roles. Communicating with a supervisor or team leader to ensure the responsibilities have been correctly interpreted is important. If the conflict resides in the employee's perception rather than in external expectations re- framing the roles might be useful. For example, a mother is asked to put in extra hours until her department replaces an employee who abruptly left. She believes her twins will feel abandoned if a caregiver takes some of her home responsibilities temporarily, and also fears refusing her boss's request. However, her twins may love the idea of increased independence, and the boss may willingly share her new responsibilities with another employee.

GROUP NORMS

Work group performance norms control the amount of effort, time and resources employees who are members of the group contribute to any given task. Managers may wish they could control these values, but the reality is, they can at best only hope to influence the group's most powerful members to some degree. Establishing and maintaining a given set of norms is extremely beneficial to the group in that when all members are in compliance, output conforms to specific measures that guarantee expectations of the group will not be raised or work increased. For example, a group member who increases production might cause a manager to assign more work to the entire group with the expectation they can all increase production. Performance norms are typically very overtly expressed. Group members can become aggressive toward members who violate this norm through the use of ridicule, mocking, insults, sarcasm, gossip, and closing ranks against violators.

APPEARANCE NORMS

Appearance norms, as the name suggests, control the multiple types of impressions individuals within an organization make. Clothing, jewelry, hair, and hygiene are perhaps the most obvious area which appearance norms control, but there are others. For example, the degree of respect for the organization that must be demonstrated both within and outside of its walls are typically well under the control of appearance norms. A new hire quickly learns from observation which members of senior staff it's important to impress by looking busy, and which are more relaxed. Appearance norms might control how distraught a tardy employee need appear, as well as how humble or gloating one who has just received a reward. Even both the dress and behaviors at a holiday party are influenced by appearance norms; while they are likely to be somewhat more relaxed, they are still limits beyond which the wise employee doesn't venture.

TWO OR MORE GROUPS WITH CONTRADICTORY NORMS

An individual who is a member of professional and social groups with differing values and norms can be faced with a dilemma. For example, a member of a conservative religious group that preaches abstinence, a risk-taking investment club, a company softball team with beer-drinking members who swear, and a literary book club that serves wine and reads controversial books has two choices. She can behave as if she subscribes to each group's norms in the presence of those group members, but this will compromise her own values and expose her as a fake if members of two groups are present at the same time. Alternatively, she can pay greater attention to her reference groups, which are the groups she most closely identifies with, wants the respect of, and hopes to continue a relationship with. While doing so will probably devalue her standing in the non-reference groups, her integrity is intact.

Independent Group Member

Much research has been done in the areas of psychology, sociology and organizational behavior to deepen an understanding of norms. Nearly all of it agrees that norms are an extremely effective way a group can convince an independent group member to curtail undesirable behavior. Every organization, regardless of size or degree of sophistication, is composed of one or more groups that exert control over members' appearance and behavior through norms. There are two primary reasons an individual participates in a group. The first is because she wants in for personal reasons. In this case, that individual is likely to pay careful attention to determining what is acceptable and unacceptable in terms of behavior, work efforts and appearance, and act accordingly so as not to antagonize the group. The second reason is that membership, as the expression goes, has its rewards. If the group offers power or protection, a free- thinking individual who sees the benefits of membership will willingly subscribe to the group's norms in order to obtain those benefits. In this second case, sacrificing some independence in order to obtain power or protection is a trade- off that provides a different sort of independence.

Conflict

Most types of conflict can be reduced to a handful of categories, including interpersonal, intrapersonal, group and inter- organizational conflict. Interpersonal conflict involves interaction between multiple individuals who hold differing views or values regarding the same thing. In the state of opposition held between them is the field for conflict. Intrapersonal conflict are internally held conflicts arising from ideals or expectations that cannot simultaneously coexist. Intrapersonal goals can be perceptual or external. They include approach- approach, approach- avoidance and avoidance- avoidance conflicts. Intergroup conflict rises between different teams or group participants, often for reasons as simple as identity. Inter- organizational conflict is the result of sharing a limited market among companies, groups or other organizations with limited resources and limited customers; rises from the struggle between unions and organizations for control of members; occurs between governmental regulations and groups being watched; and can be found in sources of raw materials and the organizations who need them.

Conflict is inevitable in any situation for several reasons. First individuals' priorities and desires cannot always be in concert for the simple reason we all have diverse needs, desires and beliefs. Secondly, as situations change, needs change in response, opening the door to potential conflict. There are as many distinct types of conflict as there are distinct individuals; however, it is possible to reduce most kinds of conflict into two fundamental types. Emotional conflict is rooted in feelings such as a resentment, mistrust, neglect, irritation, hurt, anger, and so forth; and often has little to do with the task at hand. Emotional conflict can rise out of a memory of a similar situation or encounter; once it has made its presence known, it can be difficult to uproot since it responds primarily to past action and is more concerned with resolving the emotion. Substantive conflict, on the other hand, locates an essential, absolute disagreement concerning the exact nature of the goals to be pursued, and how best to design and implement a plan to accomplish those goals. Substantive conflict is meaningful in that it is tangible and addresses current concerns and is more concerned with resolving the matter.

Not All Conflict Is Destructive

Conflict can be seen as the inevitable physical result of two or more forces attempting to occupy the same space at the same time. In such cases, something must give way, usually in a forceful, conflicted manner. Until the sources of conflict are resolved (through dialogue, physical confrontation or reorganization) a state of uneasy equilibrium is established. Looked at in this light, all conflict is potentially useful and potentially destructive. Truly constructive conflict exhibits certain characteristics. It offers a field of opportunity in which the sources of conflict can be aired and examined in an accepting, non- conflictive manner. It invites new or deeper information that may not have been available in the first place.

Constructive conflict asks participants to revisit and give careful consideration to particular decisions that were made, as well as to give equally careful consideration to new pieces of information that arise in the future that help shape future decisions.

MANAGING CONFLICT

Conflict that is not well managed, whether on an individual, interpersonal or organizational level, can quickly between toxic, resulting in dysfunction. Conflict that is ignored or repressed rather than dealt with can rapidly become a negative force that infects the ability of a group of proceed toward a healthy solution. While functional conflict invites dialogue, respects others' points of view and works toward healing anger and aggression, dysfunctional conflict seeks only to 'win' by establishing its preferred position above all else. Dysfunctional conflict employs a number of strategies designed to dis- integrate any sense of all- for one necessary to group consensus. Dysfunctional conflict first attempts to distract and scatter energies chaotically. It is important that no strong sense of group identity or solidarity exist, and so dysfunctional conflict pits factions against one another, especially promoting disagreement, hostility and disappointment between particular members for either personal or professional reasons. Dysfunctional conflict thrives in a work environment that is stressful, uncomfortable or unsafe.

POSSIBLE CAUSES OF CONFLICT

Vertical conflict occurs between individuals functioning at different levels of power, such as a top manager and a middle manager, while horizontal conflict happens between two individuals who are working at the same level, such as two team leaders. Disagreements concerning the control or management of a specific area are called line staff conflicts. When difficulties arise regarding communication about tasks, such as information that is not adequately or clearly explained, role conflicts are likely to be the result. Another type of conflict, work- flow independency, can occur when individuals or teams are assigned goals of a challenging nature, and must work together to achieve them. Domain ambiguity is another type of conflict common when a situation becomes ambiguous enough that participants aren't clear as to their responsibilities. Resource scarcity is a conflict that develops over a struggle for insufficient materials.

DIRECT CONFLICT RESOLUTION

Avoiding conflict by minimizing argument, stepping out of a disagreeable situation and maintaining neutrality may seem like conflict management, but it is, at best, simply evasion. While it still fails to address and manage the conflict, the practice of smoothing (also called accommodation) is a slightly more assertive position. Smoothing involves flexibility and a willingness to cooperate with an assertive leader in order to create the appearance of accord. A still more assertive position is one of compromise, where cooperation is still central but is offered with certain limits and conditions. Compromise requires all parties to give up something in order to arrive at a common ground for all. Further down the spectrum of conflict management is a position of authority and control. This position does not ask for, nor offer, cooperation, and seeks to resolve conflict with domination. The healthiest position is one that seeks to collaborate to resolve issues.

STAGE THE CONFLICT

In order to resolve a conflict, it's necessary to identify at what stage the conflict currently exists. Before conflict manifests, conditions must be right for it. Opposing positions, views, standards or goals with equally strong supporters create the necessary conditions. This first stage is not technically yet a conflictive one, in that it can exist without any sense of conflict. Next, is perceived conflict. In this stage, at least one of the participants becomes aware of differences in terms of feeling or meaningful intent, and a sense of conflict begins to arise. By the next stage, felt conflict, enough tension has been generated that those involved feel the need to change behaviors by acting or responding to perceived or actual action. The next stage is manifest conflict, and is the stage at which conflict has fully emerged and must now either be resolved or contained, and the situation returned to what is was prior to the disruption.

Variables of Conflict Resolution

When a manager is able to subtly, invisibly 'heal' a disagreement, it gives those involved a stronger sense of unity and shared goals. A few simple strategies can be put in place in order for an indirect resolution to take place. If the origin of the conflict is work- flow related, minimizing interdependence will shift control and dissolve conflict. Reminding individuals in conflict that they share important, common goals is most effective when the people in question agree as to what the goals are and the best way to attain them; this effect is increased if past work together has been successful. Another strategy is to refer the issue to someone hierarchically positioned; however, unless the superior truly understands the situation and the individuals, this may simply result in a superficial fix. Asking participants to break the routine, habitual way of thinking through the problem and come at it from another angle is another approach.

Negotiation

Negotiation can be defined as two or more parties with disparate needs, desires, or points of view working together to jointly reach a position that is acceptable to all. Negotiation is a necessary skill for all organizations, regardless of type. With negotiation everyone leaves the table with at least some of what they want, turning them into willing participants. There are different negotiation approaches. In distributive negotiation, a clearly defined limited amount of resources must be divided; individuals or negotiating groups seek the greatest portion they can claim. If the position taken by a negotiator is inflexible and uncompromising, it is considered hard negotiation. A willingness to compromise in order to complete a step in the process is soft negotiation. Integrative, or principled, negotiation attends not to who gets what limited resources, but rather focuses on the qualities and virtues at stake. In integrative negotiation, participants seek to increase resources so that all can gain, rather than dividing up limited and finite resources.

Leadership

Among effective leadership styles are charismatic, situational, transactional, transformative, servant, participative and quiet leadership styles. Charismatic leaders depend upon their personal charm to gather followers, pay attention to environmental clues and individual moods, and present themselves with chameleon like dexterity. Situational leaders understand that different situations require different leadership skills. They consider followers' abilities, followers' willingness, available resources and how the work is organized in their leadership decisions. Transactional leaders operate using reward and punishment under clear directives. Transformational leaders offer uplifting guidance to inspire followers, while servant style leaders base their leadership in service to others, especially to those who are at a disadvantage. Participative leaders believe that followers who are directly involved with decision making are more likely to be committed to the decisions that come as a result. Quiet leaders are humble, and do not seek or accept credit that belongs to the group.

Quiet Leaders and Servant Leaders

Both quiet and servant leaders are little driven by ego. Quiet leaders are inwardly focused, consulting thoughts to determine actions. Actions are important to quiet leaders; recognizing work that needs to be done and encouraging followers to accept the challenges is the goal. Their primary persuasive tool is rationality, and they will not employ forceful intimidation, threats or other forms of bullying. Quiet leaders bond and identify with their followers, to whom they feel responsibility. They are idealists who believe in social responsibilities which are best fulfilled through leadership. Servant leaders, like quiet leaders, have a visionary commitment to helping others. Servant leaders believe such help can come in one of two ways; by leading others to improve themselves, or by leading them to achieve goals. The more self- sufficient and psychologically balanced followers become, the better able they are to then step into a leadership position in turn.

Similarities and Differences Between Management and Leadership

Examining similarities and differences between leadership and management is something of a chicken- egg question. Leaders need managers, and managers need leaders. They share certain characteristics, most obviously authoritative responsibility, but their specific roles are ultimately different. Management primarily deals with structure, and leadership primarily deals with change. Management inherits a vision for the future from a leader, and sets about creating and fine- tuning a structure to make it operational. It can be said that if leadership deals with the ideal, management deals with the very real. Conflict, obstacles, insufficient resources, information loss, miscommunication, staffing, coordinating departments or work teams are all the work of managers. Leaders are the visionaries who see the 'big picture', if not the details. They not only visual what can be, but how it can happen; they are strategists and communicators who breathe life into their visions by inspiring followings to fall in line.

Charismatic and Transformational Leadership Styles

On the surface, charismatic and transformational leadership styles seems to share much in common. Both are inspiring and visionary, projecting images of concern for others, righteous action, and high ethical standards. However, upon closer examination, both charismatic and transformational leaders are, at base, salespeople whose product is themselves. Charismatic leaders are mirrors who project the images followers demand, and have no problem with switching from one image to another, even when they are mutually exclusive. Their ultimate goal is to draw as much power to themselves for their own use as possible. Transformational leaders are passionate and committed. While charismatic leaders can be narcissists, transformational leaders are driven by what they believe is best for all concerned; however, many find belief itself to be equivalent to truth, and can lead followers astray because they cannot see the difference between their own visionary beliefs and external evidence to the contrary.

Trait Theory

Trait theory attempts to define what makes a good leader based upon the presence of certain personality characteristics. Recently, researchers have begun to give attention to emotional intelligence (IE) as a desirable trait. Trait theory has tried (and often failed) or define great leadership in terms of certain personality traits or characteristics. While the 80 or so characteristics repeatedly surfaced in a wide range of studies, there was very little crossover from study to study. The Big Five framework gave a broader structure, and allowed types of personality traits to be subsumed under five umbrella categories. More recent research suggests that leaders who have traits from these categories, such as innovative ideas, an ability to think analytically, a substantial vision for the future, and considerable specific training, might fail to become a leader without the addition of emotional intelligence. Emotional intelligence allows a potential leader to empathize with the needs of others, 'hear' what they are trying to say even when it is not clearly stated, and react in such a way that followers feel understand and appreciated.

OHIO STATE STUDIES

Research on leadership has taken a number of forms. Early trait theories of leadership met with limited success. After the introduction of the Big Five framework, traits were found to be somewhat predictive regarding leadership, but not in terms of effectiveness. Trait theories are based upon the belief that since leaders are born and not nurtured, with an understanding of their basic traits, they can be chosen from out of a group. Behaviorist theory assumes that once behaviors exhibited by great leaders are identified, others can be trained in them. The Ohio State University studies tried to recognize dimensions in leadership behaviors, eventually winnowing 1,000 dimensions into two categories, called initiating structure and considerations. Initiating structure looks at how a leader characterizes and organizes roles in order to realize goals. Included in this dimension are behaviors whose purpose is to organize work relationships, tasks, and outcomes. A high initiating structure leader specifies standards and goals, determines deadlines and allocates specific tasks to specific employees. The dimension of consideration focuses on professional relationships demonstrating respect, trust, and concern for humane aspects like physical comfort, emotional tranquility, job satisfaction, and social connection.

THE TWO DIMENSIONS MODEL OF LEADERSHIP BEHAVIORS DESCRIBED BY THE UNIVERSITY OF MICHIGAN.

Like studies done at Ohio State University, the University of Michigan's Survey Research Center defined two leadership behavior dimensions which they named employee- oriented and production- oriented. Employee- oriented leaders prioritized relationships with employees of a personal nature, appreciated unique distinctions between them as individuals and understood their personal needs. Production- oriented leaders were those whose primary concern focused upon technology or the accomplishment of the task at hand. For production- oriented leaders, employees were functionary and not personalities; the bottom line is the speed with which a goal is reached, product is manufactured or distribution made. Interestingly, the University of Michigan study found the employee- oriented leaders, who focused not on production but on people, showed substantially higher numbers in terms of both productivity and job satisfaction. Conversely, (and ironically), production- oriented leaders consistently exhibited lower production numbers and higher overall job dissatisfaction.

DIFFERENT LEADERSHIP STYLES

A number of contingency theories of leadership have been developed in the last few decades, which try to determine situational conditions fundamental enough to affect the best choice of leadership style. Among these models are the Fiedler contingency model (which includes the well documented least preferred coworker [LPC] questionnaire); the leader- member exchange theory, the path- goal model, situational theory (Hersey and Blanchard), and the leader- participant model. Fiedler contends leadership success combines leader- follower relationships with situational control. The leader- member exchange theory finds leadership success is dependent upon choosing a cadre of capable and loyal favorites rewarded with exceptional treatment. Path- goal theory hypothesizes leader success is contingent upon providing followers with resources to reach the goal. Situational theory suggests successful leadership is designed around followers' readiness. The leader-participation model offers a formulaic rule set that indicates how followers can contribute to decision making in various situations.

LEADER- QUALITIES

Their Leadership Practices Inventory offered a list of leadership qualities and asked 75,000 people over a 20 year time span which characteristics were most likely to inspire them to follow. The list of important leadership characteristics generated over a 20 year time frame from 75,000 participants ranked characteristics which would inspire them to follow a particular leader. The list included the following in order of importance. Leaders must be honest, forward- looking, competent, inspiring, intelligent, fair- minded, broad- minded, supportive, straightforward, dependable, cooperative, determined, imaginative, ambitious, courageous, caring, mature, loyal, self- controlled, and independent. Additionally, Kouzes and Posner determined that successful leaders walk the walk; they demonstrate behaviors they expect from others. Successful leaders explain their vision and invite others to share it via vibrant, energetic communication. They do not shirk from challenge, but invite it as a way to purify their vision. They inspire action, and facilitate it. Above all, the most successful leaders lead with the heart. They believe passionately in their message, open themselves vulnerably and ask their followers to respond with their own passion, faith and trust.

Managerial grid

Graphic organizer created by Black and Mouton, is called a managerial grid or leadership grid, and was influenced by the studies at the University of Michigan's Survey Research Center and Ohio State University. The managerial grid is a two- dimensional model that visually demonstrates dimensions like those described by studies from the University of Michigan's Survey Research Center and Ohio State University. The grid charts information in two directions. The vertical grid ranks a leader's concern for people, with 1 being low and 9 being high. The horizontal grid ranks a leader's concern for production, again with 1 as the low point and 9 as the high point. With 9 distinct placements in each direction, there are a total of 81 possible leadership positions. The managerial grid does not attempt to chart results, but is concerned instead with how a leader thinks about the desired results. The managerial grid's usefulness lies in its ability to succinctly present a visual model of where a particular leader's thought processes place her, rather than as an interactive design into which new information can be added.

Leadership styles

Six emotional leadership styles as identified by Goleman, Boyatzis and McKee include the visionary leader, the coaching leader, the affilliative leader, the democratic leader, the pace- setting leader and the commanding leader. Visionary, coaching, affiliative, democratic, pace- setting and the commanding leaders collectively compose the six emotional leadership styles. Visionary leaders provide direction toward a shared vision by offering information and knowledge. The coaching leader identifies personal desires, strengths and weakness as tools toward career goals. Affiliative leaders are collaborators within an organization, focusing on creating a harmonious work environment. The democratic leader is participative, and wants to hear it all—the good, the bad and the ugly, so that it any issues or problems can be dealt with and any successes can be celebrated. The pace- setting leader creates challenges in order to inspire his employees to reach further and work harder to achieve them. He's looking for the best possible performance, which he demonstrates himself. Commanding leaders require emotional self- control from both herself and her followers. Her instructions are soothingly clear and must be given 100 percent compliance.

Differences between how power functions and how leadership functions

Effective leadership depends in part upon using power judiciously. Leaders who force power are rarely successful in the long run, but neither are leaders who fail to use it forcefully enough. One difference between the two is found in the area of goals. Attaining a leadership position depends in part upon followers perceiving a shared goal with the leader. Attaining power, however, does not require a shared goal, but simply the dependence of the less powerful upon the more powerful. Leadership is concerned with controlling influence so that it flows from the top (the position the leader holds) downward. Power, however, is equally concerned with a reversal of influences, since such a reversal can radically change the power relationship. A third difference is in the types of research each inspire. Leadership research is largely interested in style, while research that is focused upon power reviews strategies for obtaining acquiescence.

Influencing Others

There are a number of strategies that people employ when attempting to use their power to convince others to behave as they wish. Among the tactics frequently employed by people trying to influence others are legitimacy, inspirational appeal, consultation, reward, personal appeal, rational persuasion, pressure, coalition and ingratiation. Legitimacy is power granted by authority, and usually concerns rules and regulations. Inspirational appear targets the values, desires or needs of an individual or group in an emotional way. Consultation invites participation with decision making so increase support. Reward, also called exchange, trades specific benefits for support. Personal appeal depends upon a previously established friendship or social relationship, and asks for commitment based upon that. Rational persuasion uses logic, facts and evidence to seek the granting of a request. Pressure involves threats, warnings, withholding, and demands in order to force agreement. Coalition is the coming together of several individuals or positions to increase the importance or visibility of a request. Ingratiation attempts to influence an individual by pleasing them through compliments, favors, helpfulness and flattery.

Five Stage Group Development Model

The five stage group development model reduces the phases groups pass through from a task's initiation to its completion to a linear series. The length of time a group spends forming, or arriving at a group consensus regarding purpose and roles; storming, or resolving various conflicts within the group; norming, or accepting norms for behavior; performing, or addressing the assigned task; and adjourning, or disbanding, can vary significantly. A group might spend more time forming, resolving conflict or determining and accepting group norms if it contains several highly confident members with strong internal loci of control. Conversely, a group in which most members have external loci on control and low self- esteem will be more willing to accept the leadership of a confident member. A group with several highly social members is likely to spend more time in the norming stage than will a group composed of a group of task-focused scientists.

Power

Power is about dependency. The greater the dependency, and the more limited the sources available to alleviate the dependency, the greater the potential power. The more important, scarce and unique a resource is, the greater the potential power to the entity that controls it. Perception plays a very big part in organizational power. While it isn't strictly true that the resource being guarded must be important, it must be perceived as such, a perception that is the work of marketing departments. A resource gains value the less easily available it is. Whether the resource is tangible, such as an element required to a product, the completed product, or another physical resource, or intangible, such as knowledge, a skill or an idea, the more closely protected it is, the greater the potential power it can bestow. A resource that has ready substitutes is far less valuable as a power source than one that cannot be imitated. The more unique, distinct and original a resource, the less opportunity there is for others to recreate it.

Power Strategies

Power strategies include legitimacy, inspirational appeal, consultation, reward, personal appeal, rational persuasion, pressure, coalition and ingratiation. Of the power tactics of legitimacy, inspirational appeal, consultation, reward, personal appeal, rational persuasion, pressure, coalition and ingratiation, the ones that are consistently effective in a greater number of situations are rational persuasion, inspirational appeal and consultation. The success or failure of a strategy is somewhat dependent both upon organizational culture and national culture. For example, in the United States emphasis is placed upon 'proving' something by providing factual evidence, while in Asian countries, such a tactic might be too direct and be replaced by a softer one, such as coalition.

Inspirational appeal is generally successful as a tactic because individuals can be convinced to make emotional commitment when their values and hopes are addressed. Involving others in decision making is a strong tactic, because they are far more likely to support a decision they've helped make.

SUCCESSFUL POWER TACTICS

Most of the nine power tactics are effective depending upon appropriateness to a situation. For example, personally appealing to a relative to forgive a debt might be successful, at least in the short term. However, asking the loan officer at the local bank for the same favor is very unlikely to succeed, regardless of how long- term the relationship is. Certain strategies, such as rational persuasion, inspirational appeal and consultation, have a fairly high degree of success regardless of situation, but only one, pressure, has a very low degree of success more often than not. It is almost never effective except when employed by a boss over a subordinate, and even then, if support or compliance is given, it is given reluctantly and without commitment. The party that has been coerced feels belittled and responds with resentment and a determination to, at a later point in time, get back'.

The appropriateness of the power tactic but in terms of specific situation and in terms of directionality is indisputable. However, there are other factors that contribute to how well a particular strategy is likely to work. Which tactics are used in combination, how they are sequenced, the degree of power the individual wielding the strategy has, their skill in executing the strategy, and how the receiver perceives the appeal are also contributing factors. Soft strategies are subtler and easier to accept. Their source of power is personal, and they include rational persuasion, consultation and personal and inspirational appeal. The target feels invited by these strategies, rather than manipulated. If soft strategies don't work, those that reference formal power sources and have a clear cost/ risk ratio are the next step. The greater grace with which hard tactics are offered, the greater the likelihood they will be perceived in a favorable light.

DIRECTIONALITY

Of the nice power strategies, (legitimacy, inspirational appeal, consultation, reward, personal appeal, rational persuasion, pressure, coalition and ingratiation), only rational persuasion is appropriately used in all three possible relationships, between supervisors and subordinates, subordinates and supervisors, or laterally, among peers; no doubt because rationality is both logical and depends upon irrefutable fact. Other strategies that can be successful both top- down between supervisors and subordinates and laterally among peers include consultation, ingratiation, exchange, and legitimacy. Appropriate from supervisor to subordinate, but not among peers is inspirational appeal and pressure. Laterally acceptable strategies add personal appeal and coalition to the list. The only power tactic useful in a situation of upward influence is rational persuasion.

SHARING POWER

Every individual involved in an organization wants some degree of power, whether for ego gratification, productivity or social reasons. Whether an individual wants to boost status, improve self- esteem, increase influence or gain resources, wanting power is human nature. While there are those whose desire for power is insatiable and who will pursue it by all means necessary, most are content with power sufficient to insure a degree of comfort. Joining a group to gain power has a cost associated; in joining, one must share her own. Joining a coalition is the second step in attempting to grow personal power, and is resorted to only with doing so as an individual is unlikely or has failed. The more power an person privately holds, the greater its worth, but if that person has tried and failed to extend her influence, then joining a coalition of others with similar goals makes sense.

It's easier to ignore one that a group, and combining forces can exponentially increase the power of individual members.

TEAMS

A team is composed of people with skills, abilities and training responsible for achieving a shared goal in such a way that all members believe themselves to be equally responsible. Formal and informal teams are both concerned with accomplishing the goals of an organization. A team made up of departmental managers given the responsibility of organizing work teams must arrange long term employee groups focused on a single area or department. Quality circles are composed of a selection of employees from a single department who gather according to a schedule to review, discuss and resolve issues in the work environment. A virtual team is fluid, adding or subtracting members as needed using the internet, office networks, and other such sources. Product development teams consist of work and problem- solving teams who develop product designs and services. Problem solving teams, which are short- term in nature, address specific workplace issues.

COALITIONS

Coalitions form as need becomes apparent. They are a power- sharing strategy with the goal of extending the power base as efficiently as possible. Coalitions are generally organized around a single issue (or an umbrella that houses a number of interrelated issues), and while members may have different, even conflicting goals in other areas, in this their purposes are close enough to be seen as identical. Coalitions are not social groups. They are extremely fluid in character, taking shape when a group of individuals recognize a common goal that none have been able to realize independently. By coming together to gain increased influence, members are able to accomplish what they could not as individuals. Once the goal has been achieved, coalitions quickly dissolve. First, though, they seek the broadest base of power possible in order to not only influence decision making, but to see it through to implementation.

COMMUNICATION APPREHENSION

Communication apprehension is estimated to affect between 5 and 20 percent of the population, and is far more than simple discomfort at speaking in public. It is not limited to anxiety over speaking to another individual or group, but can also include a fear of communicating using writing. Individuals who suffer from just the fear of communicating orally must resort to email or fax to avoid face- t0- face communication or communicating by telephone. Those who suffer from a fear of written communication aren't comfortable with any form of writing, from hand- written notes to emails, memos, faxes and so on. They are most at ease in jobs in which they can remain highly independent, schedule their own time, and make most of their own decisions, and will tend to work with greater efficiency to make up for their inability to communicate.

SILENCE IN COMMUNICATION

Much information comes, not in the form of written or spoken words, but as attachments through facial expression, tone of voice, speed of delivery, and silence. In truth, silence speaks louder than words. Just as the pauses between notes give rhythm, shape and identity to music, so does silence inform a message's meaning. Silence is often a conscious decision to withhold an opinion, idea, support or objection for personal or political reasons. Silence can also indicate a response is being prepared, but is still in a state of contemplation. Managers should listen carefully to the sound of silence, because the message is often clear. Lack of response from a group can indicate groupthink, or it can indicate dissatisfaction or discouragement. The failure of two individuals to communicate can point to personal differences that need resolution, while ignoring the attempts of one speaker indicates a loss in that person's status. It's important to hear silences for what they are, rather than treating them as an open invitation to fill them with speech.

Ideal Organizational Communication Structure

Elements of an ideal organizational communication structure are described by Harris and Hartman. Ten characteristics must be present for an ideal organizational communication system to potentially exist. First, a pathway must be in place for communication to move top down, bottom up, or laterally. Secondly, top down communication must be received without preconceived perspectives that might change the true intention of the message. Third, bottom up communication must be correct. Fourth, managers must have an intimate understanding of issues employees face. Fifth, communications are not selective in who they benefit; their ultimate purpose is to improve situations for everyone. Sixth, all necessary information required for top performance is communicated; information is not limited to just what was requested. Seventh, issues and disagreements are openly addressed and resolved in a healthy manner, not ignored. Eighth, individual interpretation is avoided, so that the message's true meaning is received. Ninth, regular feedback informs employees of results, and tenth, information is delivered in a timely manner.

Miscommunication

Clear communication is utterly important within any organization. While complete transparency will always remain an unrealized ideal, it's important to strive for it nonetheless. One area where miscommunication is especially common is that between women and men. From the time they first learn to communicate, girls and boys use language differently and for different purposes. In general, feminine conversation, whether social, professional, political and informational in nature, is characterized by the desire to create connection and inclusion. Masculine communication, on the other hand, is by and large driven by the desire to stake territory, compete, and gain status. In short, women use communication to join together, while men use it to individualize. It should be noted that these tendencies are not absolute positions. Generally, women understand women because the 'language' they speak is designed for intimacy. Men understand men because they 'language' they speak is designed for power. Just as a native Japanese speaker has difficulty hearing the difference between the phonemes /r/ and /l/ in English, so do men and women have difficulty distinguishing differences that are clear within a gender group but indistinct across it.

MIS and the Organization

SKILL BASED PAY PLANS

Skill based pay plans offer both managers and employees advantages. Managers gain a deeper pool of capabilities in the same number of employees, simplifying scheduling. Skill based pay rewards motivated employees who are willing to develop expertise but given little chance of promotion, with pay raises. In a changing technological world, skills needed today may become obsolete tomorrow. When companies are willing to offer a skill based pay increase to employees to acquire a needed skill, problems arise when the skill becomes obsolete. Either the organization reduces pay to an employee who, in good faith, learned the skill, or continues to pay for a skill no longer needed. To employees, skill based pay plans can seem like the perfect solution to what some consider dead-end jobs with no possibility of advancement. Continuing to develop their skills makes them increasingly valuable to the company with a commiserate increase in pay. This solution is extremely motivating to the type of employee businesses want; achievers. However, at some point any organization will run out of needed skills. This presents a built- in frustration for achievers who gain job satisfaction from developing new talents to apply to increasingly challenging tasks.

Organizational Processes and Characteristics

Job Responsibilities

Job responsibilities require decisions on a daily basis. Some decisions are made by a team or other group, but many large and small decisions must be made by an individual. Even without being conscious of it, individuals make hundreds of decisions every day. At its most basic, a decision is simply choosing between two or more possible alternatives. The more alternatives available, or the more complex alternatives are, the more difficult it is to make a decision. The higher on the corporate ladder a job resides, the more weight decisions tend to carry. Top managers might be responsible for deciding which old products to eliminate and which new ones to introduce; where to go for operations monies; or what her organization's vision should be. Among their many job responsibilities, middle managers hire and fire; decide how to distribute rewards and raises; and how to schedule production for the greatest productivity. Non- managers might decide how to schedule tasks; how thoroughly to perform them; which can be combined, postponed or eliminated; and even whether to come to work in bad weather.

Group Decisions

Many organizational decisions are made by groups that have been designated for just that purpose. Whether a decision made by a group is a stronger one than a decision made by an individual is contingent upon a wide range of factors. It is logical to assume that a group decision is likely to be more conservatively made for a number of reasons. The tendency of any individual to lean toward an irresponsible decision is theoretically balanced by the presence of other group members; however contributing circumstances might render this theoretical position moot. On the plus side, a group is likely to consider a wider range of data with more input sources. Diverse points of view must be considered, which can minimize or eliminate problems that might arise later.

Alternative Decisions

Some people seem fearless when it comes to making even major decisions, while others feel immobilized over decisions that are minor and carry no long- term effects. While some people seem to enjoy making major and minor decisions, for many decision- making is fraught with uncertainty, anxiety or fear. They may be worried that making a bad choice will reflect badly upon them, open them to ridicule, devalue them in the eyes of peers or supervisors. A bad decision can result in a loss of bonuses or other incentives, a drop in pay, the loss of a job, and even the crippling or destruction of an entire organization. People who have made a reckless, careless or thoughtless decision in the past that backfired might have learned the lesson too well, and no longer be willing to assume the responsibility decisions come with. Worse are those who made a carefully considered choice, only to have unforeseen conditions negatively affect the outcome, leaving them feeling they have little control over outcomes, regardless of how rational their decision making process may be.

Rational Decision Making

Most people would say that the best decisions are thoughtfully and rationally made. Well made decisions are generally believed to be the result of rational, carefully thought out consideration. While this is not always the case, a model composed of six steps can be used to describe the most rational approach to making decisions. In this model, the first step is to find a definition that fits the problem and narrows the focus to consider only what is essential. Next, identify the necessary criteria to use in resolving the problem. It's essential in this step to consider all significant criteria;

any left out of the equation at this point cannot be considered at a later point. Third, prioritize the criteria to consider the most important first. Fourth, look at all possible alternatives. Fifth, assess each alternative in terms of each of the criteria, remembering that some criteria have greater weight than others. Finally, select the alternative with the greatest collective weight.

Bounded Rationality

Bounded rationality involves the reduction of a model to its most basic elements in order to make a decision. The human mind is complex, but not nearly complex enough to entertain all the information present in even a simple problem. Making decisions requires selecting specific criteria to a narrow, manageable field upon which to focus. Complexity simplified to its most fundamental form provides a model of bounded rationality. This model, though simplified, retains the essence of a problem or situation while refusing the many layers of complexity that exist in the problem itself but are extraneous to its solution. Bounded rationality provides an environment in which a problem or situation has been purified of information that is not useful or distinct, and that would only serve to muddy the waters. Bounded rationality requires one to identify the problem; consider the most obvious features; intuitively review them for similar problems in which a solution was found; and creatively consider these solutions until an acceptable one is found.

Biases

Because managers and other decision makers are sometimes forced to make a decision in very little time, they may resort to short cuts such as basing a choice on a gut feeling, or allow a preconceived idea or bias about a group of people lead them toward a choice. Sometimes decision makers don't have the time or sufficient information to make a rational decision and depend instead upon gut instinct, previous experience with a similar situation, or other biases. Among the common types of biases are overconfidence, anchoring, confirmation, availability, hindsight and representative biases, as well as well as erroneous positions such as the winner's curse, randomness error and escalation of commitment. While it is understandable that, under stress, a manager may feel forced to make a decision that is not based on rational components, it is important that the manager understand the types of distortions that commonly arise from depending too heavily upon a variety of biases. If a supervisor is inclined to take an unnecessary shortcut because there are too many options and criteria to consider, he should move forward with caution and interject as much rationality to the decision making process as possible.

Overconfidence, Anchoring, and Confirmation Biases

Overconfidence refers to faith in one's ability to be correct that exceeds the reality. Numerous studies indicate that people who insist they are 100% certain about something are actually correct only 75-80% of the time. It is interesting to note that the tendency to be overconfident is greater the less real knowledge an individual has about a subject. There is a human inclination to absorb preliminary information about a situation or subject and give that initial knowledge undue anchor at the expense of later, equally important information. For all practical purposes, this means that decisions are often made on the basis of incomplete data, because later facts are not given the same depth of consideration. The inclination to focus on data that supports previous, somewhat similar decisions while ignoring data which challenges past decisions is known as the confirmation bias; this bias is one of selective inattention.

Distorting Information During the Decision Making Process

In the process of making decisions the most accessible information is considered first. The availability bias is caused by the fact that since recent memories and highly dramatic or emotional situations are more accessible, decision makers rely upon them rather than giving equal weight to past events or those that lack emotion or drama. The representative bias assumes that a highly unlikely event in the past is identical to a current situation (which is, in fact, not identical) that will most likely have the same outcome. An example is the man who buys ten lottery tickets on Tuesday and Friday without fail, because he heard of a winner who did the same. The hindsight bias is the tendency to believe an event that has occurred could have been predicted, although certain information wasn't then available. A decision maker who believes she can accurately predict outcomes is less likely to learn from prior experience.

Over the objections of the family, a young woman moves in with her unemployed boyfriend. She offers an alibi when he is accused of robbery and waits when he goes to prison. Her decisions are based on escalation of commitment; as negative information accumulates that an earlier choice was bad, her escalating commitment allows her to avoid admitting a mistake in judgment. Randomness error, the belief that seemingly random or unpredictable events can be predicted if conditions are right, is at the root of superstitions. Gamblers are victims of randomness error, convinced that there's a way to analyze data that will lead to a predetermined outcome, regardless of how unlikely it is. The winner's curse is the conviction that the winning bid is always one that has overestimated actual value. When an organization prepares a bid for goods or services, the idea of the winner's curse can distort the bid amount.

Making Choices

Making choices causes some people to fall into a quandary, while others seem to have an instinct for arriving at decisions both rapidly and with good results. Intuition, while unconscious, is not mind reading, although someone who operates with a great deal of intuition can seem almost psychic. While many people believe that intuition is the opposite of reason, it is, in fact, one unique application of reason. Intuitively attuned individuals have found common patterns in sets of experience and internalized them to the point where they are felt, rather than thought. An intuitive decision- maker assesses a new problem and may almost immediately 'feel' it to be an instance of a very familiar, though unconscious, pattern. Once the pattern is identified, information associated with those previous experiences becomes available. Almost without thinking, an intuitive decision maker is then able to

confidently make a choice. While she may not be able to explain her process, that doesn't mean that there wasn't a rational process involved; it merely means she had internalized it to the point she needn't be fully conscious of it.

Intuitive Problem Solving

Some problems lend themselves to intuitive choices, and certain conditions make purely rational decisions too difficult to arrive at. Intuitive choices are more readily made when there is a high degree of uncertainty as to the outcome. In situations lacking a precedent it is easier to feel one's way to a decision. Scientifically unpredictable variables and a limited body of facts can create an environment allowing an intuitive selection. A situation containing contradictory data, statistics or other facts invites an intuitive response. A problem that could be resolved in a number of equally viable ways might, when no single approach rises above the others, call for an intuitively arrived at decision. Possessing data regarding a problem without a logical way to apply the data is more likely to permit an intuitive choice. Finally, a decision that must be made without the luxury of time is far more likely to be made intuitively.

Gender Roles Within Organizations

In the last few decades, much study has been given to gender roles within organizations. One area of particular interest is concerned with the differences in how men and women are trained or biologically inclined toward particular styles of decision making. Research indicates that women are more likely than men to contemplate a decision over a longer period of time and to give thoughtful consideration to a wider range of variables. While this might suggest that women are better decision makers, in fact, these tendencies can make them less likely to efficiently and effectively arrive at a decision. Because women typically focus on relationships to a greater degree than do men, they typically see more value in drawing on information gleaned from past experiences, in considering the potential outcomes of alternative decisions in the present, and in being concerned with the effects of a decision on the future. Over analyzing a problem can make it harder, rather than easier, to resolve; because women are, by and large, more conscious of the continuity of time, they also tend to second guess themselves regarding a decision that has already been made.

Decision-making

Hundreds if not thousands of decisions are made on a daily basis within any organization. While grave decisions are typically given considerable forethought, many decisions are not given the time a rational model requires. In an ideal world, all organizational decisions would be rational, as well as in the organization's best interests. In reality, decision making is far messier. Attention must be given to what criteria to consider or ignore; how to prioritize information; and how alternatives would affect the organization. Decision makers are human beings, subject to external influences that affect them, if not the decision. Managers necessarily base their decisions upon the standards that are used to evaluate them. If a manager knows her supervisor values a low incidence of workplace accidents, she will make decisions giving consideration to safety components. The organization's reward system is another influence. In a company that gives bonuses to employees who retain customers, a manager will give careful consideration to a problem and likely select a customer-friendly solution. Other constraints are rigid sets of rules, policies or regulations that limit creative solutions to unique problems.

Ethical decisions

Ethical decisions can be difficult to make for the simple reason that the most ethical decision is too often not the most useful one. Ethical decisions are made using three types of criteria. The first is the principle of utilitarianism. Utilitarianism is ultimately practical, and holds that a decision is ethical to the degree that it serves the greatest good for the greatest number. This is the approach most in sync with organizations that value profit, production and efficiency. Utilitarianism in concerned with the protection of the many over the few. The second principle used in making ethical decisions is rights. This position prioritizes fundamental rights and freedoms, such as the right to free speech, due process under the law, and the right to privacy, and protects employees who report illegal or unethical business practices to the outside world. The third principle called upon when making ethical decisions is that of justice. Ethically just decisions are, above all, fair and impartial. They distribute costs, benefits and rewards equitably, regardless of gender, age, race, ethnicity or other considerations.

Positive and negative attributes of the criteria of utility, human rights and justice in making ethical decisions

Ethical decisions can be based on utilitarianism, individual rights, justice or a combination of these. It is easy to consider these three principles in terms of ideal benefits. Utilitarianism is often said to provide the greatest good for the greatest number; itself a virtue. Additionally, a utilitarian standard encourages high productivity that is efficiently accomplished, which results in greater results for the greater number of people. However, these positive outcomes are nearly always at the expense of the rights of certain individuals. Using the principle of individual rights in an ethical decision protects individuals as the Bill of Rights intended, but it can create a legalistically entangled environment where little gets accomplished. Prioritizing justice when making an ethical decision means the 'little people' who lack power are protected, but it can encourage a lack of innovation and a sense of entitlement that is incongruent with the goals of business.

Restrictions Placed on Managers

It is not always possible for managers to make decisions based on the rational decision- making model in which the problem is examined and clearly defined; decision criteria is then identified; next, the criteria weighted; all possible alternatives developed; all possible alternatives reviewed; and last, the best alternative chosen. Managers must be careful to make decisions that align with the performance evaluation and reward system of the organization; to act in accordance with organizational policy, rules and regulations; and to meet necessary organizational time constraints. In addition, managers must consider the weight of prior decisions, in that they act as precedents. These limitations can affect the manager's decision making process by limiting the length of time permitted to draw a rational conclusion. This can result in managers being forced to apply short cuts, or basing the decision in part upon subjective or personal attitudes, values and perspectives.

Traditional Relationship Problems

Issues of competition, fragmentation, and reactiveness plague traditional relationships, encourage divisiveness and discourage a sense of unity and single vision in traditional organizations. Traditional organizations have historically seen themselves as an individual entity composed of separate systems. Just as medicine once saw the mind and body as entirely unrelated, so have organizations seen their various departments as unrelated. When departments don't work together, they work in competition with one another, concerned only that their particular contributions are appreciated and prioritized, that they receive necessary resources, which manager has more power, and which employees are most influential. This competitive attitude not only discourages collaborative efforts, it destroys them. The departmentalization of organizations is the result of fragmentation. Fragmentation is created by specializations that establish themselves and their functions as independent. Increased specialization leads to further and further divisions, which further fragments the organization. Fragmentation gives rise to competition; competition gives rise to a multitude of problems. Reactiveness results, by forcing managers to focus on endless rounds of problem solving rather than on creative, new endeavors.

Learning Organization

A learning organization can be described as one which has consciously evolved itself to be continuously open to learning and continuously willing to adapt to fit new information. Learning organizations which employ double loop learning, are considered to be more effective than those who employ single loop learning. In order to continue to exist, all organizations absorb new information and learn lessons, regardless of whether the learning is intentional or not. Learning organizations consciously create and nurture a shared vision that is agreed upon by all its members. Learning organizations encourage their members to shed outmoded ideas and step out of habitual routines when new information requires a new way of responding. Thirdly, learning organizations are seen by members as a single system of a multitude of interrelationships that include processes, environmental relationships, activities and functions. Fourth, Learning organizations foster a culture in which everyone feels free to communicate fully and openly with peers as well as with supervisors or supervisees without danger of reprimand or censure. Finally, learning organization members prioritize their shared organizational vision above individual interests, self- interest or personal preference. Supporters of learning organizations believe it remedies the problems of competition, reactiveness and fragmentation in traditional groups.

STEPS MANAGERS CAN TAKE TO HELP THEIR ORGANIZATIONS TRANSFORMATION TOWARD THE LEARNING IDEAL

All learning organizations exist in the real world, and as such, cannot perfectly embody the five characteristics of learning organizations. This fact, coupled with the learning organization ideal of constant evolution through learning, creates a model that can only be realized through continual growth and continual development. Managers can pursue three specific directions in their efforts to help their organization evolve from a traditional learner to a learning organization. The first step is to launch a line of attack. Managers must aggressively address the necessary role of innovation in meaningful change. They must take a clear stand committed to letting go of stale, fruitless habits in favor of fresh new vision. Secondly, the more rigid and formal an organization's structure, the more difficult it will be to introduce meaningful, continuous learning. Just as modern architecture has merged rooms that served single, narrow purposes in favor of open, flowing space that encourages a multitude of activities, so must managers work to reshape the organization's structure by merging or discarding departments, creating multifunctional teams, encouraging interdependence and creativity. Third, the organizational culture must undergo a transformation. Learning organizations embrace risk, respect open communication, and welcome growth; traits managers must exemplify.

TEAM PERFORMANCE

Teams perform best when they are supplied with sufficient resources; agree on how the team will structure itself; develop an atmosphere of confidence in one another; and undergo performance evaluation that reflects the involvement of all members of the team. Because teams are never given a free hand with budgeting, equipment and supplies, they must depend upon other sources for these things as well as for information, administrative support and encouragement from other parts of the organization. Team structure is vital, as is the need to establish or share leadership roles and work responsibilities; decide how to determine the best solution to problems; and share in both the work and the appreciation. Trust breeds cooperation, and cooperation breeds collaboration. The product of teamwork is synergistically greater than the sum total of its parts. Finally, establishing a single performance evaluation for the whole team emphasizes the need for shared responsibility, and shared rewards.

ALTERNATIVE WORK MODELS

Many organizations have begun to look at ways of restructuring traditional organizational models to increase job satisfaction, productivity and quality. Flextime, which is an increasingly popular alternative to traditional office schedules, permits employees some discretion in deciding their own work hours. Flextime typically requires all employees to be at work during core hours, which are the five or six hours in the middle of the workday. Employees are required to work a certain number of weekly hours, but can choose to come in early and leave early, come in later and leave later, or work one or two very long days and one or two shorter days. Job sharing is an option in which two employees share a full time job. Any number of combinations are possible, such as one employee working only mornings while the other works only afternoons; or both employees working every other day, so that one has a two day week followed by a three day week, while the other's schedule is exactly opposite.

TELECOMMUTING

Telecommuting is only an option for employees when it's an option for their organization. While not every job can realistically be done by a telecommuter, there are some employment areas which are well suited. Many employees would like telecommuting, but most wouldn't be good candidates because of the nature of their work. Three professional areas that adapt well to telecommuting include employees who habitually work with information processing, organizing and sharing; employees whose job responsibilities include a good portion of the work week spent traveling either locally or at a greater distance; and highly trained professionals who are already working with considerable autonomy. Telephone marketing and sales work, travel agents, product and technical support representatives, and appointment schedulers are primarily focused on information processing, organizing and sharing. Salespeople who make visits in person and employees responsible for delivering goods or services typically spend the bulk of the work week in transition; for them, telecommuting for the remainder of their work week makes sense. Writers, researchers, architects and other highly trained specialists are already working with less supervision and might find telecommuting a more efficient way to work.

Points That Demonstrate Telecommuting Might Be Worthy of Consideration

Some organizations are more conservative by nature or by necessity than others. Certain arguments have been raised in opposition to permitting employees to complete some or all of their work responsibilities from the home. While transitioning some workers to telecommuting positions would require changes to the organization's structure that would need to be well thought out, there are several very clear benefits to telecommuting that should be considered as well. Telecommuting can offer an organization a significant reduction in office expenses in terms of utilities, parking, office furniture, office machinery and space and so forth. It can broaden the pool of high quality employees. If employees who are given the option of telecommuting are wisely chosen, it can increase job satisfaction, reduce absenteeism and slow turnover. Greater job satisfaction will almost certainly lead to a higher level of production, as well as greater on the job efficiency.

Collateral Downside to Telecommuting

It is important to understand that not all employees are good candidates for telecommuting. An employee who works efficiently inside the office might not fare as well working from home if his past work required few decisions on his part, included considerable feedback, or was limited in scope. Some employees chafe under a lot of supervision; others thrive in such an environment. Those who enjoy interaction with supervisors and other members of the team may feel isolated and lost when working from home. This is not to suggest that all employees who dislike being managed are good candidates, either. Their desire for greater autonomy must be balanced by their work ethic, a strong sense of responsibility and a history of making good independent choices. As well, managing teams consisting of employees who are all working out of different locations can burden supervisors; this is no small objection, and must be carefully considered.

Support Resources

All jobs require support of one kind of another. Support can come in the form of explicit directions, clarifications, praise, rewards, sufficient materials, a work environment that is both comfortable and lacks distractions, and more. One way to look at support is by defining obstacles to best performance as 'negative support'. Employees who are sufficiently trained, share an organization's values and vision, and are eager to succeed at the job can still be hindered by computers, printers and other machinery that are slow or fail to function; by a supply room that lacks sufficient stock due to someone's failure to order, or to budget cuts; by the failure to provide these employees with the information, data, research results or other facts required to make intelligent decisions or complete the job in a timely manner; or by a hostile or negative work environment or indeed, simply by the absence of a positive one.

Participative Management Programs

Participative management programs are made up of supervisors and subordinates who make collective decisions. This model does not assign extra weight to input from supervisors or other employees with a greater degree of office power; all input is equally received, evaluated and considered. As an ideal, participative management makes sense. Its supporters believe participative management will improves office self- esteem and will result in a greater willingness to commit to decisions made within the group. However, research studies of real life applications suggest that the program works best when the decision being made has relevance to the employees, when all participants are sufficiently knowledgeable to make intelligent contributions, and when subordinates trust their supervisors and supervisors respect their subordinates. Even then, employee motivation, productivity and satisfaction are not guaranteed outcomes of establishing participative management programs.

Representative Participation Programs

Representative participation is designed to restructure organizational control to give employees power in decision making similar to shareholders' and managers'. Representative participation is common in Europe, where some countries have legislated that companies must include representative participation programs. Board representatives and works councils are two types of programs. Board representatives are members of an organization's board of directors; their main function is to protect employee interests. Work councils are composed of members who have been selected by nomination or election. Management decisions that affect personnel must include a consultation with the organization's works council. However, like the participative management model, representative participation gets mixed reviews in real life applications. The tendency of managers to dictate at meetings undercuts the program's intentions. Furthermore, many researchers have noted that while employee representatives may experience an amplified sense of job satisfaction or motivation, this increased satisfaction does not pass from the representatives to those they represent.

Salaries

Making a decision regarding salary is complex. Every type of business is part of a greater market, which includes other businesses of the same type. There are no industry absolutes regarding pay; organizations must decide whether to offer a salary that matches industry averages, one at the high end of the scale, or a salary lower than the average. This decision is based in part upon internal equity, or what value the position has to an organization, and external equity, or how competitive an offering is in relation to similar companies' offerings. Pay decisions also include whether to incorporate a variable or a skill based salary arrangement. Benefits are another important consideration, and within the area of benefits is a further question of whether employees will be offer flexible benefits. A final consideration is to decide the manner in which employees will receive financial recognition for work well done.

Salaries Above or Below Industry Standard

It seems logical that any business would ideally want to attract the best talent by paying employees at or above industry standard. While no business would consider paying their employees at the bottom of the pay scale a wise long- term decision, it might be a temporary necessity than can offer benefits to both the company and the employees. A business in the process of establishing itself might very well be one that has youth, vitality and vision on its side. If the business has identified a niche or approach that has been unexplored by competitors, it might be able to draw employees who are able to see the potential and want to be involved from the outset. Offering stock in addition to salary (if the business has gone public), ownership interest, or other incentives that might pay off in the long run might be sufficient to attract less experienced but highly competent employees who would expect to start at another, more established company at the lower end of the pay scale in any event.

Middle Range Salaries

While it might seem common sense to aim a pay decision toward the middle range of what the market pays, there can be a number of variables that contribute to a company's decision to pay at a higher or lower rate. For example, a financially healthy company that can afford to offer pay that leads the trade will draw talent to the job in the form of industry leaders who have already demonstrated outstanding competence. A company that needs to restructure might also be convinced to offer a salary at the higher end for employees who can help to implement the restructuring as efficiently as possible. On the other hand, a company that is just starting out will most likely not possess resources necessary to lure the market's finest and best. Their offering might, of necessity, be at the bottom of the scale.

Merit Based Pay

Merit based pay, like piece rate pay, offer compensation that is specifically tied to how well an employee performs. Piece rate plans base pay on objective, measurable, identical units; employees know exactly what must be accomplished in order to reach a specific pay goal. Merit based pay, however, is based upon a far more subjective measure. An employee's performance is evaluated and salary is linked to how well her performance appraised. This form of variable pay is favored by managers for employees whom they consider at the top of the performance ladder; higher salaries are justified by superior reviews. Properly handled, this version of variable pay has proven itself to be highly motivating to employees, who recognize their individual performances determine their pay. Merit plans typically are organized around annual reviews; if the review is inaccurate, the employee can gain or suffer unfairly as a result.

Compensation Based upon Production

Pure and modified piece rate plans have been used for well over a century in factories and other businesses that produce and sell individual unit items. Both pure piece rate plans and modified piece rate plans offer strong incentive to workers, in that the greater their output, the higher their pay. Employees in jobs where there is little opportunity to advance find piece rate pay gives them the opportunity to increase their salaries as their experience, and thus their production, increases. While they aren't being formally recognized with a promotion, a better title and higher pay, their experience and effort is paying off nonetheless. A pure piece rate pay plan gives no base salary. Everything the employee earns is based solely upon how many units he creates. More common are modified piece rate plans, in which employees earn a low but constant salary, plus an additional amount that is directly tied to production.

Profit Sharing Plans and Gainsharing Plans

Profit sharing organizations compensate all employees or members of an organization based upon how profitable the organization has been in a specific period of time. An established formula determines how each type of employee will be rewarded. Profit sharing is often made in the form of cash, although some companies offer stock as an alternative to employees at certain levels. Most companies offer stock options to top managers in addition to or instead of a cash payment. Gainsharing variable pay programs, on the other hand, reward members of a team or other group for increased production rather than on profits, during the course of a particular time period; the amount of the incentive each position receives is also based upon a pre- determined formula, with the company receiving a certain percentage and employees receiving a certain percentage. Gainsharing encourages desirable behaviors regardless of company profit.

Flexible Fringe Benefits Packages

Organizational fringe benefits are worth as much as 40% of an average employee's pay. Traditional benefits packages are tailored to a 1950s husband with a wife who worked inside the home, and two or three children. Today, this description fits only one employee in ten. Benefits packages can consist of a variety of options. Life insurance, health insurance, death benefits, vacation or personal time, and company paid training are perks that can appeal to one employee and not to another. The contemporary workplace is indeed a world of individuals. Childless individuals or couples, those with young children, gay couples whose union, though long-term, isn't recognized by institutions, older employees with grown children, employees who prize personal development and those who prize financial security reflect the nation in which we live. Flexible benefits allow employees to select what fits. An employee whose wife is a long-time well placed CEO may not need health insurance, but his teammate, a young, single woman with a history of cancer in her family, considers it essential. Flexible plans are just that; they offer a combination of benefits that are relevant to the lives of the individuals for whom they are tailored.

Myth of Rationality

Traditionally, the position on showing emotion in the workplace has been, don't. Employees tiptoe around angry managers, and politely turn their faces away from an obviously upset coworker. Proper employees remain firmly in control of their feelings, because they've been taught that strong feelings have no place at work. Researchers, too, have been fooled by the myth of rationality, so much so that until recently the only emotions studied in regards to organizational behavior were negative ones. No one was surprised to discover that exhibits of anger or depression disturbed efficiency and contributed to low morale. The myth of rationality locates feeling at one end of the spectrum and rationality at the other. Aligned with feeling were irrationality, foolishness, lack of control, and chaos. Aligned with rationality were wisdom, thought, control and calm. The myth of rationality is a myth precisely because thought and feeling aren't diametrically opposed but absolutely interrelated.

Management by Objectives

Management by objectives programs sound good, and in practice they are often successful. However, these programs contain areas of weakness that can result in failure. Management by objectives programs require four traits for the program to succeed. They are specificity of objectives, meaning goals must be narrow, specific, and clear; temporal boundaries, meaning the goal must be achieved within a specified time period; goals established by all employees who will be affected; and ongoing feedback as workers progress toward achievement of the goal. While management by objectives programs are becoming increasingly accepted, they can fail. First, if the established goal is idealistic to the point of being unrealistic, the program's success is unlikely. Including employees in goal setting is useful only to the degree that these employees have sufficient knowledge and experience, so the goals are reachable. Secondly, higher levels of management must be as committed to the program as workers at ground level, rather than passing off design and implementation. Third, these programs aren't compatible with low risk cultures that focus on long term goals.

Cascade of Objectives

Cascade of objectives is a model that demonstrates how management by objectives is most effectively structured. Management by objectives programs begin by translating organization-wide goals into explicit aims for teams and individuals. The model which demonstrates how management by objectives programs are able to condense an organization goal (which is by its nature wide-reaching and generalized) into goals that are meaningful on an individual level, is called a cascading of objectives. This model considers objectives at the organizational level (the broadest), the divisional level, the departmental level, and the individual level (the most specific). The beauty of the approach is that it works both from the top down—with goal requirements cascading from the organization through top, middle and lower managerial levels to the workers themselves—as well as from the bottom up, because teams at the ground floor participate in setting realistic goals. In this fashion, goals are shared from level to level, with each level fine- tuning goal applications to be relevant to them.

Rapid Changes in Workforce

The world has become both larger and smaller from a business viewpoint. Larger, in terms of global issues, and smaller, because fast moving information means business decisions must be made efficiently and appropriately or the negative response will be potentially crippling. One development has been changes within the workforce. Where once males of European descent dominated the workplace, now people of every race and age work side by side. Technology becomes increasingly less expensive and more sophisticated. Thirdly, many parts of the world are currently rocking in small boats on unpredictable economic waters. Competition abroad, coupled with the growing presence of ecommerce means many businesses must consolidate or merge in order to survive. Discount retailers who also offer inexpensive goods for online or telephone orders, bloggers who praise or blast products, and other social trends present a fifth development. Finally, uneasy world politics plays a role in how organizations must behave.

Organizational Theories

Traditionally, studies of micro organizational behavior have examined the ways in which both individuals and groups relate to one another within an organizational setting. For example, a study at the micro level might look at the channels through which office rumors spread. Macro organizational theory has traditionally focused on analyzing how entire organizations structure themselves and adapt to change. A study of how large organizations restructured their safety regulations following 9/11 would be the work of a macro organizational behavior theorist. Meso organizational behavior theory is a relatively new field, and is interested in issues of workplace culture, distributions and uses of power, and communication networks within an organization. Someone interested in the ways newly hired managers go about learning which employees will be most reliable, which employees seem to represent their peers, which employees are highly respected, and which are given greater clearance, is observing behavior on the meso level.

Mintzberg's Organizational Configurations Framework

Mintzberg's organizational configurations framework is built upon six classifications. These groups include adjustment, which refers to the use of informal communication to create synchronic action between two or more people; direct supervision, which involves a leader or manager who instructs a group doing interrelated step by step work; standardization of work processes, by which work involving interconnected, particularized tasks is given a standard form; standardization of outputs, in which synchronization is reached by detailing results of a number of tasks; standardization of skills and knowledge, in which different work is coordinated due to similarity in training; and standardization of norms, which involves controlling norms in order to synchronize work. Standardizing actions, processes, outputs, skills, knowledge and norms is a bureaucratic concept characterized by highly formalized and functionalized organization designed for greatest efficiency.

Mintzberg's Organizational Configurations Model

Mintzberg's six essential components required to create a formal structure for tasks within an organization include the operating core, which is composed of individuals whose job it is to be responsible for ensuring products and services are produced as planned; the strategic apex, which is composed of employees working at the top managerial level; the middle line, which is composed of employees working at the middle managerial level; techno structure, which is composed of analysts responsible for creating standardizing systems to be used with work processes and products; and support staff, who are responsible for organizational support that is outside of operating workflow. The relationships among these six groups are tightly structured and controlled for optimum efficiency. Communication moves from the operating core to the strategic apex, and if appropriate, to the middle line level. If appropriate, information moves from the middle line level to the techno structure and, less often, support staff.

COMPETITION

Rapid changes in technology have resulted in global markets and increased competition. Where once a company could create a business model that included proven systems of production and distribution, understood customers needs, could anticipate the number of units and types of services customers would purchase in a specific time period, and knew who their competitors were, all of these parameters have changed. Because the internet and other types of technology have opened up the world, competitors can come from any corner at any time. Competitors are no longer other established businesses operating on traditional models; some of the goods and services they provide are the result of innovative approaches. Smaller, entrepreneurial businesses can force a larger, more established business's hand by getting new product to the marketplace much faster. To survive, established companies often must downsize and rapidly restructure; the more traditional and established an organization is, the harder to accomplish this.

RESISTANCE TO CHANGE

While radical, unexpected or overtly threatening change might induce an immediate response which is clearly tied to the change itself, resistance to change can surface in unexpected ways or at times distant to the change being made operational. Overt, immediate change is easiest for managers to respond to, in part because specific objections can be anticipated and a 'party line' response crafted in advance. Deferred resistance, or resistance that is not overt, is more difficult for managers to diffuse. Employees who respond to change with a loss of company trust, with increased tardiness or absenteeism, who become depressed and unmotivated, who begin making a higher percentage of errors or whose production slows down may not even known themselves that the change in behavior reflects resistance to the change in organization. Unless a manager identifies the source as resistance to change, it could build to the danger point.

TERMS RELATING TO ORGANIZATIONAL STRUCTURE

Divisionalized form is a typical design structure used in extremely large organizations that are less contemporary. In this design structure, the business's organization conforms to the various markets it identifies and serves. Divisions and company headquarters are horizontally and vertically specialized, and production is standardized.

Environmental complexity refers to how many environmental elements are imposed upon decision making.

Environmental dynamism is a term that describes how those environmental elements that impose upon decision making can change.

Environmental uncertainty manifests when there is little data available to managers in regards to events or situations in the environment, or information regarding their affect upon the organization.

The term general environment refers to the range of considerations that create the organizational setting, including political, cultural, legal, technological, economic, and global considerations.

The task environment includes particular groups, associations, and people that have influence within the organization.

Organizational downsizing has, in recent years, become an often used option in organizations that need to decrease staff size at the corporate and middle management levels in an attempt to control skyrocketing costs.

The term organizational environment refers to individuals, groups, economic considerations, material goods, cultural considerations, events, activities, situations and all other possible influences existing outside the limits of the organization that can impact it negatively as a threat, or positively as an opportunity.

Organizational technology is a term used to describe all processes, including those that are automated, programmed, conceptual, or psychological, which are involved in the process of turning organizational resources and contributions into products. Organizational technology is concerned with efficiency, innovation, and improved productivity.

Action Research Model

The first two steps of the action research plan include gathering information relevant to an anticipated change (diagnosis), and then organizing and examining that information in order to determine as scientifically as possible the best course of action (analysis). In the diagnostic phase, the change agent is looking at every possible source within the organization to collect data, information, numbers and opinions regarding issues and problems. A number of collection forms might be used, including formal interviews, informal questions raised in conversation, record reviews and polls. The analysis phase of an action research plan organizes this data into three areas; primary concerns, problematic areas, and action possibilities. Primary concerns can include organizational elements that employees find unclear or unsettling but which have not coalesced into an identifiable 'problem'. These initial two steps correspond to the first two steps in the scientific method; X AND Y

Formal Organizations

Formal organizations are more rigid than informal ones. Their establishment is intended to carry on into the future, to remain strong in the face of opposition. Formal organizations typically operate from the top down, high level executives making decisions which are handed to middle management, whose job it is to implement them intact. Historically, formal organizations could be described as static. Organizational visions in traditional formal organizations are absolute, and change is the enemy. They are mission oriented, and exist to accomplish goals by whatever means necessary. Power in formal organizations is hierarchically held, with those nearer the top holding a unequal percentage which they share cautiously and to effect collaboration when needed. Formal organizations are very much rule oriented, and rules are clear, simple and codified. Within a formal organization, it is the role or work, rather than the individual that has priority. Formal organizations excel in situations where all parameters are consistent and known.

Informal Organizations

Formal organizations use informal organizations for certain tasks. Informal organizations nurture and protect organizational norms, preserving a sense of unity through daily connection on a personal level. They also encourage a sense of identity and status to employees who may not get recognition from formal channels; this contributes to a sense of personal worth and appreciation, which contributes to job satisfaction. Informal organizations also enhance communication within its members. An informal group spontaneously creates its own channels whereby information, including important work information, is informally shared. It's not unusual for managers to send information via informal channels that can be dismissed as rumor or innuendo if necessary, or that can prepare employees for future changes. Informal groups also supply social control by influencing activities within the group. Group members are more likely to adhere to certain behaviors expressed by the group than to the same behaviors regulated by management.

Group Decision Making

In recent years, many organizations have tended toward assigning decision making to teams or groups, rather than to individuals. While group decision making has advantages in that decisions are based upon a wider data base and consider heterogeneous points of view, there are also some disadvantages to decisions made by groups. While at first glance, a group decision making process might appear to offer numerous advantages and no disadvantages. Multiple points of view and a much wider and deeper information base mean decisions will in all likelihood be better informed. However, drawbacks to a group decision making process do exist and must be considered. Unless the circumstances surrounding the decision under consideration aren't time- constrained, the speed at which groups move can hinder the process, meaning a problem may not be resolved and a decision reached in a timely manner. Secondly, while a group is likely to rein in a member whose contributions and suggestions might lead to an unwise decision, it is just as likely that the group could be controlled by one or two strong members who do not solicit nor consider input from others. Additionally, members are less likely to feel accountable, and may therefore accept riskier decisions.

Efficiency and Effectiveness of Group and Individual Decisions

When considering whether group or individual decisions are more efficient and effective, various criteria need to be considered. For example, an individual charged with making a decision will arrive at one more rapidly than a group assigned the same task. Groups take longer in part because they are considering more information and thus, it is also true that a group decision might be more deeply considered. On the whole, decisions arrived at through group consensus prove to be more accurate than those made by an average individual within the group—but less accurate than decisions made by the most accurate member of the group. Groups consider a decision with more creativity than do individuals, for the simple reason that multiple thinkers are actively looking for contributions and solutions other group members haven't considered. Groups that have collectively arrived at a decision are also more likely to accept and support its implementation.

Inner Circle of Groups

Leader- member exchange theory hypothesizes that successful leadership is contingent upon a leader being supported by a core in- group of favorites who are loyal and exceptionally capable. Leader-Member Exchange Theory, also called Vertical Dyad Linkage Theory, describes how group leaders control power by making exchange trades. Nearly all groups, regardless of how egalitarian they profess to be, contain an inner, trusted cadre with greater responsibility. This inner circle has a higher ability to influence decisions, clearer access to resources, are more loyal, more responsible, and harder working than those in outer groups. In payment for their unquestioning loyalty and hard work, they have more ready access to the source of power, and greater influence. Leaders must determine who is in the inner circle early on, and nurture the relationship with those individuals. Inner circle members negotiate with the leader to determine the role they will serve and what benefits they will receive in return for their support. Members who reflect the leader's style are most likely to succeed, but only if they demonstrate no betrayal whatsoever.

Emotional Leadership Styles

The visionary leader, the coaching leader, the affilliative leader, the democratic leader, the pace-setting leader and the commanding leader as described by Goleman, Boyatzis and McKee are all emotional leadership styles offering particular strengths for particular situations. The visionary leader expects her followers to struggle toward vision; she tells where the goal is, but gives no direction. Visionaries are most useful when a change in direction is required. Coaching leaders don't limit inspiration to the workplace. With great faith in their followers, they delegate tough work that inspires a high degree of loyalty. Coaches who lack skill micromanage. Affiliative Leaders connect people amicably, prioritizing human over task needs, but an unskilled affilliative leader may avoid emotionally unpleasant occasions. Democratic leaders are good listeners who value input. Unskilled democratic leaders can be ineffective action initiators. Pace- setting leaders demand excellence, a good short- term position but offers too little guidance to go the distance. Commanding Leaders are very clear in what they expect, and are excellent in a crisis. They don't worry about hurting feelings, but do what must be done. However, they can be cold.

Authority

With authority comes responsibility. Whether authority is legitimately assigned in terms of decision making or influencing others, it carries responsibility. Formal job definitions and coordinating strategies are not enough to get the work done. Managers must use influence to encourage workers to action. If they are to succeed, managers must possess the ability to influence organization members. Influence is the ability to bring about change and produce results; people derive influence from interpersonal power and authority. Interpersonal power allows organization members to exert influence over others. In some respects, everyone has power—the power to either push forward or obstruct the goals of the organization by making decisions, delegating decisions, delaying decisions, rejecting decisions, or supporting decisions. The effective use of power does not mean control. Power can be detrimental to the goals of the organization if held by those who use it to enhance their own positions and thereby prevent the advancement of the goals of the organization. Successful managers are able to use power ethically, efficiently, and effectively by sharing it. Power can be used to influence people to do things they might not otherwise do. When that influence encourages people to do things that have no or little relationship to the organization's goals, that power is abused. Abuses of power raise ethical questions. For example, asking a subordinate to run personal errands is an abuse of power. People who acquire power are ethically obligated to consider the impact their actions will have on others and on the organization.

In order for managers to achieve goals in an efficient manner, part of their work may be assigned to others. When work is delegated, tasks and authority are transferred from one position to another within an organization. The key to effective delegation of tasks is the transference of decision-making authority and responsibility from one level of the organization to the level to which the tasks have been delegated. In order to effectively delegate work, some guidelines should be followed: Determine what each worker can most effectively accomplish; decide whether the worker should just identify a problem or also propose a solution; consider whether the person can handle the challenge of the task; be clear in the objectives of the task; encourage questions; explain why the task is important; determine if the person has the appropriate resources—time, budget, data, or equipment—to get the job done on a deadline; create progress reviews as part of the project planning; and be prepared to live with less than perfect results. Authority should be delegated in terms of expected results. The more specific the goal, the easier it is to determine how much authority someone needs.

Authority gives legitimacy to power. Within organizations, legitimate authority can be given for the purpose of making decisions, of influencing others, of providing guidance, for hiring purposes, or dealing with resources. Each instance of authority carries its own responsibility, and organizational structure formalizes the responsibility- authority relationship within the different types of authority it allows; line authority, staff authority and functional authority. Line authority can be found in the chain of command, and is concerned with where individuals stand hierarchically in relationship to one another. Higher positions have the authority to make decisions, assign tasks, and expect their orders will be carried out. Staff authority is advisory in nature. It offers advice, makes suggestions and proposes alternatives. Staff authority gains power from the specialized knowledge the individual possesses. Functional authority gives supervisors the authority to manage specific activities that may have a bearing upon other departments, regardless of hierarchical relationship.

Employees may desire a greater balance of power or a redistribution of authority within the existing formal authority structure. People can share power in a variety of ways: by providing information, by sharing responsibility, by giving authority, by providing resources, by granting access, by giving reasons, and by extending emotional support. The act of sharing information is powerful. When people don't share information, the need to know still exists; therefore, the blanks are filled in with gossip and innuendo. People need the legitimate power to make decisions without having to clear everything first with someone higher up in the organization. People who have power must also have the necessary range of resources and tools to succeed. Access to people outside as well as inside the organization should be provided and encouraged. People should be told why an assignment is important and why they were chosen to do it. Emotional support can come in the form of mentoring, appreciation, listening, and possibly helping out. Sharing power or redistributing authority does not necessarily mean moving people into positions of power; instead, it can mean letting people have power over the work they do, which means that

people can exercise personal power without moving into a formal leadership role. The ability to influence organization members is an important resource for effective managers. Relying on the title "boss" is seldom powerful enough to achieve adequate influence.

Some employees resist delegation. Initiative and responsibility involve risk that some people try to avoid. People tend to play it safe if risk results in criticism. Those who feel they already have more work than they can do avoid new assignments. Some people doubt their own abilities and lack the self-confidence to tackle new assignments. Delegation is an excellent professional development tool so long as it expands a worker's expertise and growth. Delegation can also compensate for a manager's weakness. A successful team is developed by building on the strengths of its members. People develop most when stimulated to broaden themselves—when challenged. More authority can add challenge; too much challenge, however, can frustrate people and cause them to avoid new responsibilities. Delegation should involve acceptable challenge—enough to motivate but not so much as to frustrate. Managers are compelled to rely more on persuasion, which is based on expert and referent power rather than reward, coercive, or inappropriate use of power. A manager who shares power and authority will be the one with the greatest ability to influence others to work toward the goals of the organization.

Structures

Simple structure, bureaucracy and matrix structure organization types are commonly found in a variety of organizational models. Simple structure organizations usually have an owner who is also the manager; authority and decision making rests in that individual. Simple structure are not hierarchical, and are typically small both in number of employees and in production or services offered. Bureaucratic organizations are generally large, concentrate on standardizing, coordinating and controlling every aspect of the business. These organizations take specialization, formalization and departmentalization to the extreme, follow a strict chain of command, and are highly efficient. Matrix structure organizations combine functional departmentalization and product departmentalization. Functional departmentalization groups specialists in order to share resources; product departmentalization synchronizes efforts for efficiency and increased accountability. Matrix structure organizations break the single commander model; employees must respond to both the functional supervisor and the product supervisor.

The structure of an organization determines the arrangement and synchronization of tasks. Six areas must be adequately addressed in order to create a functional system. They include work specialization; departmentalization; command chain; span of control; centralization/ decentralization; and formalization. Work specialization involves dividing a task with numerous steps into distinct tasks, each of which is accomplished by one individual. Departmentalization organizes specialized tasks into related groups; common ways of departmentalizing are by function performed; by product created; by geographical location; by process accomplished or by type of customer. The concept of command chain, a foundation in traditional organizational models, names the links of authorization and determines responsibility. Span of control is concerned with the number of employees a manager can supervise. Centralized organizations concentrate decision making in one location without input from the outside. Decentralized organizations contribute to decisions. A highly formalized job is one that is profoundly standardized.

SIMPLE STRUCTURE ORGANIZATION

Organizations can be structured in any number of ways, but three of the most common are simple structure, bureaucracy and matrix structure. Simple structure organizations are streamlined; they are not highly departmentalized, most of the authority and decision making power resides in a single individual, the span of control is narrow, and there is little need for formalization. At most, simple organizations contain no more than three hierarchical levels, and employees flow comfortably from level to level. Commonly, the owner is also the manager. Because simple structure organizations are so sleekly designed, decisions can be made quickly, they are as flexible as a situation requires them to be, accountability is transparent, and cost to operate is low. The biggest drawback to an organization based on a simple structure is that remaining small is the only way it can be managed; there is literally no room for substantial growth.

ORGANIZATIONAL DESIGNS THAT MEET THE CHALLENGES OF THE 21ST CENTURY

The world has changed rapidly in the last 40 years, and with it, organizational designs. Team structure, virtual organizations and boundryless organizational structures have taken hold. Team structure operates vertically, horizontally, or both; teams share burden of responsibility along with freedom of choice, an alternative to a bureaucratic, heavily controlled structure. Virtual organizational structure, also called modular or network organization, is about leaving the office, along with the bulk of costs, behind. A virtual organization has a small, well- controlled core and outsources most of its requirements. There is no need to departmentalize with a virtual organization. The boundaryless organization (coined by GE chair Jack Welch) can be enormous in terms of employees and output, but tries its darnedest to limit boundaries, including those between supervisors and employees, horizontal boundaries from department to department, and boundaries that are external, such as between company and customer or company and suppliers.

ORGANIZATIONAL DESIGN CONCEPTS

One way of looking at the differences in organizational design structure is in terms of extremes. At one end stands the mechanistic model, which characterizes a highly departmentalized approach featuring a high degree of formalization, rigorously controlled communication pathways, low decision- making participation and numerous hierarchical levels. In the mechanistic model power is tightly controlled and centralized, and a clearly established chain of command controls all information regarding decisions by passing it in prescribed fashion along predetermined paths. High specialization and a narrow span of control complete the model. At the opposite end stands the organic model, which characterizes the boundaryless approach, with flattened hierarchy, teams that are both cross- functional and cross- hierarchical, open communications, low formalization and high participatory decision making. In this model, power is not only decentralized, it rests in more than one location, and the span of control is wide.

Cost- minimizing strategies

Cost- minimizing is a strategy many organizations are forced into, while others see it as a wise choice and a good fit for the type of business they do. Cost- minimizing examines every avenue to determine ways to reduce expense. Innovative strategies are banished as too risky and too costly, as are expensive marketing campaigns. Jobs are highly specialized and streamlined, resources and information shared whenever possible. Cost- minimizing requires tight control throughout the organization. It does not invite participation in decision- making, is not open to bottom- up communications, and firmly controls changes as it sees fit. Money is not only saved by such a strategy, it is made by passing along lower costs to consumers. Cost- minimizing is the essential strategy employed by big- box companies such as Wal- Mart, as well as of buyers' clubs like Costco or Sam's.

Boundaryless organization

The concept of boundaryless organization was coined by former General Electric chairman Jack Welch and can make a mega- organization more intimate. Currently, the concept of boundaryless organizations remains an ideal; but one that companies like IKEA, AT&T, Motorola, Hewlett-Packard and others are embracing. In a boundaryless organization, limitations, whether vertical, horizontal, internal or external, are minimized or eliminated. With the reduction of boundaries, rank loses importance as well. Participatory decision making rules the day, with teams that contain members of every level working as one. Departments vanish and are replaced by teams, whose work is coordinated as required by any particular project. Traditionally, functional departments establish boundaries between equals, minimizing resource or information sharing, networking and other sharable resources. By replacing functional departments with multidisciplinary teams whose primary concerns are processes, those who were previously specialists can function globally. Some boundaryless organizations reduce cost by assigning responsibilities that previously belonged to the company, to the customer, for example, by shipping on- line orders to a local retail store for pick up.

Innovation

Some organizations depend to a high degree upon a strategy of innovation to gain an edge over competitors. True innovation is more than simple changes to a product's surface design; it is a profound re-imagining of function. Innovation revises by re- visioning. It can be a risky position to attempt, because there is little to no prior models upon which to base decisions, and depends entirely on a vision based upon anticipated outcomes. When it is successful, however, it is generally wildly so, bringing to market not only a new product that stands alone and fills a previously unidentified need, but a strong and positive sense of the visionary company that saw that need and designed a product to perfectly answer it to the degree that the company itself develops a mythology. Apple Computer is the perfect example, having created innovation after innovation to the point where consumers want a new Apple product before it is produced, and even before they fully understand its purpose.

Three strategies that are commonly used by organizations today as they consider their structure designs are an innovative strategy, a cost- minimizing strategy and an imitation strategy. While organizations that use innovative strategies gain consumer respect when those strategies are successful, organizations that depend upon imitation prefer to remain invisible. Their purpose is not to be lauded as design leaders, but to capitalize on designs other organizations have already proven successful. These types of companies are often labeled rip- offs, selling everything from generic foods and medicines to fashion that appears to be original but is anything but. While imitation organizations lack consumer respect, they nonetheless manage to gain enough consumer dollar to justify their tactics. With a safety- first motto, imitators move into a new market once an innovator has proven it is viable. While many imitator products are of lesser quality, such as generic medications and paper goods, some companies invest their dollar not in unique design but in improving that design to create an imitation that is actually superior to the original.

Technology

In common parlance, the term 'technology' is used to discuss everything from electronics to the internet, from DNA charting to MRIs. Technology suggests specialized knowledge of a mechanical or scientific nature. In terms of organizational design, the term has a broader definition. While technology commonly is used as a catch- all for specific knowledge that is scientific or mechanical in nature, and includes IT, medicine, scientific research and the like, in terms of organizational structure technology has a broader meaning. The most basic definition of technology within organizational design terms is the ways in which inputs are translated into outputs. Inputs include all resources at an organization's disposal, including information, human resources, physical resources, and financial resources. Much research has attempted to understand how organizational technology affects organizational structure, and have found that technologies that are highly routine, unwavering and predictable are typically standardized or automated, and found in structures with centralized control, or in decentralized structures but only if they are highly formalized. Technologies that are not routine in nature are customized, adapt to the needs of a particular situation, and generally belong to decentralized structures with flattened hierarchy.

Dimensions in organizational environments

Environmental uncertainly is found in the dimensions of capacity, volatility and complexity. An organization's environmental capacity describes how well it supports growth. An abundance of resources that permit growth can also offer a cushion should the situation reverse. With abundance, organizations have the luxury to attempt innovations that may fail or to take other risks. The dimension of volatility refers to the degree of instability in the environment. An unstable environment makes prediction impossible, which changes the way decisions must be made since probabilities attached to alternative possibilities cannot be ascertained. A stable environment, however, allows a greater degree of risk- taking, communication that flows in all directions and decentralized control. The third dimension, complexity, if found in environments with considerable variety of widely dispersed environmental elements. Complex, dynamic environments with scarce resources require organic structures capable of customized responses. Stable, rich, simple environments work best with mechanistic structures.

Elements of organizational structure

According to Richard Daft, organizational structure contains two basic dimensions, structural and contextual. Structural dimensions includes centralization, or with how organizational tasks are distributed; formalization, which considers how structured organizational procedures and guidelines are; hierarchy, or the composition, type and degree of organizational levels; routinization, which is concerned with the degree of standardization in organizational procedures; specialization, or how profoundly actions, behaviors and other activities are fine tuned; and training, meaning the degree to which the organization offers employees activities, education and hands- on experience to increase their skills and competency in terms of their work obligations. In the category of contextual dimensions are grouped the elements of culture, or shared values as indicated by work place norms; environment, which refers to technical, social, political and economic influences from outside the organization; goals, which can be described as individually described end states; size, both human and resource; and technology .

External Environment

Organization's external environment can affect the efficiency of its performance. Customers, government regulations, competitors, suppliers, watchdog groups, and marketing groups can be strong external forces affecting an organization's successful performance. If these external institutions and groups were predictable an organization would be able to factor them into their bottom line; but not only are they each unpredictable on their own, the interactions of some of these groups exponentially increases their indeterminable potential. Some types of organizations face far less environmental uncertainly than others. When few competitors exist, watchdog groups aren't concerned, and suppliers available, there is little environmental reason for internal structural change. But when an organization's external environment is highly dynamic rather than static, internal structure will have to adapt quickly to minimize the threat of uncertainly. Changes can occur by reducing the size of work force in order to gain greater control; by adapting hierarchical relationships; by responding with public announcements or marketing, or in other ways.

Stalemate

Negotiations that take place directly between bargaining parties is not always successful

When negotiating parties are unsuccessful, one possible solution is third party help. Among third party roles are mediators, arbitrators, conciliators or consultants. Mediators favor neither side; their goal is to convince parties to reach an agreement by offering alternatives, logical reasoning, and reminder of possible outcomes of particular positions. When all parties are motivated to arrive at a compromise, mediation can be highly successful. Arbitrators do not need to convince; they are invested with the authority to determine an agreement that conforms within a range previous agreed to by negotiating parties. A conciliator is an uninvolved individual who is trusted by both negotiating parties, and who research relevant facts, work to persuade and interpret the messages they carry between parties in disagreement. Consultants are armed with special knowledge in the area of conflict management. His role is to heal the relationship between conflicting parties, rather than resolve issues.

Resolving Issues Causing Stagnation

When managers are faced with the responsibility of resolving a issue that has reached the point of stagnation, a number of steps can be taken to return the group to the greatest level of productivity. It is always in the organization's best interest to resolve apathy or aggression as efficiently as possible. No single approach works best across the board; the situation and personalities must be carefully considered. Situations that require a firm, decisive hand, such as emergencies, decisions likely to be unpopular, or confrontation of those who attempt to control nonaggressive behavior, require a firmly competitive stance. Collaboration is appropriate when both sides are equally important, when the goal is to gain knowledge or commitment, or to deal with emotional issues. A third position is avoidance; appropriate when the issue is of minor importance or there is little hope of settling the issue. Accommodation works in situations when there is a question as to who is right and when tranquility must be returned. Compromise is the best choice when working with negotiators who have equal power and are firmly committed to opposing positions.

Employee Attitude and Behavior

Organizations that are highly centralized, formal, specialized and with a strict chain of command do not offer members much in terms of freedom of expression. Creativity is limited and discouraged, and unless an individual knows and fits his proper peg, job dissatisfaction, high absenteeism and high turnover can be the result. On the other hand, organizations that are tightly controlled are typically clear from the outset about their expectations. Employees are less often surprised by what expectations turn out to be, and are more likely to fulfill them without rocking the boat. The more mechanistic the structure, the more specialized the individual's role. For those who like knowing what is expected, this can be a perfect fit. The more organic the structure, the more creative, customized, and relational the individual's role will be. This is a good fit for employees who enjoy autonomy, have a strong sense of self- worth and appreciate a challenge.

RESPONSIBILITY

Responsibility is part of every job. It is the obligation to complete tasks that have been directly or indirectly assigned. Managerial responsibility, regardless of what hierarchical level they occupy, holds several common characteristics. Among the obligations managers must fulfill are assigning tasks, directing projects, keeping an eye on work progress, be conscious of possible areas of conflict and resolve them quickly; and complete the information circle by notifying the manager's supervisor of all necessary information. Managers must remain in service to the organization's guiding principles, be aware of potentially useful innovations, and alert to company culture, norms and communication networks. Good managers know how to delegate, and very good managers know how to delegate increased responsibility as a form of reward, which results in a happier employee who feels appreciated and is likely to be more committed to the company vision. Managers have the responsibility to hide noting of importance from their superiors, but they have an equally important responsibility to first try to resolve conflict, negotiate compromise, enhance production and handle employee dissatisfaction before passing the buck up.

DSST Practice Test

1. Which of these is not one of Henry Mintzberg's main groupings of roles that managers play in the workplace?

a. Interpersonal
b. Informational
c. Decisional
d. Leadership
e. All are correct

2. A manager gives a new intern a tour of his facility; the president of a community college gives diplomas to students at the graduation ceremony. These are both examples of which type of managerial role according to Mintzberg?

a. Leader
b. Liaison
c. Figurehead
d. Disseminator
e. Spokesperson

3. Which of the following is not included by Robert Katz as being a basic skill required of managers?

a. Decisional
b. Technical
c. Human
d. Conceptual
e. They all are required.

4. Psychologists have found that in work as in life, it is human nature that we tend to overestimate the power of internal (personal) factors and to underestimate the power of external factors. This mistake is known as the:

a. self-serving bias
b. fundamental attribution error
c. error of selective perception
d. error created by contrast effects
e. error created by the halo effect

5. Sally is a very honest person and employee. She tends to assume automatically that all of her coworkers and customers are equally trustworthy. If another lies or cheats in the workplace, Sally never expects it and, as a result, is caught by surprise and ends up feeling betrayed. Malcolm is a manager who was so impressed by the technical expertise of several Asian American employees he had hired that when faced with a choice of three new candidates, he hired another Asian American, but was then disappointed to find that this new hire was not as technically proficient on the job as he had expected. Which statement correctly identifies the errors of Sally and Malcolm?

a. Sally engaged in stereotyping, and Malcolm engaged in projection.
b. Sally and Malcolm both engaged in projection.
c. Sally and Malcolm both engaged in stereotyping.
d. Sally and Malcolm did not engage in stereotyping or in projection.
e. Sally engaged in projection, and Malcolm engaged in stereotyping.

6. According to the Myers-Briggs Type Indicator (MBTI) instrument, which of these is not one of the bipolar pairs of classification terms used to arrive at a personality type?

a. Extroverted vs. introverted
b. Sensing vs. intuitive
c. Active vs. reflective
d. Thinking vs. feeling
e. Judging vs. perceiving

7. The Big Five model of personality traits has in common with the Myers-Briggs Type Indicator the dimension of extroversion, or how outgoing a person is. Which is not one of the other four dimensions of the Big Five?

a. Agreeableness
b. Locus of control
c. Conscientiousness
d. Emotional stability
e. Openness to experience

8. Don is very successful in his job. He is very good at convincing others. He is willing to do whatever it takes to achieve his aims. He is not very concerned with the ethics of all of his actions. He is not a stickler for following the rules if they do not serve his purposes. Based on this description, Don would best be characterized as a:

a. narcissistic type
b. risk-taking type
c. Type A personality
d. Machiavellian type
e. proactive personality

9. Julia recently started working for a business running a large chain of stores. She has been proud and enthusiastic about the low prices in her company's stores, which customers love, making the stores more successful than others. Then one day she discovers reports by outside observers that her company underpays its store employees and denies them certain basic employee rights. She is very disturbed at these reports of business practices that she personally condemns. Until or unless she comes up with a solution to resolve the conflict she is now feeling, Julia can be said to be experiencing:

a. cognitive dissonance
b. employee dissonance
c. organizational dissonance
d. employee engagement
e. perceived organizational support

10. Cris manages a team of ten employees in a corporate office. He observes that his team members do not all consistently arrive on time for work in the morning. He implements these new practices: He gives verbal praise and small daily rewards to every team member who comes in on time; he reports and acknowledges the number of team members who were on time all week during team meetings; and he gives a larger reward, like taking the whole team to lunch, anytime that all team members have come in on time every workday for an entire month. As a result, soon all of his team members are consistently arriving on time and his team has the highest rate of timeliness of all the teams in the office. What Cris has done is an example of:

a. classical conditioning
b. operant conditioning
c. social learning
d. shaping
e. none of these

11. In social learning theory, the effect a model has on a learner is subject to certain processes. Which of these is not one of these processes?

a. Attentional
b. Retention
c. Motor reproduction
d. Reinforcement
e. Extinction

12. There is a very old (and bad) joke: "Hey Joe, why are you hitting yourself on the head?" "Because it feels so good when I stop." In behavioral terms, this would be an example of:

a. negative reinforcement
b. negative punishment
c. positive reinforcement
d. positive punishment
e. extinction

13. Which of the following schedules of reinforcement is most likely to elicit the highest levels of performance and take the longest time to extinguish the desired behavior?

a. Fixed-interval schedule
b. Variable-interval schedule
c. Fixed-ratio schedule
d. Variable-ratio schedule
e. Continuous schedule

14. Which statement is not correct regarding Abraham Maslow's theory of motivation?

a. Someone who is homeless will not focus on meeting social needs like friendships.
b. Maslow's theory of a hierarchy of needs is supported by much empirical research.
c. Clayton Alderfer's ERG theory is actually a revised variation of Maslow's theory.
d. Maslow's theoretical hierarchy of needs has remained popular with management.
e. Maslow's theory is popular because it is easy to grasp and intuitively makes sense.

15. Douglas McGregor's Theory X describes four assumptions of management about employees. Which of these is not one of those assumptions?

a. Employees innately dislike and avoid work.
b. Employees must be controlled to meet goals.
c. Employees value comfort over job security.
d. Employees prefer direction to responsibility.
e. Employees value job security over ambition.

16. Douglas McGregor's Theory Y describes four assumptions of management about employees. Which of these is not one of those assumptions?

a. Employees are able to see work as coming naturally.
b. Commitment to goals enables workers' self-control.
c. Average people can accept and seek responsibilities.
d. Making original decisions is restricted to managers.
e. All of these are assumptions described in Theory Y.

17. Which of the following is true about Herzberg's Two-Factor Theory?

a. The theory aligns with earlier research by accounting for situational variables.
b. Herzberg's research measured satisfaction both with parts of jobs and with jobs overall.
c. Herzberg's method limits his theory's application due to the self-serving bias.
d. The methodology is reliable, as it is not subject to interpretations by the raters.
e. A proven high correlation of satisfaction and productivity supports the theory.

18. Which is not one of the needs identified by David McClelland in his Theory of Needs?

a. The need for achievement
b. The need for flexibility
c. The need for power
d. The need for affiliation
e. These are all identified.

19. Hackman and Oldham's Job Characteristics Model (JCM) describes five core dimensions of all jobs. Which of these does not correctly represent one of the dimensions?

a. Skill focus
b. Task identity
c. Task significance
d. Autonomy
e. Feedback

20. Which of the following statements is incorrect regarding theories of motivation relative to work?

a. Management by Objectives (MBO) programs are applications of goal-setting theory.
b. Self-efficacy in work is a key concept from Albert Bandura's social learning theory.
c. Equity Theory compares job inputs with outcomes; an equal ratio means that equity exists.
d. Expectancy Theory relates work effort to performance to rewards to personal goals.
e. In Cognitive Evaluation Theory, intrinsic rewards lessen existing extrinsic rewards.

21. Potential sources of work stress include environmental factors, organizational factors, and personal factors. Of the following choices, which one represents environmental factors?

a. Economic uncertainty, political uncertainty, and technological changes
b. Demands of the task(s), demands of the role(s), and interpersonal demands
c. Problems in the family, economic problems, and personality problems
d. Different perceptions, job experience, social support, or motivation
e. All of these choices represent various environmental stress factors.

22. Jack has been subject to excessive ongoing hindrance stress at work. He now has high blood pressure, often feels anxious or depressed, is less satisfied with his job, has become less productive, and misses more days of work. The consequences of work stress to Jack include which of the following types of symptoms?

a. Physiological
b. Psychological
c. Behavioral
d. Physiological and psychological
e. Physiological, psychological, and behavioral

23. One motive that people have for joining a group at work is to meet their social need for affiliation. Another is to gain a greater sense of security than they would have as a single employee. Which of these is not another motive people have for joining a group at work?

a. Power
b. Status
c. Self-esteem
d. Assignment
e. Meeting goals

24. In the five-stage group development model, at which of the stages is a group said to attain cohesiveness?

a. Forming
b. Storming
c. Norming
d. Performing
e. Adjourning

25. Of the following identified characteristics or properties of groups, which one was directly involved in the unexpected outcomes of psychologist Philip Zimbardo's Stanford prison experiment?

a. Norms
b. Roles
c. Size
d. Status
e. Cohesion

26. What type of conflict is the most likely to be dysfunctional at any level?

a. Task conflict
b. Relationship conflict
c. Process conflict
d. All are dysfunctional.
e. All are functional.

27. Competing, collaborating, compromising, avoiding, and accommodating fall into which stage of the five-stage conflict process?

a. Potential opposition or incompatibility
b. Cognition and personalization
c. Intentions
d. Behavior
e. Outcomes

28. Martin, a corporate manager, finds excessive conflict among several of his higher-level employees. This is interfering with getting work done, meeting company goals, and maintaining a pleasant work atmosphere. Martin resolves the problem by taking the following actions: He transfers one employee to another department, where the types of tasks and practices and the personalities of the workers seem more compatible with the transferred employee's personality. Martin redesigns the job of another employee, changing its duties to eliminate the source of conflict with a third employee, whose job duties formerly overlapped with those of the second worker. He also changes two other employees' jobs so that they now coordinate with one another, whereas they previously were separate and independent of one another. Martin's actions best illustrate which of these conflict-resolution techniques?

a. Problem solving
b. Expansion of resources
c. Authoritative command
d. Altering human variables
e. Altering structural variables

29. Research at the University of Michigan identified two dimensions of leadership: employee-oriented leadership and production-oriented leadership. These correspond to two dimensions identified in research at Ohio State University: consideration, which is similar to the employee-oriented dimension, and initiation of structure, which is similar to the production-oriented dimension. Blake and Mouton's managerial grid (or leadership grid) also identifies styles of "concern for people" and "concern for production." All of these theoretical constructs belong to:

a. behavioral theories of leadership
b. trait theories of leadership
c. contingency theories of leadership
d. the leader-participation model
e. They don't belong to any of these.

30. According to business experts, which of the following is not included in the role of a leader?

a. Dealing with change
b. Establishing direction
c. Developing a vision
d. Implementing a vision
e. Providing a strategy

31. Contingency theories have identified situational elements that apply to analysis of leadership. One of these elements is the intelligence and experience of the leader. Which of the following is not one of the others?

a. Structure of the tasks in the job
b. Level of stress in the situations
c. The level of support in a group
d. Characteristics of the followers
e. These are all relevant elements.

32. Regarding bases of power, which of the following is not considered a type of formal power?

a. Coercive power
b. Reward power
c. Legitimate power
d. Referent power
e. All of these are

33. When people perceive business politics as threatening, they can react with defensive behaviors. Of the following defensive behaviors, which one is not a behavior to avoid taking action?

a. Overconforming
b. Passing the buck
c. Playing too safe
d. Playing "dumb"
e. Stretching tasks

34. There are individual factors and organizational factors affecting political behavior in the workplace. Which of these is an individual factor rather than an organizational factor?

a. High pressure to perform
b. Expectations of success
c. Promotion opportunities
d. Ambiguity around roles
e. None of these factors is.

35. Impression Management (IM) techniques include conformity, or agreeing with someone to garner approval; making excuses to minimize the seriousness of something; and apologizing for something and seeking forgiveness. Which of these is not an additional IM technique?

a. These are all IM techniques.
b. Promoting oneself to others
c. Flattering others to be liked
d. Getting approval via favors
e. Utilizing one's associations

36. Which of the following is not one of the major functions of communication in an organization?

a. Control
b. Meaning
c. Motivation
d. Information
e. Emotional expression

37. In models of the communication process, the components necessarily include the sender, the message, and the receiver. Which of the following is not one of the other components?

a. Encoding
b. The channel
c. Transmission
d. Noise
e. Feedback

38. Which of these is not considered a form of nonverbal communication?

a. Body language
b. Facial expression
c. Tone and emphasis
d. Interoffice memos
e. Physical proximity

39. Of the following channels of communication, which pair represents the highest and lowest, respectively, in channel richness (or media richness)?

a. Face-to-face conversations and formal reports
b. Voice mail messages and online discussions
c. Memos or letters and live videoconferencing
d. Speeches made live and prerecorded speeches
e. E-mail messages and telephone conversations

40. Klaus and Fred both work for the same multinational corporation. Klaus is German and Fred is American. Kim is Korean and is the corporation's chief of Korean operations. Li is Chinese and is in charge of the corporation's Chinese subsidiary. All of these individuals speak fluent English. But when they take a meeting, they experience some communication difficulties despite their equally excellent command of the same language. Two of them want directness, are used to giving or taking explicit orders, and rely on written contracts; the other two value oral agreements as proof of high commitment, are more comfortable with subtlety, and are more likely to suggest an action than to order it. Which statement correctly explains these differences?

a. Klaus and Kim come from high-context cultures, while Fred and Li are from low-context cultures.
b. Kim and Li come from low-context cultures, while Fred and Klaus are from high-context cultures.
c. Klaus and Li come from high-context cultures, while Fred and Kim are from low-context cultures.
d. Fred, Kim, and Klaus all come from high-context cultures, while Li is from a low-context culture.
e. Fred and Klaus come from low-context cultures, while Kim and Li are from high-context cultures.

41. In the rational decision-making model, the first step is to define the problem. Of the remaining five steps, which of the following is incorrect?

a. Identify decision criteria.
b. Give the criteria weights.
c. Develop the alternatives.
d. Give alternatives weights.
e. Pick the best alternative.

42. The rational decision-making model operates on six assumptions. One assumption is that the problem is clear. A second assumption is that all of the options are known; i.e., the decision maker knows all the pertinent criteria, knows all the alternatives feasible for addressing those criteria, and knows all the potential consequences of using each of those alternatives. Of the following, which is not one of the other assumptions of this model?

a. Choices are clear for ranking criteria and rating alternatives.
b. Criteria and their weights are constant or stable over time.
c. There are no limitations in time or costs that may be needed.
d. The alternative chosen will pay off with the greatest value
e. These are all assumptions of the rational decision-making model.

43. In organizational structure design, six elements are important to address. One of these is work specialization, also known as division of labor into separate jobs. Which of these is not correct as one of the other five key elements of organizational structure?

a. Departmentalization
b. Chain of command
c. Unity of command
d. Span of control
e. Formalization

44. Which of the following does not correctly describe a characteristic of a simple structure?

a. Low departmentalization level
b. High level of decentralization
c. Not much formalization
d. Wide spans of control
e. These are all correct.

45. What do the structures of the bureaucracy and the matrix have most in common?

a. Departmentalization by function and by product
b. Departmentalization by product and by territory
c. Departmentalization by function and by territory
d. Centralization of powers and unity of command
e. Increased formalization of jobs and role clarity

46. Six forces for change in business have been identified. For example, the nature of the workforce is one force for change. Currently the nature of our workforce has become culturally more diverse and older due to the aging population and is being entered by more new workers with skills insufficient for the work, who thus require training by employers. Of the five other forces for change listed, the rising use of chat rooms on the Internet is an example of which one?

a. Trends in society
b. Economic shocks
c. Global politics
d. Competition
e. Technology

47. There are individual and organizational sources of resistance to change. Which of the following is an organizational rather than an individual source?

a. Security
b. Economic factors
c. Threat to expertise
d. Fear of the unknown
e. Selective information processing

48. Which of these tactics for overcoming resistance to change would be most informed by the results of personality testing for certain traits or characteristics?

a. Negotiation
b. Participation
c. Education and communication
d. Picking those who accept change
e. Building support and commitment

49. Regarding organizational change, what statement correctly compares Kurt Lewin's model of change with John Kotter's model for implementing change?

a. The two models represent distinctly different viewpoints of organizational change.
b. The only difference is that Kotter's model has fewer steps and Lewin's has more.
c. The steps in Kotter's model incorporate Lewin's steps expanded with more detail.
d. Kotter's model incorporates Lewin's three steps but then adds five different steps.
e. None of these statements correctly compares Lewin's model with Kotter's model.

50. Which of the following does not accurately describe one of the values on which organizational development (OD) is based?

a. Respect for people
b. Trust and support
c. Equalizing power
d. People's participation
e. Avoiding confrontation

Answer Key and Explanations

1. D: **Leadership** (d) is not one of Mintzberg's *main groupings* of roles managers play but a subcategory, or one of the roles found in each grouping. The role of leader falls under the interpersonal (a) grouping of roles. The three main groupings of roles are interpersonal, informational (b), and decisional (c). Since (d) is the incorrect item, making it the correct answer, answer (e) is incorrect.

2. C: These are both examples of (c) the **figurehead** role, which falls into the interpersonal grouping of managerial roles according to Mintzberg. The leader (a) role also falls into this group; this is the role responsible for inspiring motivation in and providing direction for workers. The liaison (b) role also falls into the interpersonal grouping. This is the role responsible for staying in touch with resource people outside the company who can supply information and assistance. The disseminator (d) role falls into the informational grouping. This is the role responsible for giving information, from those outside the company or from other workers, to members of the workplace. The spokesperson (e) role also falls into the informational grouping of roles. This is the role responsible for communicating information about the firm's policies, programs, activities, and outcomes to those outside the company and for functioning as an expert on the company's specific industry.

3. A: **Decisional** (a) is not named by Robert Katz as a skill managers must have. Mintzberg's managerial roles include the decisional grouping of roles (see explanation to #1), which includes the entrepreneur role, the disturbance handler role, the resource allocator role, and the negotiator role. The basic skills found by Katz to be necessary for managers are technical (b) skills, or the capacity to apply knowledge and/or experience in a specialized field; human (c) skills, or the capacity to function well on an interpersonal basis, communicating with, delegating duties to, and motivating other people in the workplace; and conceptual (d) skills, or the intellectual capacity for analysis, interpretation, diagnosis, problem solving, and decision making. Since (a) is not included by Katz and is thus the correct answer, answer (e) is incorrect.

4. B: The term for underestimating outside forces while overestimating the influence of individuals is known in psychology as (b) the **fundamental attribution error.** We are more likely to attribute failure, for example, to our employees' deficiencies than to a competing company's superior product or to our own company's inferior product. The self-serving bias (a) describes our tendency to attribute success to our own hard work or talent but to attribute failure to other people's actions or to bad luck. So we tend to take personal credit for positive outcomes but blame negative outcomes on outside forces. The error of selective perception (c) is our tendency to notice more salient features while disregarding others because we cannot possibly observe everything at once. For example, we are more likely to notice others' cars of the same make, model, and color as our own car. This occurs commonly in the workplace when employees perceive the functions of their own department as more important than those of other departments, where they have less involvement and interest. The error created by contrast effects (d) is caused by comparison of one person with others, as we do not perceive a person in a vacuum. For example, a job applicant can get a higher rating when interviewed immediately following several less qualified applicants, or a lower rating if interviewed immediately after several more qualified applicants. The error created by the halo effect (e) refers to the phenomenon of allowing a single attribute of an individual to color one's perception of all the individual's other attributes. The halo effect can result in a supervisor giving an employee favorable evaluations on all job criteria because of outstanding performance on just one criterion. For example, a salesperson with superior sales figures may also be perceived through the halo effect as being superior at keeping records and interacting with coworkers, even though the salesperson is actually deficient in these areas.

5. E: Sally engaged in projection, and Malcolm engaged in stereotyping. Sally herself was honest and projected this trait onto other people, so she unrealistically expected everybody else to be honest. Malcolm had hired several technically proficient Asian American employees and then saw all Asian American employees who were qualified for technical jobs as being equally proficient; i.e., he stereotyped *all* Asian Americans in technical job fields as always being superior in technical ability/performance to technical workers who were not Asian American. In both cases, these errors distorted Sally's and Malcolm's perceptions. Answer (a) reverses Sally's error with Malcolm's error and is thus incorrect. Sally and Malcolm did not both engage in projection in these examples (b); only Sally did. Sally and Malcolm did not both engage in stereotyping in these examples (c); only Malcolm did. Since Sally engaged in projection and Malcolm engaged in stereotyping, it is incorrect that (d) they did not engage in either one of these.

6. C: Active vs. reflective (c) is not one of the Myers-Briggs pairs of classification terms. The MBTI classifies individuals as either (a) extroverted or introverted—outgoing and social versus inward and reserved; (b) sensing vs. intuitive—practical, orderly, and detail oriented versus more reliant on the unconscious than order and more interested in the "big picture"; (d) thinking vs. feeling—more reliant on logic and rational approaches versus more reliant on emotional and personal approaches; and (e) judging vs. perceiving—preferring control and structure versus preferring spontaneity and flexibility. Note: A choice of one out of each of these pairs does not by itself constitute a personality type in the MBTI. Rather, this instrument, after identifying which pole the individual best fits in each pair, combines all four choices within each dimension to arrive at one of 16 specific personality types. Using E for extroverted, I for introverted, S for sensing, N for intuitive, T for thinking, F for feeling, J for judging, and P for perceiving, an individual may be categorized as either ESTJ, ESTP, ESFJ, ESFP, ENTJ, ENTP, ENFJ, ENFP, ISTJ, ISTP, ISFJ, ISFP, INTJ, INTP, INFJ, or INFP. Each combination of traits yields a different type, such as visionary, organizer, etc.

7. B: Locus of control (b) is not one of the Big Five personality traits. Locus of control is identified by psychologist Julian Rotter as how much an individual attributes his or her outcomes to internal or external factors, described as having an internal locus of control or an external locus of control. Individuals who attribute their failures to their own lack of ability and/or effort and their successes to their own ability and/or effort are said to have a predominantly internal locus of control. Those who blame their own failures on things outside of themselves, like bad luck, sabotage by coworkers, or an unfair boss, and credit their own successes to good luck, help from coworkers, or a boss who favors them are said to have a predominantly external locus of control. (Note: A person operating under the self-serving bias would appear to have an internal locus of control for his or her positive outcomes and an external locus of control for his or her negative outcomes.) In addition to extroversion, the other four of the Big Five personality traits are agreeableness (a), or how cooperative and trusting one is; conscientiousness (c), or how responsible and reliable one is; emotional stability (d), or how secure, confident, and calm one is (as opposed to neuroticism, or how insecure, unconfident, and nervous one is); and openness to experience (e), or how comfortable with novelty one is (as opposed to disliking anything new or different).

8. D: Based on the description, Don is best characterized as a (d) **Machiavellian type.** Named for Niccoló Machiavelli, the 16th-century author of *The Prince,* who wrote that "the ends justify the means," this personality type in the workplace will do whatever is needed to succeed, regardless of the ethical ramifications or the rules, and shows talent for the persuasion and manipulation of others to realize his or her goals. Under the right circumstances, Machiavellian types can be very successful. A narcissistic type (a) is likely to be less successful than a Machiavellian type. Narcissists are selfish, arrogant, likely to exploit others, and unlikely to help others. They need and demand excessive attention and have an inflated sense of their own importance. They tend to rate themselves higher on their job performance, while their bosses tend to rate them lower. A risk-taking type (b) is a personality type more comfortable with uncertainty, more willing to take chances, and quicker to make decisions than one more averse to risk. This type is more successful in certain types of enterprises than in others. Speculative positions such as those of stockbroker, entrepreneur, or manager in a large corporation are more suited for risk takers than positions requiring more thoroughness and deliberation, such as accounting or auditing. A Type A personality (c) is highly ambitious, competitive, impatient, driven, and aggressive. This type is usually not creative, as Type A personalities are more concerned with speed and amount of production and tend not to vary their responses when faced with new challenges. A proactive personality (e) is a type that displays initiative rather than remaining passive, and persists until the desired changes are effected. Though they are more likely to challenge existing conditions and to express any dissatisfaction, these personality types tend to be successful in work and desirable to employers for their initiative and positive actions. They are also more likely to depart from those employers to start their own businesses due to their high initiative.

9. A: Julia is experiencing (a) **cognitive dissonance.** Identified and named by psychologist Leon Festinger, cognitive dissonance is a discrepancy between or among attitudes, or between attitudes and behavior. Festinger stated that we naturally find cognitive dissonance uncomfortable and seek to reduce it. Julia's perception of her company in positive terms is inconsistent with the reports of behaviors by her company that she finds negative. There is no such term as employee dissonance (b); there is a recent term called employee *engagement*, or how involved, enthusiastic, and satisfied an employee is with his or her job. There is no such term as organizational dissonance (c); organizational *commitment* is one of several terms used to describe job attitudes, along with job satisfaction and job involvement. It refers to how much an employee identifies with his or her employing organization (rather than with his or her individual job, which is job involvement). Employee engagement (d) is defined above in the explanation to (b). This is a real term but is not what Julia is experiencing. Perceived organizational support (e), or POS, is also a real term but is not what Julia is experiencing. It refers to how much a worker feels the organization cares about his or her welfare and values his or her contributions to it.

10. B: Cris' practices are an example of (b) **operant conditioning.** His employees' timely behavior increased after he gave positive consequences or reinforcement for this behavior. Reinforcement is a consequence of a behavior that strengthens its likelihood of recurring. Classical conditioning (a) also conditions behavior to recur in the presence of certain stimuli with which the behavior becomes associated, but it conditions passively; i.e., it is known more for learning with reflexive behaviors (like Pavlov's dogs salivating to a bell once they came to associate it with food, even without the food; or the pupils of a person's eyes contracting at a bell once they come to associate it with a bright light, even without the light). Operant conditioning involves a choice by the learner. Coming to work on time was a voluntary behavior by the employees. They were more likely to do it after being rewarded for it. Social learning (c) is observational or vicarious learning: An individual can learn from observing and imitating a model without directly experiencing what the model experiences. While both operant conditioning and social learning theory subscribe to the idea that behavior is changed by the consequences it receives, in operant conditioning the learner learns through direct experience with consequences, while in social learning the learner can learn indirectly through observing consequences experienced by others. Shaping (d) is a type of behavior modification that also uses the operant conditioning paradigm, but it refers specifically to the use of successive approximations. In other words, behavior is changed incrementally in smaller, more achievable steps. For example, if some of Cris's team members were often 30 minutes late, and he first rewarded each of them for being only 20 minutes late, then for being only 15 minutes late, then only 10 minutes late, then only 5 minutes late, and finally for being on time, with the rewards improving as they moved closer to the goal, this would be shaping. Since (b) is correct, answer (e) is incorrect.

11. E: Extinction (e) is not one of the processes identified in social learning theory as determining the influence of a model on a learner. Extinction is the behavioral term that refers to the phenomenon of a behavior eventually ceasing when the reinforcement that has maintained it is no longer present. For example, if students raise their hands and the instructor never calls on them but ignores them, eventually the students will stop raising their hands. The processes affecting social learning are (a) attentional: A learner will learn from a model only if the learner is paying attention to the model's salient features; (b) retention: How strong a model's influence is on a learner depends on the learner's remembering the model's behavior once the model is no longer available for observation; (c) motor reproduction: Once a learner observes a model, the learner must make a transition from observing the model's behavior to physically doing the behavior; (d) reinforcement: If a learner imitates a model's behavior and receives positive reinforcement (consequences) for performing that behavior, the learner is more likely to repeat the behavior.

12. A: This is an example of (a) **negative reinforcement,** or the removal of an aversive (unpleasant) stimulus. Negative punishment (b) is the removal of an appetitive (pleasant) stimulus. An example would be if a mother is stroking her toddler's hair, which feels good to him, and when he misbehaves she stops stroking his hair; i.e., "It feels so *bad* when she stops" is negative punishment, instead of "It feels so *good* when I stop" (negative reinforcement), as in the question. Positive reinforcement (c) is the introduction of a pleasant stimulus as a consequence to a behavior. For example, if our toddler does something the mother likes and she strokes his hair, which he enjoys, she is positively reinforcing his behavior so he will be more likely to do it again. Positive punishment (d) is the introduction of an unpleasant stimulus as a consequence to a behavior. This is more popularly known simply as punishment. It makes the behavior less likely to recur. If our toddler misbehaves and his mother sharply reprimands him, this would be an example of punishment. Extinction (e) also makes a behavior less likely to recur until it completely stops. Extinction does not involve the introduction of a stimulus, pleasant or unpleasant, but the removal of a reinforcing stimulus that has been maintaining a behavior. Once the learner no longer receives any reward for the behavior, there is no more motivation to keep doing it, and the learner will eventually stop.

13. D: The **variable-ratio schedule** (d) yields the highest performance levels and slowest extinction due to its unpredictability, which keeps people "on their toes." Reinforcement is given for production rather than at time intervals, as with interval schedules, so performance responses are higher. With intermittent reinforcement, the behavior is not quickly extinguished, as another reward could come at any point. An example of this schedule is with salespeople who work for commissions. A fixed-interval schedule (a) gives reinforcement regularly at fixed time intervals. This schedule yields average rather than high levels of performance and is quickly extinguished. One example is receiving a paycheck every two weeks. Payment is not directly associated with performance but time periods, so the work behavior this schedule produces will be quickly extinguished if the rewards stop. A variable-interval schedule (b) gives rewards irregularly like a variable-ratio schedule, but the variation is in time periods, not production. This schedule yields moderately high levels of performance; response rates are stable and resist extinction. Levels of response are higher than with fixed schedules owing to unpredictability, but not as high as with ratio schedules because the reinforcements, though irregular, are associated with time periods, not production. Examples include surprise visitors to the workplace from corporate headquarters, or pop quizzes given in school. A fixed-ratio schedule (c) gives rewards based on regular quantities of production rather than time periods. This schedule yields high performance levels, as reinforcement is associated with performance, and response rates are stable. While these high rates are achieved quickly, they are also extinguished quickly. An example is the piecework method of payment. In a continuous schedule (e), reinforcement is given every time the target behavior occurs. This results in rapid learning of new behaviors but also rapid extinction when reinforcement is withdrawn. An example is complimenting a person. People respond quickly to such positive reinforcement because they like compliments; but if these are discontinued, there would be no residual motivation to continue the behavior.

14. B: The incorrect statement is (b) that **Maslow's theory of a hierarchy of needs is supported by much empirical research.** Actually, research has not borne out this theory's assumptions at all. However, this theory continues to be popular among business managers (d) despite the lack of concrete evidence to substantiate it, because it is easy to understand and it makes intuitive sense (e) to people. According to Maslow's theory, higher-order needs, such as social needs for belonging, acceptance, and friendship, cannot be addressed until lower-order needs, such as physical needs for food and shelter, and safety needs for protection from harm, are met first, so a person without shelter and safety would not focus on friendships (a) according to this theory. It is true that Alderfer's ERG theory is a variation of Maslow's (c): The initials stand for existence, relatedness, and growth—three groupings of basic needs similar to those of Maslow. (In Alderfer's version, needs in the hierarchy are not met in an invariant sequence; they can be addressed in different orders or simultaneously, and regression is possible.) In reworking Maslow's theory, Alderfer was trying to come up with a version more compatible with empirical research. However, the research did not find any evidence to support ERG theory either.

15. C: McGregor's Theory X does not include an assumption of management that (c) **employees value comfort over job security.** The assumption that employees value job security over ambition (e) not only is true, but also states that employees value job security above all else related to work. The other three assumptions of managers according to this theory are that employees basically dislike work and will avoid it if possible (a); that management must control employees, coerce them, or threaten them with punishment to get them to meet work goals (b); and that employees do not want responsibilities and would rather have the direction of management (d). (Note: You may have noticed that all the assumptions of managers in this theory are negative. McGregor formulated Theory X and Theory Y to describe negative and positive views, respectively, of employees by managers.)

16. D: It is not an assumption of McGregor's Theory Y that (d) **making original decisions is restricted to managers.** One assumption of Theory Y is that this ability to be innovative is spread throughout the population and is not limited to those with managerial roles. The other three assumptions are (a) that employees have the ability to regard work as coming just as naturally to them as play; (b) that employees are able to use self-control and self-direction as long as they have a commitment to the job's and/or company's goals; and (c) that an average person is capable of learning to accept responsibility and even to seek it out. Because (d) is an incorrect statement and thus the correct answer, answer (e) is incorrect. (Note: McGregor formulated two theories, X and Y, to describe negative and positive assumptions, respectively, about employees made by managers. This question is about Theory Y's positive assumptions.)

17. C: It is true of the Two-Factor Theory that (c) **Herzberg's method limits his theory's application due to the self-serving bias.** According to the self-serving bias, people will personally take credit for positive results but blame negative results on external factors. It is not true that this theory aligns with earlier research by accounting for situational variables (a); in fact, one of the criticisms of Herzberg's theory is that it does not take situational variables into account. If circumstances differ, the theory may not apply. It is not true that this theory measured satisfaction both with parts of jobs and with jobs overall (b); another criticism of Herzberg's work is that he did not measure overall job satisfaction, and a person may be dissatisfied with certain parts or aspects of her job but overall may be satisfied with the job as a whole. It is not true that Herzberg's methodology is reliable, as it is not subject to interpretations by the raters (d). In fact, another criticism of this theory is that the raters are required to interpret the responses, and they cannot possibly be totally consistent in their interpretations, which could contaminate the instrument's findings. This makes the methodology less reliable. It is also not true that this theory is supported by a proven high correlation between job satisfaction and job productivity (e). This theory requires a strong correlation between satisfaction and productivity for it to apply, yet such a correlation has not been proven but must be assumed for Herzberg's research to relate to the realities of work.

18. B: McClelland's Theory of Needs does not include (b) **the need for flexibility.** While researchers do find in surveys that employees want flexibility in their choices of assignments and their working hours, flexibility was not a need identified in McClelland's theory. The needs McClelland describes are for (a) achievement—to succeed and excel; for (c) power—to have control over others' behavior; and for (d) affiliation—to have good interpersonal relationships at work. Since (b) is not one of the needs identified in this theory and is thus the correct answer, answer (e) is incorrect.

19. A: **Skill focus** (a) is not one of the JCM's core job dimensions. Skill *variety* is the first of the dimensions described, i.e., how many different skills are required by a job. Some jobs involve multiple skills, such as keeping records, supervising workers, interacting with customers, and reporting to upper management, while other jobs might involve only one skill, such as typing data entries all day. The other four dimensions in the JCM are (b) task identity, or how much a job involves a holistic process from beginning to end, as opposed to being just one piece, step, or cog in the larger process; (c) task significance, or how much impact a job has on other people's lives (contrast the job of a cardiac surgeon who saves lives with the job of one person out of hundreds answering the phone in an amply staffed call center); (d) autonomy, or how much independence and freedom a job affords the worker (contrast a job where the employee is assigned specific tasks, a specific schedule to follow, and is supervised closely versus a job where the employee decides his or her own activities and schedule with no supervision); and (e) feedback, or how much or little feedback a worker gets about his or her job performance (e.g., a worker who must test every unit he assembles gets higher feedback, while a worker who assembles units that are tested by a separate inspector in the quality assurance department gets lower feedback).

20. E: The incorrect statement is that (e) **in Cognitive Evaluation Theory, intrinsic rewards lessen existing extrinsic rewards.** The opposite is true in this theory: Researchers have found that when a person finds an activity so internally rewarding that she will do it by choice for enjoyment rather than only for external rewards like payment, and then this person is given external rewards like payment for what she previously did for its own sake, the person's existing internal rewards will lessen. This is explained by the idea that the extrinsic reward causes people to lose control of their own behavior and no longer feel autonomous in choosing to perform the activity. Some psychologists have termed this phenomenon "turning play into work." It is correct that MBO programs are applications of goal-setting theory (a). It is correct that Albert Bandura's concept of self-efficacy, or a person's perception of how able she is to perform a task successfully, is a key concept in his Social Learning Theory, applied to the topic of work motivation (b). People with greater self-confidence are more motivated to undertake a task or job, to make more effort, and to perform better. It is correct that Equity Theory compares how much you put into a job and how much you get out of it, and if the ratio of the two is equal, there is equity (c). Workers who feel underrewarded or overrewarded relative to their efforts perceive inequity. It is correct that Expectancy Theory relates work effort to performance, performance to rewards, and rewards to personal goals (d). How much a person expects causality in each relationship, i.e., how much that person's effort will lead to performance, how much that person's performance will lead to reward, and how much the rewards will meet the person's own goals, determines how much effort the person will be motivated to expend.

21. A: The choice representing environmental factors that are potential sources of stress is (a). **Economic uncertainty, political uncertainty, and technological changes** are all features in the environment that can contribute to work stress. Demands of tasks, roles, or between people (b) at work are classified as organizational factors rather than environmental factors. Family, economic, and personality problems (c) are classified as personal factors rather than environmental ones. Individual differences in perception, job experience, social support, or motivational factors (d) such as locus of control, self-efficacy, or hostility are classified as individual differences as factors, rather than environmental factors. Because (a) is the correct choice for environmental factors, answer (e) is incorrect.

22. E: Jack is displaying symptoms that are **physiological, psychological, and behavioral** (e). His high blood pressure is a physiological (a) symptom. Other common physiological symptoms that are consequences of unhealthy work stress include frequent headaches, more frequent colds or other upper-respiratory problems, immunosuppression, and metabolic changes. His anxiety, depression, and decline in job satisfaction are psychological (b) symptoms of work stress. Other psychological consequences of job stress include irritability, boredom, and putting things off at work. His decline in productivity and increased absences are behavioral (c) symptoms of work stress. Other behavioral symptoms of work stress include increased (or new) smoking or drinking or both, fast or "pressured" speech, sleep problems, and increased (or new) fidgeting. Because Jack has symptoms falling into all three categories, answers (a), (b), and (c) listing only one category are incorrect, and answer (d) listing only two of the three is also incorrect.

23. D: Assignment (d) is not considered a motive people have for joining a group at work. Although certainly it is not unusual for management to assign employees to a work group or task group, and often in this situation the employees have no choice but to be in that group, this would not be a motive, as the workers are not joining the group voluntarily. Therefore, they are in the group whether they are motivated to be or not. When people are motivated to join a group voluntarily at work, it may be for power (a): The common expression "power in numbers" means that what one cannot achieve individually, a group can often achieve. Or it may be for status (b): Being included in a group others perceive as important or influential confers status on each of the group's individual members. People are also motivated to join groups at work for self-esteem (c): Belonging to the group can confer an enhanced sense of self-worth on the individual. (Status is an extrinsic reward of group membership, and self-esteem is an intrinsic reward.) Another motive for joining a group at work is to meet goals (e): As with the power motive, many things cannot be achieved by a single individual. If a goal desired by the company and/or the individual requires a group to attain it, management will often utilize a formal group. Individual workers would be motivated to join such a group (when not assigned to it) if they were motivated to help achieve the group's goal.

24. C: The **norming** (c), or third, stage is when the group has developed close relationships within it and a strong sense of group identity; at this stage, the group is said to have cohesiveness. In the forming (a), or first, stage, group members have not yet developed norms for acceptable group behaviors, and the aim, organization, and leadership of the group are not certain yet. Members are testing out the new group. When they begin to perceive themselves as part of this group, the forming stage is considered to be completed. The storming (b), or second, stage is characterized by the conflict associated with development. While members see themselves as part of the group, they still resist group constraints, and until a leader for the group (or a hierarchy of leaders) is identified, this is another source of conflict. When leadership issues are resolved, the storming stage is complete. In the performing (d), or fourth, stage, members have already gotten acquainted, and the organization and leadership of the group are already established. The energy of the group in this stage is then directed toward performance of the group's task(s). The adjourning (e), or fifth, stage applies only to time-limited groups rather than those that may continue indefinitely. Groups designed for finite existence need the adjourning stage when their tasks are completed, to wrap things up and achieve a sense of closure as preparation for disbanding.

25. B: The group property or characteristic involved in Zimbardo's prison experiment was (b) **roles.** In Zimbardo's simulation, students were given the roles of either guards or prisoners. The experiment had to be terminated prematurely because it was "too successful"; i.e., the subjects adapted so extremely to their roles of guards or prisoners that it was deemed unsafe to continue without risking psychological harm. The experiment clearly showed how rapidly people can learn new roles. But nobody expected that the mock guards would display behavior so abusive, that the mock prisoners would display behavior so passive, and that they would do so as soon as they did. (The simulation was planned to last for two weeks but was stopped after only six days.) Even though they all knew the situation was not real, none of the subjects protested or tried to interrupt the proceedings; this was also unexpected. Norms (a) refer to established standards of behaviors that are acceptable within a group. While the behaviors adopted by the prison experiment's subjects may have conformed to what they perceived as norms for a prison, they were not in a real prison, so norms were not as directly involved in their behavior during the simulation as roles were. Size (c) refers to the size of a group. There were 24 subjects in the Stanford prison experiment. There have been no significant conclusions about the sizes of the groups having any impact on their behavior. Status (d) refers to social ranking of individuals or groups. While one source of status is power, and the mock guards in the prison experiment had power over the mock prisoners, again this was not a real prison but a simulation, so the groups did not have any real-world status. More direct involvement was with the roles each group learned, roles they did not play in real life. Cohesion (e), or cohesiveness, refers to a sense of group identity. Neither the mock guards nor the mock prisoners were found to enjoy a sense of group cohesion during the simulation. The most salient aspect of behavior in this experiment was the speed and extremity with which the students learned to assume unaccustomed roles.

26. B: The type of conflict most likely to be dysfunctional at any level—low, moderate, or high—is (b) **relationship conflict.** Because relationship conflict involves interpersonal friction and hostility, even a low level of it can derail achieving an organization's goals Task conflict (a), which is conflict over the content of the work and its goals, can be functional at low or moderate levels. Task conflict actually has a consistently positive influence on the performance of groups when it is at low to moderate levels. This is because the conflict generates group discussions with members contributing various ideas, and this improves the performance of the group as a whole. Process conflict (c) is conflict over the work process, i.e., the way in which the group's task(s) will be completed. Process conflict can be functional if it is maintained at a low level. If the level of process conflict is moderate or high, it will create dysfunction as group members argue about task roles, i.e., who will do what. Too much process conflict will cause confusion over task roles and make task completion take longer and can cause group members to work against one another. Since (a) can be functional at low and moderate levels and (c) can be functional at low levels, answer (d) is incorrect. Since (b) is nearly always dysfunctional at any level, answer (e) is also incorrect.

27. C: The stage of **intentions** (c), stage III of the conflict process, refers to decisions we make to engage in certain behaviors. Intentions come between our feelings and perceptions and our observable behaviors. Intentions related to the desire to handle conflict are competing intentions, collaborating intentions, compromising intentions, avoiding intentions, and accommodating intentions. Potential opposition or incompatibility (a), stage I of the conflict process, refers to the existence of conditions under which conflict has the potential to develop. Such conditions are classified into three categories: communication, structure, and personal variables. Cognition and personalization (b), stage II of the conflict process, is the stage wherein conflict is perceived or felt. If realized, the element in stage I occurs in stage II. Behavior (d), stage IV in the conflict process, refers to observable conflict; i.e., the parties involved actually do something outwardly that is seen to initiate or participate in a disagreement or conflict. (Making demands, arguing, challenging, questioning, being verbally or physically aggressive, making threats, and issuing ultimatums are some examples of actions in stage IV, in ascending order of escalation.) Outcomes (e), or stage V in the conflict process, refers to the results of the behaviors of stage IV: greater or lesser group performance. Conflict can stimulate functional, constructive outcomes or dysfunctional, destructive outcomes depending on the individual situation and its variables.

28. E: Martin's actions best exemplify (e) **altering structural variables.** This is defined as changing the formal structure of the organization and the patterns of interaction among coworkers experiencing conflict. Transfers, reassignments, and job redesign are examples of this technique. Problem solving (a) is defined as having a face-to-face meeting among the employees experiencing conflict to identify and solve the problem(s) via open discussions. Expansion of resources (b) is defined as addressing a conflict over inadequate resources by expanding those resources. If the cause of conflict is the fact that a resource such as money, office space, or advancement opportunity is scarce and it is feasible to increase that resource, providing more of something that has been in short supply will resolve such a conflict. Authoritative command (c) is defined as using one's formal authority within the organization to end the conflict and then communicating one's wishes to the individuals who had the conflict. Altering human variables (d) is defined as implementing behavioral techniques to change those attitudes and behaviors causing conflict among employees. An example of such a technique is human relations training.

29. A: All three of these theoretical constructs regarding people versus production belong to (a) **behavioral theories of leadership.** In each, the two dimensions describe observable, measurable behaviors of leaders. Observable behavior is the focus of behaviorism, which does not concern itself with inner states but only with outward responses which can be taught, learned, unlearned, changed, and shaped. Trait theories of leadership (b) focus on personal characteristics, qualities, or traits of leaders as contrasted with those of nonleaders. The Big Five personality traits have proven quite useful to researchers in identifying traits of leaders. More than one characteristic identified in a leader can be grouped under one of the Big Five (e.g., energy and ambition can both be grouped under extroversion). Use of the Big Five personality traits has been found to be very predictive of leadership. Contingency theories of leadership (c) seek to remedy the failures of both trait and behavioral models to account for situational variables that cause variation in the results of research on the effectiveness of leadership. The leader-participation model (d) is just one of quite a few contingency theories of leadership. Others include Fred Fiedler's contingency model, the situational theory developed by Hersey and Blanchard, the leader–member exchange theory, and path-goal theory. Since (a) is correct, answer (e) is incorrect.

30. D: The activity not included in the role of a leader is (d) **implementing a vision.** According to professors at the Harvard Business School and the Wharton School, the role of a leader includes dealing with change (a), as contrasted with the role of a manager, which includes providing order and handling daily issues. It is also the role of a leader to establish direction (b) for an organization, to develop a vision (c) for the company, and to provide a strategy (e) or strategies for the employees to use to realize the leader's vision. Implementing the vision (d) is not the role of the leader but of the manager, who implements the strategy provided by the leader. Leadership has been defined as a person's ability to influence a group in the interest of accomplishing a vision (or a group of goals). Leaders establish direction when they communicate their vision to employees and inspire them to overcome obstacles. Management's role is to help to actualize the leader's vision by implementing strategies and providing and maintaining organization and structure.

31. E: These are all relevant elements (e) to understanding leadership. Research done to develop contingency theories, which address differences owing to situational factors, has identified these as applying most to studying leadership in work environments. How structured or unstructured the tasks are in a given job (a) is one of three situational variables that, according to Fiedler, are key determinants of the effectiveness of leadership. (The other two are leader–member relations and position power.) In their leader-participation model, Vroom and Yetton also contend that leaders need to adapt their behavior to the given task structure. The degree of situational stress (b) is an element emphasized by Fiedler and Garcia in Cognitive Resource Theory. They found in their research that leader intelligence has a positive correlation with performance under conditions of low stress and a negative correlation with performance under conditions of high stress. They also found that leader experience correlates negatively with performance when stress is low and correlates positively with performance when stress is high. So, according to Fiedler and Garcia, situational stress levels dictate whether leader intelligence or leader experience will enhance performance in leadership. The level of support in a group (c) relates to Hersey and Blanchard's Situational Leadership Theory (SLT) in that followers' "readiness" to get a task done determines the effectiveness of leadership. SLT also focuses more on the characteristics of followers (d) than do most other leadership theories. And focus of the leader–member exchange (LMX) theory on "in" groups that it posits are chosen by leaders also puts some emphasis on the characteristics of followers as well as those of leaders.

32. D: Referent power (d) is not considered a type of formal power but a type of personal power. A person others admire, identify with, and hence want to please is said to have referent power. Coercive power (a) is power based on fear of negative consequences for noncompliance, and is a type of formal power. Reward power (b) is the opposite: It is power that elicits compliance via positive consequences or rewards. It is also a type of formal power. Legitimate power (c) is conferred by having a position of formal authority within an organization which is accepted by members of that organization. It is a type of formal power with wider influence than coercion or reward, as the authority of the position itself is respected, as contrasted with having power over individual instances of punishment (or its threat) or reward. Since (d) is not a type of formal power, answer (e) is incorrect.

33. C: Playing too safe (c) is not a defensive behavior to avoid taking action but rather a defensive behavior to avoid being blamed. Only undertaking tasks likely to succeed, requesting managerial approval of decisions with any inherent risk, putting qualifications on any judgments one makes, and maintaining neutrality during any conflicts are some examples of this behavior. Defensive behaviors to avoid acting include overconforming (a), or interpreting one's roles and responsibilities in an overly strict or literal way (e.g., saying you cannot do something because of the rules); passing the buck (b), or dumping the responsibility to do something on another person; playing "dumb" (d), or pretending not to know how to do a task or pretending to be unable to do it; and stretching tasks (e), or extending the time it takes to perform a task beyond what is actually required in order to appear too busy to undertake another task one wishes to avoid.

34. B: Expectations of success (b) fall in the category of individual factors affecting political work behavior. What an individual expects in terms of his or her success in the organization will influence whether or not s/he engages in political behavior. High pressure to perform (a) is an organizational factor. The more pressure an individual feels to "look good," the more likely that individual is to engage in political behavior to ensure this result, but this is an organizational factor rather than an individual one, since that pressure is put on individual workers by the organization. Promotion opportunities (c) also fall in the category of organizational factors, since it has to do with the organization whether or not opportunities for promotion exist within it. Ambiguity regarding roles (d) is an organizational factor as well. Job roles may or may not be well defined within any particular organization; this is not a variable determined by the individual worker. Since (b) is an individual factor, answer (e) is incorrect.

35. A: These are all IM techniques (a). Self-promotion (b) is pointing out your strengths and accomplishments and minimizing your weaknesses in order to give others the most positive impression of you. Flattery of others to get them to like you (c) is another IM technique. By giving others compliments, you can give them the impression that you are a likable person with good judgment. Many people would rather believe that your high opinion of them is due to your discernment rather than that their own opinion is inflated or false! Doing favors for other people at work to get their approval (d) is like flattering them, only in terms of taking actions rather than in verbal terms of paying compliments. Utilizing one's associations (e) is a technique of IM that involves managing or using information you may have about how people and things are associated. For example, you could curry favor with a superior by pointing out that you were both members of the same fraternity or sorority in college (this was illustrated in, among others, the movie *Legally Blonde II: Red, White & Blonde*).

36. B: Meaning (b) is not one of the major functions of communication in an organization or group. The transmission of meaning is part of the definition of communication. Another part is the understanding of that meaning by its recipients. The functions of communication in an organization are (a) control—formally, by having employees follow company policy, work according to their job descriptions, and communicate grievances to their immediate supervisors; and informally, by the expression of approval or disapproval from coworkers and workplace culture; (b) motivation—by managers communicating work expectations, job goals, feedback on work progress, and verbal reinforcement for performance to employees; (c) information—by providing information to employees that they need to make decisions and perform tasks; and (e) emotional expression—by employees meeting needs for sociability and being able to relieve frustration.

37. C: Transmission (c) is not a component of the communication process model. The message is indeed transmitted, but this fact is assumed in the model. Transmission occurs via the channel (b) that is used. Depending on the medium, the channel in a company may be formal, i.e., professional actions that follow the chain of authority in that company; or informal, i.e., spontaneous actions resulting from individual choices. Encoding (a) is done by the sender, who encodes his or her thought into a message, which may be spoken, written, or gestural. (A component missing from the answer choices here is decoding, which is done by the receiver, who converts the symbols used in the message to a form he can understand.) Noise (d) refers to obstacles distorting or interfering with a clear message. Noise can be caused by problems with perceiving the message; information overload; and differences in semantic distinctions or cultures. Feedback (e) is how the sender finds out whether the receiver understood the message as the sender intended. The feedback the receiver gives the sender will show that the message was or was not received correctly.

38. D: Interoffice memos (d) are not considered nonverbal communication. Though a written or typed memorandum is not *oral,* it is still *verbal,* i.e., it uses words. Body language (a), such as shrugging the shoulders to indicate that one does not know or care, drumming the fingers to show impatience, or sitting with arms and legs crossed to seem unapproachable, is a form of nonverbal communication. Facial expressions (b) display various emotions and can substantially alter the meaning of the spoken words they accompany, and are another form of nonverbal communication. Tone and emphasis (c) can also change the meaning inferred by the listener about what is said (e.g. "I want YOU to do it" may mean "I prefer you for this task over another person" or "Don't delegate this to somebody else," while "I want you to DO it" may mean "Stop procrastinating already!") and are another form of nonverbal communication. Spoken tone can make a message completely different from the same words when written, as when the speaker uses a sarcastic tone of voice. "You're a real go-getter" may seem like a literal compliment on paper, but if spoken with an ironic tone, it may mean "You're a slacker." Physical proximity (e) is a form of nonverbal communication. If somebody moves away from you while you are trying to talk to them, it can indicate that the person lacks interest in what you are saying or dislikes the message. It can also mean that the person dislikes you, doesn't want to talk to you, is in a big hurry, or is in the midst of a big problem. Conversely, someone who is trying to intimidate you may move too close, such as when delivering a reprimand or verbal attack. And physical-distance parameters vary with cultures. For example, most Americans would be uncomfortable with how closely Italians stand to one another in a normal conversation, and most British people would likewise find the Americans' most comfortable distance to be too close.

39. A: Face-to-face conversations and formal reports (a) represent the richest and the least rich channels of communication, respectively. The most information can be communicated in the face-to-face scenario because it allows for speech, nonverbal communication, instant feedback, and the personal factor of communicating in person physically. Formal reports or bulletins are not spoken, do not afford nonverbal communication or immediate feedback, and do not take place in person. Voice mail messages and online discussions (b) are both around the midpoint of channel richness and are neither highest nor lowest in rank. A memo or letter is very low in richness, the only lower channel being the formal report, while live videoconferencing is very high in richness, being second only to the face-to-face conversation (c). Live speeches are less rich than videoconferences but more rich than online discussions; prerecorded speeches are less rich than online discussions and are richer only than formal reports or memos (d). E-mails are richer than memos or letters but are still low in richness, while telephone conversations are higher, being less rich than only face-to-face conversations and live videoconferences (e)

40. E: The correct explanation for the cultural differences these four employees experienced in their meeting is (e): **Fred and Klaus come from low-context cultures, while Kim and Li are from high-context cultures.** Low-context cultures place more value on explicit communication, precise wording, getting things in writing, and giving and taking direct orders. Low-context cultures find words to be the most important indicators of meaning. European and North American cultures are typically low context. The lowest of the low-context cultures is the German culture. (This is evidenced in their language, which is very literal and commonly connects series of shorter words to build longer words to convey more complex concepts.) The North American culture is close to the German culture in being low context; only the German, Swiss, and Scandinavian cultures are lower context. High-context cultures are found in Asian countries. (The Mediterranean cultures—those of Italy, Spain, Greece, and Arab nations—are in the middle.) The highest-context culture is the Chinese culture; next is the Korean culture, then the Japanese culture, followed by the Vietnamese culture. High-context cultures put more emphasis on nonverbal cues, situational signals, and other subtleties in their communications. A person's identity, company status, social status, reputation among others, age, etc., have more effect on that person's credibility when communicating in high-context cultures. High-context cultures find oral agreements to be signs of trust and great commitment, unlike Western cultures, which devalue oral agreements as unenforceable and having no concrete proof. And high-context cultures are much more likely to make suggestions or recommendations than to give orders. Answers (a), (c), and (d) give partially incorrect descriptions of which cultures correspond to which individuals, and answer (b) gives a completely incorrect one.

41. D: Give alternatives weights. After developing the alternatives, the next step is to *evaluate* the alternatives. Assigning weights for prioritization is done only with the criteria identified (b) in this model. Once you have generated some alternatives, the next step of evaluating them is to *rate* (not weight) each alternative according to each of the criteria you identified and weighted. The correct steps of this model are:

- Define the problem (stated in the question).
- Identify criteria for the decision to be made (a).
- Weight the criteria to rank them in order of priority (b).
- Develop a number of potential alternatives (c) for solving the problem.
- Evaluate the alternatives by rating them with respect to each of the criteria identified.
- Choose the best alternative (e) out of those developed.

42. E: These are all assumptions of the rational decision-making model (e). In addition to the assumptions of problem clarity and known options named in the question, the other four of the six assumptions are: clarity of preferences (a), constancy of preferences (b), no constraints of time or cost (c), and maximum payoff (d). All of these conditions are assumed to exist in order to apply the rational decision-making model.

43. C: Unity of command (c) is not one of the six key elements to consider in the design of organizational structure. Unity of command is a concept related to chain of command (b). It refers to having an unbroken chain of command, meaning that each worker should report directly to only one manager. If there is not unity of command or it is disrupted, a worker could have to deal with contradictory commands from more than one superior. The six important elements of organizational structure are work specialization or division of labor, stated in the question; departmentalization (a), or the grouping of certain jobs together—by their functions, by the product they deal with, or by territory; chain of command (b), or the vertical line of authority in the organization; span of control (d), or how many workers a supervisor can manage in a productive way; centralization and decentralization (omitted from the choices here), meaning how much the decision making is focused at the next higher level within the organization (centralization) versus how much input into decision making, or actual power to make decisions, employees at lower levels have (decentralization); and formalization (e), or how much standardization of jobs there is in the organization (i.e., specific job descriptions, clear definitions of procedures, etc.). Formalization correlates negatively with employee freedom, discretion, and input about procedures, but correlates positively with clarity of duties and uniformity and consistency of outcomes.

44. B: High level of decentralization (b) does not correctly describe a characteristic of a simple structure. Simple organizational structures tend to have their authority centralized in one person who is in charge. They also tend to be less departmentalized (a), have less formalization of jobs (c), and have wider spans of control (d), corresponding to their high levels of centralization. Since (b) is incorrect, answer (e) is incorrect.

45. A: Bureaucracy and matrix structures most commonly share (a) **departmentalization by function and by product.** The matrix design combines the strengths of functional departmentalization and product departmentalization while avoiding the weaknesses of both. The bureaucracy design is characterized by high levels of functional departmentalization. Bureaucracies can also use product departmentalization depending on the individual organization. These two structures do not both use (b) departmentalizations by product and by territory or (c) by function and by territory, as the matrix design does not typically departmentalize according to geography. Centralized authority and unity of command (d) typically exist to a high degree in bureaucracy, but the matrix clearly breaks unity of command because each employee has both a product manager and a functional department manager. It follows that matrix structures will not have increased role clarity (e) but increased role confusion or ambiguity. Bureaucracies eliminate ambiguity or confusion by increased job formalization, making jobs and roles more predictable. Matrices have less formalization owing to their coordination of specialists across complex, interrelated work activities.

46. A: The rising use of chat rooms on the Internet is an example of (a) **trends in society**. Other examples of social trends include baby boomers retiring and the rise in discount and big box retail businesses. (Note: If you got this question wrong by answering "Technology" (e), this may clarify it: Although the existence of the Internet and its chat rooms are the results of technology, the rising use of the chat rooms is a social trend rather than a technological trend, as it reflects changes in social behaviors.) Economic shocks (b) are events such as the rapid ascent and decline of stocks in dot-com businesses, collapses in the stock market, and drastically lowered interest rates in lending. Global politics (c) include wars—in the United States especially, wars in other countries in which the United States is involved; the historical advent of access to the Chinese market; or the post-9/11 "war on terrorism." Competition (d) has changed with the increase in international commerce as businesses now have more competitors in other countries; it has changed with the advent of e-commerce which formerly did not exist; and it has been affected by numerous mergers and consolidations of companies due to economic necessity. Technology (e) has created cell phones; has made computers available and then less expensive, more portable, and faster; has enabled the sharing of music online, with a great impact on the music industry; and has enabled successful research into the human genome, with significant impact on the pharmaceutical and insurance industries.

47. B: Threat to expertise (c) is an organizational source of resistance to change. Change in the way an organization does things can present a threat to the expertise of specialized work groups if those changes mean that their expertise will no longer be needed, may be replaced by different expertise, or must be substantially modified to continue to be useful. Individual sources of resistance to change include habit, i.e., people have learned to do certain things automatically and if they continue to do so rather than consciously adopting different behaviors, their habits present resistance to change; security (a), since change is a threat to people's sense of safety; economic factors (b), since changes at work can initially decrease productivity and hence pay; fear of the unknown (d), since previous procedures are known quantities, while change brings new, unknown quantities; and selective information processing (e), which people use to defend their perceptions by attending to things that fit and ignoring things that threaten or challenge those perceptions.

48. D: Picking those who accept change (d) would be most informed by results of personality tests. There are measures to indicate openness to experience, risk tolerance, flexibility, positive self-concept, and positive attitudes regarding change. Researchers suggest that selecting people with these qualities can ease the process of change. Negotiation (a) is an exchange method of reducing resistance to change. The change agent offers rewards valued by resistant employees in return for not resisting change. This tactic is not typically used in conjunction with personality tests. Participation (b) is based on the principle that it is harder for people to resist decisions for change when they participate in the decision process. Personality testing is not required to recruit participation. Using education and communication (c) is a way to overcome resistance by giving workers the information they need to understand the reasons for change. Also, communicating with employees helps to "sell" the change or convince them. Personality tests are not needed to educate and communicate with employees. Building support and commitment (e) helps employees to align emotionally with changes while reducing the anxiety and fear that often motivate resistance. The various forms this can take, like training in new skills, employee counseling, or short paid leaves, do not require personality testing to be effective. (Note: The main difference between the correct and incorrect choices is that the four incorrect tactics are used with employees who already resist change, and personality tests are not needed to see this, while the correct tactic would use such tests to aid advance selection of individuals unlikely to resist change. The tactic of selection based on personality traits seeks to *prevent* resistance to change, while the others seek to *remedy* existing resistance.)

49. C: The statement correctly comparing Lewin's model with Kotter's model is (c): **The steps in Kotter's model incorporate Lewin's steps expanded with more detail.** Kotter's model has more detailed directions to guide change agents, but his eight steps can be grouped into three categories corresponding to Lewin's three steps: unfreezing the status quo to permit change; effecting movement to realize the change; and refreezing the changed status to make it last. Kotter's first four steps—establishing a sense of urgency, forming a coalition, creating a new vision, and communicating the vision throughout the organization—correspond to Lewin's unfreezing the status quo. Kotter's fifth, sixth, and seventh steps—empowering others to act on the vision; planning for, creating, and rewarding short-term successes approximating the new vision; and consolidating improvements, reassessing changes, and making needed adjustments—correspond to Lewin's movement toward the change. And Kotter's eighth and last step—reinforcing changes achieved by showing how the new behaviors correlate with the organization's success—corresponds to Lewin's third and last step of refreezing the new status for permanence. So, these two models do not represent distinctly different views of organizational change (a). Kotter's model has more steps than Lewin's, so answer (b) has it backward. Kotter's model does not *add* five *different* steps to Lewin's three (d). Kotter's eight steps all cover some aspect of each of Lewin's three, but in more detail. The two models are very similar, but Kotter's is more explicit. Since (c) correctly compares the two, answer (e) is incorrect.

50. E: Avoiding confrontation (e) is not an accurate description of one of the values on which OD is based. The opposite—confrontation—is one of the underlying values of OD. In other words, problems should be confronted openly rather than being ignored, hidden, or minimized. Other values inherent in OD are treating individual people with respect (a) and dignity; maintaining an atmosphere in the organization of trusting and supporting individuals (b); equalizing the power in the organization (c), i.e., reducing emphasis on rigid hierarchies of authority; and participation (d), because employees will be more committed to carrying out decisions to effect change when they have participated in those decisions.

How to Overcome Test Anxiety

Just the thought of taking a test is enough to make most people a little nervous. A test is an important event that can have a long-term impact on your future, so it's important to take it seriously and it's natural to feel anxious about performing well. But just because anxiety is normal, that doesn't mean that it's helpful in test taking, or that you should simply accept it as part of your life. Anxiety can have a variety of effects. These effects can be mild, like making you feel slightly nervous, or severe, like blocking your ability to focus or remember even a simple detail.

If you experience test anxiety—whether severe or mild—it's important to know how to beat it. To discover this, first you need to understand what causes test anxiety.

Causes of Test Anxiety

While we often think of anxiety as an uncontrollable emotional state, it can actually be caused by simple, practical things. One of the most common causes of test anxiety is that a person does not feel adequately prepared for their test. This feeling can be the result of many different issues such as poor study habits or lack of organization, but the most common culprit is time management. Starting to study too late, failing to organize your study time to cover all of the material, or being distracted while you study will mean that you're not well prepared for the test. This may lead to cramming the night before, which will cause you to be physically and mentally exhausted for the test. Poor time management also contributes to feelings of stress, fear, and hopelessness as you realize you are not well prepared but don't know what to do about it.

Other times, test anxiety is not related to your preparation for the test but comes from unresolved fear. This may be a past failure on a test, or poor performance on tests in general. It may come from comparing yourself to others who seem to be performing better or from the stress of living up to expectations. Anxiety may be driven by fears of the future—how failure on this test would affect your educational and career goals. These fears are often completely irrational, but they can still negatively impact your test performance.

Elements of Test Anxiety

As mentioned earlier, test anxiety is considered to be an emotional state, but it has physical and mental components as well. Sometimes you may not even realize that you are suffering from test anxiety until you notice the physical symptoms. These can include trembling hands, rapid heartbeat, sweating, nausea, and tense muscles. Extreme anxiety may lead to fainting or vomiting. Obviously, any of these symptoms can have a negative impact on testing. It is important to recognize them as soon as they begin to occur so that you can address the problem before it damages your performance.

The mental components of test anxiety include trouble focusing and inability to remember learned information. During a test, your mind is on high alert, which can help you recall information and stay focused for an extended period of time. However, anxiety interferes with your mind's natural processes, causing you to blank out, even on the questions you know well. The strain of testing during anxiety makes it difficult to stay focused, especially on a test that may take several hours. Extreme anxiety can take a huge mental toll, making it difficult not only to recall test information but even to understand the test questions or pull your thoughts together.

Effects of Test Anxiety

Test anxiety is like a disease—if left untreated, it will get progressively worse. Anxiety leads to poor performance, and this reinforces the feelings of fear and failure, which in turn lead to poor performances on subsequent tests. It can grow from a mild nervousness to a crippling condition. If allowed to progress, test anxiety can have a big impact on your schooling, and consequently on your future.

Test anxiety can spread to other parts of your life. Anxiety on tests can become anxiety in any stressful situation, and blanking on a test can turn into panicking in a job situation. But fortunately, you don't have to let anxiety rule your testing and determine your grades. There are a number of relatively simple steps you can take to move past anxiety and function normally on a test and in the rest of life.

Physical Steps for Beating Test Anxiety

While test anxiety is a serious problem, the good news is that it can be overcome. It doesn't have to control your ability to think and remember information. While it may take time, you can begin taking steps today to beat anxiety.

Just as your first hint that you may be struggling with anxiety comes from the physical symptoms, the first step to treating it is also physical. Rest is crucial for having a clear, strong mind. If you are tired, it is much easier to give in to anxiety. But if you establish good sleep habits, your body and mind will be ready to perform optimally, without the strain of exhaustion. Additionally, sleeping well helps you to retain information better, so you're more likely to recall the answers when you see the test questions.

Getting good sleep means more than going to bed on time. It's important to allow your brain time to relax. Take study breaks from time to time so it doesn't get overworked, and don't study right before bed. Take time to rest your mind before trying to rest your body, or you may find it difficult to fall asleep.

Along with sleep, other aspects of physical health are important in preparing for a test. Good nutrition is vital for good brain function. Sugary foods and drinks may give a burst of energy but this burst is followed by a crash, both physically and emotionally. Instead, fuel your body with protein and vitamin-rich foods.

Also, drink plenty of water. Dehydration can lead to headaches and exhaustion, especially if your brain is already under stress from the rigors of the test. Particularly if your test is a long one, drink water during the breaks. And if possible, take an energy-boosting snack to eat between sections.

Along with sleep and diet, a third important part of physical health is exercise. Maintaining a steady workout schedule is helpful, but even taking 5-minute study breaks to walk can help get your blood pumping faster and clear your head. Exercise also releases endorphins, which contribute to a positive feeling and can help combat test anxiety.

When you nurture your physical health, you are also contributing to your mental health. If your body is healthy, your mind is much more likely to be healthy as well. So take time to rest, nourish your body with healthy food and water, and get moving as much as possible. Taking these physical steps will make you stronger and more able to take the mental steps necessary to overcome test anxiety.

Mental Steps for Beating Test Anxiety

Working on the mental side of test anxiety can be more challenging, but as with the physical side, there are clear steps you can take to overcome it. As mentioned earlier, test anxiety often stems from lack of preparation, so the obvious solution is to prepare for the test. Effective studying may be the most important weapon you have for beating test anxiety, but you can and should employ several other mental tools to combat fear.

First, boost your confidence by reminding yourself of past success—tests or projects that you aced. If you're putting as much effort into preparing for this test as you did for those, there's no reason you should expect to fail here. Work hard to prepare; then trust your preparation.

Second, surround yourself with encouraging people. It can be helpful to find a study group, but be sure that the people you're around will encourage a positive attitude. If you spend time with others who are anxious or cynical, this will only contribute to your own anxiety. Look for others who are motivated to study hard from a desire to succeed, not from a fear of failure.

Third, reward yourself. A test is physically and mentally tiring, even without anxiety, and it can be helpful to have something to look forward to. Plan an activity following the test, regardless of the outcome, such as going to a movie or getting ice cream.

When you are taking the test, if you find yourself beginning to feel anxious, remind yourself that you know the material. Visualize successfully completing the test. Then take a few deep, relaxing breaths and return to it. Work through the questions carefully but with confidence, knowing that you are capable of succeeding.

Developing a healthy mental approach to test taking will also aid in other areas of life. Test anxiety affects more than just the actual test—it can be damaging to your mental health and even contribute to depression. It's important to beat test anxiety before it becomes a problem for more than testing.

Study Strategy

Being prepared for the test is necessary to combat anxiety, but what does being prepared look like? You may study for hours on end and still not feel prepared. What you need is a strategy for test prep. The next few pages outline our recommended steps to help you plan out and conquer the challenge of preparation.

Step 1: Scope Out the Test

Learn everything you can about the format (multiple choice, essay, etc.) and what will be on the test. Gather any study materials, course outlines, or sample exams that may be available. Not only will this help you to prepare, but knowing what to expect can help to alleviate test anxiety.

Step 2: Map Out the Material

Look through the textbook or study guide and make note of how many chapters or sections it has. Then divide these over the time you have. For example, if a book has 15 chapters and you have five days to study, you need to cover three chapters each day. Even better, if you have the time, leave an extra day at the end for overall review after you have gone through the material in depth.

If time is limited, you may need to prioritize the material. Look through it and make note of which sections you think you already have a good grasp on, and which need review. While you are studying, skim quickly through the familiar sections and take more time on the challenging parts.

Write out your plan so you don't get lost as you go. Having a written plan also helps you feel more in control of the study, so anxiety is less likely to arise from feeling overwhelmed at the amount to cover.

STEP 3: GATHER YOUR TOOLS

Decide what study method works best for you. Do you prefer to highlight in the book as you study and then go back over the highlighted portions? Or do you type out notes of the important information? Or is it helpful to make flashcards that you can carry with you? Assemble the pens, index cards, highlighters, post-it notes, and any other materials you may need so you won't be distracted by getting up to find things while you study.

If you're having a hard time retaining the information or organizing your notes, experiment with different methods. For example, try color-coding by subject with colored pens, highlighters, or post-it notes. If you learn better by hearing, try recording yourself reading your notes so you can listen while in the car, working out, or simply sitting at your desk. Ask a friend to quiz you from your flashcards, or try teaching someone the material to solidify it in your mind.

STEP 4: CREATE YOUR ENVIRONMENT

It's important to avoid distractions while you study. This includes both the obvious distractions like visitors and the subtle distractions like an uncomfortable chair (or a too-comfortable couch that makes you want to fall asleep). Set up the best study environment possible: good lighting and a comfortable work area. If background music helps you focus, you may want to turn it on, but otherwise keep the room quiet. If you are using a computer to take notes, be sure you don't have any other windows open, especially applications like social media, games, or anything else that could distract you. Silence your phone and turn off notifications. Be sure to keep water close by so you stay hydrated while you study (but avoid unhealthy drinks and snacks).

Also, take into account the best time of day to study. Are you freshest first thing in the morning? Try to set aside some time then to work through the material. Is your mind clearer in the afternoon or evening? Schedule your study session then. Another method is to study at the same time of day that you will take the test, so that your brain gets used to working on the material at that time and will be ready to focus at test time.

STEP 5: STUDY!

Once you have done all the study preparation, it's time to settle into the actual studying. Sit down, take a few moments to settle your mind so you can focus, and begin to follow your study plan. Don't give in to distractions or let yourself procrastinate. This is your time to prepare so you'll be ready to fearlessly approach the test. Make the most of the time and stay focused.

Of course, you don't want to burn out. If you study too long you may find that you're not retaining the information very well. Take regular study breaks. For example, taking five minutes out of every hour to walk briskly, breathing deeply and swinging your arms, can help your mind stay fresh.

As you get to the end of each chapter or section, it's a good idea to do a quick review. Remind yourself of what you learned and work on any difficult parts. When you feel that you've mastered the material, move on to the next part. At the end of your study session, briefly skim through your notes again.

But while review is helpful, cramming last minute is NOT. If at all possible, work ahead so that you won't need to fit all your study into the last day. Cramming overloads your brain with more information than it can process and retain, and your tired mind may struggle to recall even previously learned information when it is overwhelmed with last-minute study. Also, the urgent nature of cramming and the stress placed on your brain contribute to anxiety. You'll be more likely to go to the test feeling unprepared and having trouble thinking clearly.

So don't cram, and don't stay up late before the test, even just to review your notes at a leisurely pace. Your brain needs rest more than it needs to go over the information again. In fact, plan to finish your studies by noon or early afternoon the day before the test. Give your brain the rest of the day to relax or focus on other things, and get a good night's sleep. Then you will be fresh for the test and better able to recall what you've studied.

Step 6: Take a Practice Test

Many courses offer sample tests, either online or in the study materials. This is an excellent resource to check whether you have mastered the material, as well as to prepare for the test format and environment.

Check the test format ahead of time: the number of questions, the type (multiple choice, free response, etc.), and the time limit. Then create a plan for working through them. For example, if you have 30 minutes to take a 60-question test, your limit is 30 seconds per question. Spend less time on the questions you know well so that you can take more time on the difficult ones.

If you have time to take several practice tests, take the first one open book, with no time limit. Work through the questions at your own pace and make sure you fully understand them. Gradually work up to taking a test under test conditions: sit at a desk with all study materials put away and set a timer. Pace yourself to make sure you finish the test with time to spare and go back to check your answers if you have time.

After each test, check your answers. On the questions you missed, be sure you understand why you missed them. Did you misread the question (tests can use tricky wording)? Did you forget the information? Or was it something you hadn't learned? Go back and study any shaky areas that the practice tests reveal.

Taking these tests not only helps with your grade, but also aids in combating test anxiety. If you're already used to the test conditions, you're less likely to worry about it, and working through tests until you're scoring well gives you a confidence boost. Go through the practice tests until you feel comfortable, and then you can go into the test knowing that you're ready for it.

Test Tips

On test day, you should be confident, knowing that you've prepared well and are ready to answer the questions. But aside from preparation, there are several test day strategies you can employ to maximize your performance.

First, as stated before, get a good night's sleep the night before the test (and for several nights before that, if possible). Go into the test with a fresh, alert mind rather than staying up late to study.

Try not to change too much about your normal routine on the day of the test. It's important to eat a nutritious breakfast, but if you normally don't eat breakfast at all, consider eating just a protein bar. If you're a coffee drinker, go ahead and have your normal coffee. Just make sure you time it so that the caffeine doesn't wear off right in the middle of your test. Avoid sugary beverages, and drink enough water to stay hydrated but not so much that you need a restroom break 10 minutes into the test. If your test isn't first thing in the morning, consider going for a walk or doing a light workout before the test to get your blood flowing.

Allow yourself enough time to get ready, and leave for the test with plenty of time to spare so you won't have the anxiety of scrambling to arrive in time. Another reason to be early is to select a good seat. It's helpful to sit away from doors and windows, which can be distracting. Find a good seat, get out your supplies, and settle your mind before the test begins.

When the test begins, start by going over the instructions carefully, even if you already know what to expect. Make sure you avoid any careless mistakes by following the directions.

Then begin working through the questions, pacing yourself as you've practiced. If you're not sure on an answer, don't spend too much time on it, and don't let it shake your confidence. Either skip it and come back later, or eliminate as many wrong answers as possible and guess among the remaining ones. Don't dwell on these questions as you continue—put them out of your mind and focus on what lies ahead.

Be sure to read all of the answer choices, even if you're sure the first one is the right answer. Sometimes you'll find a better one if you keep reading. But don't second-guess yourself if you do immediately know the answer. Your gut instinct is usually right. Don't let test anxiety rob you of the information you know.

If you have time at the end of the test (and if the test format allows), go back and review your answers. Be cautious about changing any, since your first instinct tends to be correct, but make sure you didn't misread any of the questions or accidentally mark the wrong answer choice. Look over any you skipped and make an educated guess.

At the end, leave the test feeling confident. You've done your best, so don't waste time worrying about your performance or wishing you could change anything. Instead, celebrate the successful completion of this test. And finally, use this test to learn how to deal with anxiety even better next time.

Review Video: Test Anxiety
Visit mometrix.com/academy and enter code: 100340

Important Qualification

Not all anxiety is created equal. If your test anxiety is causing major issues in your life beyond the classroom or testing center, or if you are experiencing troubling physical symptoms related to your anxiety, it may be a sign of a serious physiological or psychological condition. If this sounds like your situation, we strongly encourage you to seek professional help.

Online Resources

Due to our efforts to try to keep this book to a manageable length, we've created a link that will give you access to all of your online resources:

mometrix.com/resources719/dsstorgbehav

It's Your Moment, Let's Celebrate It!

Share your story @mometrixtestpreparation